The Central Philosophy of The Ṛgveda

Dedicated to
the sacred memory of
Sri Aurobindo
a seer-philosopher

The Central Philosophy of The Ṛgveda

The Concept of Divine

A. Ramamurty

D.K. Printworld (P) Ltd.
Publishers of Indian Traditions

Cataloging in Publication Data — DK
[Courtesy: D.K. Agencies (P) Ltd. <docinfo@dkagencies.com>]

Ramamurty, A. (Aryasomayajula), 1935-
The central philosophy of the Ṛgveda : the concept of divine / A. Ramamurty. — 2nd rev. ed.
p. cm.
Includes bibliographical references (p.) and index.
ISBN 13: 9788124606100

1. Vedas. Ṛgveda — Philosophy. 2. Hindu gods. I. Title.

DDC 294.59212 23

First published in India, 1991
Second Revised Edition, 2012
ISBN 13: 978-81-246-0610-0 **ISBN 10: 81-246-0610-2**

Published and printed by:
D.K. Printworld (P) Ltd.
Regd. Office: 'Vedaśrī', F-395, Sudarshan Park
(Metro Station: Ramesh Nagar)
New Delhi – 110 015-11
Phones: (011) 2545 3975; 2546 6019; *Fax*: (011) 2546 5926
E-mail: indology@dkprintworld.com
Website: www.dkprintworld.com

Preface

AMONG the Saṁhitās (collections) of the Veda, the *Ṛgveda Saṁhitā* occupies a pre-eminent position as it presents comprehensively the vision or wisdom of the Vedic seers. Apart from the fact that the other Vedic Saṁhitās, with the exception of the *Atharvaveda Saṁhitā*, repeat most of the hymns of the *Ṛgveda*, they do not have much to add to the basic thought or wisdom of the Vedic seers as expressed in the hymns of the *Ṛgveda*. The importance of the *Ṛgveda* to Indian thought is foundational, and our understanding of the meaning of the *Ṛgveda* will not only help us in comprehending the thought of the Veda, but will be significant in understanding and appreciating the post-Saṁhitā or the Upaniṣadic thought also. Some of the ideas and insights, which are central to the Upaniṣads, presuppose, and are a continuation and development of the Vedic ideas and insights, which, when interpreted in their proper perspective, will be valuable in revealing the depth and richness of the Upaniṣadic ideas. For instance, the meaning of the Upaniṣadic concept of *Brahman* can be comprehended in depth and more integrally when it is viewed and understood in relation to the Vedic concept of Brahma, inspired devotion and its poetic expression in prayer. Similarly, the meaning of the Vedāntic idea "knowledge" (*jñāna* or *prajñā*) both as the essence of and a means of *Brahman* realisation, can be grasped and appreciated more fully in the light of the Vedic concepts of Vāk and Kāvya. So also is the case with the Vedāntic concept of Māyā whose positive dimension is revealed in the hymns of the *Ṛgveda*. All this depends upon our approach to Vedic interpretation. If we start with the assumption that the Veda, as a collection of primitive man's thought and wisdom, reflects his helpless condition in a hostile nature over which he had no control or mastery and hence his animistic world view, and try to interpret it in the light of certain modern theories about the origin of religion hoping thereby to find a sort of confirmation for those theories in the Veda, we not only will be prejudging the worth and significance of the Veda but by attempting a naturalistic interpretation of it we will be distorting and consequently missing the real meaning of the Veda. The meaning of almost all the hymns of the *Ṛgveda* remains unintelligible in terms of a naturalistic interpretation. And almost all the modern scholars on the Veda, with the exception of a few thinkers like Sri Aurobindo, started with such a presupposition, and tried to force a naturalistic interpretation on all the hymns of the Veda whether thereby the hymns reveal anything meaningful or not. Because of this the naturalistic interpretations of the Veda are utterly confusing and unintelligible, except in broad outline, even from a naturalistic standpoint. On the other hand, if we try to discover in the Veda a creative beginning of the later Indian thought, especially that of the Upaniṣads, though expressed in a language peculiar to the Veda which is highly symbolic, our attitude and approach to the Veda will be significantly different. This does not, however, mean that we should try to find out in the Veda some form of Vedāntic thought. And if we keep in view the traditional view that the Veda and Vedānta form an integral whole, and are hence complementary to each other — both form Śruti — it will help us in comprehending the meaning of both in relation to each other.

My interpretation of the *Ṛgveda* in the following pages is inspired partly by the writings of Sri Aurobindo on the Veda. My attempt to understand and interpret the central teaching or philosophy of the *Ṛgveda* is born out of tension which I experienced while going through and comparing the naturalistic interpretations of the Veda offered by most of Vedic scholars, both Indian and Western, and the psychological or spiritual interpretation of it offered by Sri Aurobindo. The following is a systematic attempt to reconcile both the views, and yet to go beyond them in comprehending the basic vision of the Vedic seers as expressed in the hymns of the *Ṛgveda*. Although the work is based entirely on the text of the *Ṛgveda,* in comprehending its meaning the other Vedic literature is consultued. While some of the interpreters of the Veda find it difficult to appreciate the role of Sāyaṇa as an interpreter of the Veda, I find that without his commentary on the Veda the possible meanings of a Vedic word or a hymn and hence the whole of the Veda can have remained highly unintelligible.

University of Hyderabad
Hyderabad

A. Ramamurty

Contents

1

Introduction

FROM the Brāhmaṇas down to the present times several attempts have been made, both from within and without tradition, to interpret the Vedic Saṁhitās, especially the *Ṛgveda Saṁhitā*. Each school of thought has evolved its own method of interpretation; and historically we find several such methods of Vedic interpretation. The different schools of Indian thought have developed distinct standpoints of their own, not only with regard to the nature and validity of Vedic revelation, but also in respect of its meaning. Although the revealed character and authority of the Veda are admitted by all the schools of Indian tradition, the continuous attention paid to the study and interpretation of the Vedānta texts has not been shown to the study and interpretation of the Vedic Saṁhitās. The mutual antagonism developed and sustained by certain schools of Indian thought between the Saṁhitās and the Upaniṣads in terms of ritualism and knowledge (*jñāna*), in which the Saṁhitās are seen as standing for ritualism, mainly due to the view adopted by these schools that the significance of the Saṁhitās is tied up with the ritualistic literature of the Brāhmaṇas, has led to the relegation of the Saṁhitās to a secondary position, in relation to the Upaniṣads, in respect of both importance and meaning. And almost all the traditional schools of Indian thought, which have shown concern for the Veda, have tried to understand and explain the meaning of the Vedic Saṁhitās mainly with reference to their relevance to the performance of various religious rites and duties as developed in the Brāhmaṇas. Because of their predominant concern with the notion of *dharma* which, according to them, consists chiefly in the proper performance of religious rites and duties, and as the Veda is viewed by them as the ultimate source and authority of all religious duties, the thinkers of the Pūrva-Mīmāṁsā School have not tried to understand the meaning of the Saṁhitās independently of their ritualistic relevance and significance. The thinkers belonging to the different schools of Vedānta have shown little or no interest either in interpreting the Saṁhitās, or in understanding the positive relationship between the Saṁhitās and the Upaniṣads. Their concern for the Saṁhitās has been limited to those Saṁhitā passages or hymns which fit in well with their interpretation of the Vedānta texts according to their respective standpoints; and in that they have tried to derive the authority of the Saṁhitās or the Veda to their respective positions. The other systems of Indian philosophy have not generally shown any concern for the Veda beyond accepting it as a source of valid knowledge. And even then they have not tried to understand how the revealed knowledge of the Veda has any value in understanding the problems with which they are concerned. Thus no systematic attempt was made until the emergence of Sāyaṇa to interpret the Saṁhitās systematically and comprehensively. Most of the other traditional works on the Veda have limited their scope to some of the scholastic and technical aspects of it like the nature and source of its origin and its general validity as a source of valid knowledge; and in those cases wherein attempts to explain the meaning of the Saṁhitās have been made, they are not systematic and comprehensive. In most cases the purpose of interpretation is either to elucidate the meaning of certain difficulit Vedic terms and expressions, or to impose one's own sectarian views on the Veda. Thus in general the concern traditionally shown to the Saṁhitās has been nothing more than paying them formal and sentimental homage. Beyond this the basic vision informing the Saṁhitās has not been an object of comprehensive study.

Although the Brāhmaṇas form an integral part of the corpus of Vedic literature, they are the earliest historically known attempts at interpreting the Vedic Saṁhitās. However, the peculiarity of the interpretation available in them is that it is not an interpretation for the sake of interpretation, or for elucidating the meaning of the Veda. Some of the Vedic hymns are interpreted in the Brāhmaṇas chiefly by way of adapting them for religious or ritualistic purposes, which is done with a view to consecrating and organising the life of man, both at the individual and social levels, in the light of Vedic revelation. They have evolved, though not in a systematic manner, different methods to interpret the Saṁhitās which are later on developed individually and systematically by different thinkers and schools of thought. One such method is to explain the meaning of Vedic hymns by means of analysing the meaning of the key Vedic words etymologically.

We find in the Brāhmaṇas etymological definitions of several Vedic words which vary from context to context, as the words are etymologically defined mainly to render meaningful the adaption of certain Vedic hymns to the performance of various rituals and ceremonies. They have also developed the method of explaining the significance of some of the hymns in terms of their mythico-historical content. But the most significant and enduring contribution of the Brāhmaṇas towards Vedic interpretation consists in their providing a broad perspective and direction for understanding the meaning of the Saṁhitās. This they have done by introducing the interpretative concepts of *ādhidaivika, ādhibhautika* and *ādhyātmika*. Althougth these concepts are to be found in the Vedic literature in general, they are systemetically developed and employed in the Brāhmaṇas. The main purpose of these concepts is to guide and help the later generations in understanding the meaning of the Vedic Saṁhitās, as well as to explain the significance and justification of the broad division of the Veda into Saṁhitās (*mantra* portion of the Veda), Brāhmaṇas and the Upaniṣads. Their significance and value lay in the help they render in seeing the sense in which each constituent of the Veda is a revelation of the Divine, or how in its totality the Veda stands to reveal the infinite richness and integral unity of the Divine as it reveals itself in and through the varied forms of its self-manifestation, or at different levels of human experience.

According to the scheme of interpretation, the concepts or rather the categories of interpretation are intended primarily to help us in comprehending the nature and meaning of divine revelation at all levels of human experience, the object of which is broadly divided into three distinct realms : (i) The realm of the deities (*ādhidaivika*) who as the primary and universal self-manifestations of the Divine are the inner principles or powers of nature, and manifest themselves in and through the diverse phenomena of nature and govern them. (ii) The realm of physical nature in all its aspects (*ādhibhautika*). (iii) And finally the inner reality of man (*ādhyātmika*). Now, the manner in which the divine reveals itself at all levels of human experience, or the mode of its revelation within the various realms is not the same. The nature of the Divine as apprehended by man, or as revealed to man, which depends upon the forms of its manifestation, is distinct from realm to realm. Nevertheless, the nature of divine revelation remains the same, though its meaning to man at one level of his experience may be distinct from its meaning at the other two levels. The Divine reveals itself in its infinite richness within all the realms, or at all the levels of human experience.

The basic approach of the Veda to the problem of man's knowledge of the Divine is not that of speculative understanding, whereby its nature is conceived in abstract terms, but to see its presence in all the forms of its manifestation which equally reveal its nature and glory. Thus when the basic vision of a tradition is to relate integrally the whole of human experience to its ultimate source or the Divine, or to see in all that man experiences the presence of the same divine reality, the attempts at interpreting every area of human experience in terms of the Divine will be of supreme significance and value. No sphere of human experience will then be devoid of revelatory value and divine significance.

On the other hand, every aspect of human life, as well as the various areas of his experience gain their true significance and value in their relation to the Divine.

Now, according to this approach, the Vedic Saṁhitās may be seen primarily as an interpretation of the Divine at the level of the deities, or stand to reveal the nature of the Divine in and through the various deities, its primary and universal self-manifestations, while the Brāhmaṇas are an interpretation of the Divine at the level of nature. And the Upaniṣads interpret the nature of the Divine as revealed within the reality of man. We can thus understand and appreciate the attempts made in the Brāhmaṇas to interpret nature divinely by way of finding out the identities and correspondences, either real or symbolic, between the Divine seen in the forms of its manifestation as various deities and the various phenomena of nature. And the process of integrating nature with the Divine is sought to be accomplished by the Vedic seers with the help of the concept of *yajña*. *Yajña* as representing the process of self-manifestation or self-expression of the Divine in the form of the phenomenal reality is the Vedic man's means of integrating nature with the Divine, and to consecrate nature thereby. The chief object of the Veda, as thus conceived by the Brāhmaṇas, is to integrate into Divine unity what is diversified in the process of self-manifestation of the divine.[1] Each phenomenon of nature is to be related and integrated with the Divine, so that what is diversified in the process of self-manifestation or self-expression of the divine is seen in its inner Divine unity. As every experience of man reveals the nature of the Divine, though in its own peculiar manner, no area of human experience is divinely insignificant. To a divinely inspired person or a seer the Divine is revealed in and through all that he experiences.

The unique appeal of the Upaniṣads and their immediate spiritual significance to man are, however, mainly due to their

1. *Śatapatha Brāhmaṇa* 10.4.2.2, 21; *Aitareya Āraṇyaka* 3.2.6.

being an interpretation of Divine revelation at the level of his own reality. *Ātman* is the name given to the Divine or *Brahman* as it reveals itself within the being of man, whereas revelation of the Divine at the other two levels of man's experience may not be so clearly intelligible and immediately significant to him as it is at the level of his experience of his own reality. Thus the Veda in all its constituents seeks to reveal the nature and glory of the Divine as they are mediated to man in and through the different realms of his experience. One's inability to see, therefore, the presence of the divine in any of the realms of his experience is to miss its infinite richness and integral unity. Consequently, the different areas of human experience remain unintegrated, and one area of his experience may gain supreme or even exclusive importance and meaning over the other areas of his experience. It is thus in later Hindu tradition one category of interpretation, the *ādhyātmika* one, and one area of human experience, that is the inward life of man, have gained supreme importance and meaning over others, thereby giving rise to several types of misconception regarding the value and significance of the Saṁhitās and the Brāhmaṇas, as well as to unwarranted attacks on their spiritual worth. This has also resulted in exclusive concern for the thought of the Upaniṣads, claiming thereby supreme importance and value to self-realisation, to the neglect, at times with contempt, of the study and understanding of the other two areas of human experience, and general adoptation of spiritual or subjective approach to philosophical and religious problems. The meaning of Hindu spirituality has thus been narrowed down or reduced to a single dimension and perspective which is decidedly not the case with the Veda. Thus attempts have often been made in the later Hindu tradition to interpret everything spiritually or mystically, or to reduce everything to *ādhyātmika* level to give them validity, or to render things interpreted meaningful, whereas by adopting the above three categories of interpretation we will not only be able to understand and appreciate fully the meaning of Vedic revelation, but can also comprehend the real meaning of the Vedic deities as primary and universal self-manifestations of the Divine, and their revelatory value.

The Upaniṣads are not an interpretation of the Saṁhitās, but a continuation of the same Divine revelation, though received at a different level of man's experience, and expressed in a form which is distinct from that of the Saṁhitās. The Upaniṣads express the nature of the Divine as it is experienced within the being of man. For instance, the Upaniṣadic understanding of *Brahman* as identical with the Self of man, as well as the inner controller and unity of all is a philosophical restatement of the Vedic concept of Brahma which as devotion expands till it is able to transform man's vision divinely, and inspire him to see all that is as a dynamic self-expression of the Divine. Further, the Upaniṣadic insight that what is there is here also, or the reality without man is the same as within him is also significant in this context. The Upaniṣadic assertion that the Vedic knowledge is inferior to direct and immediate realisation of the Self need not be taken too seriously, as all indirect or mediate knowledge of the Divine, including the Upaniṣadic knowledge, is inferior to direct and immediate knowledge of the Divine, and in attaining which one has to transcend all scriptural knowledge. We also find in the Upaniṣads attempts at comprehending the nature of the Divine in its abstract nature or in itself through generalised concepts, which, however, presuppose its revelation in concrete living situations. Because of this much of the symbolism and mythical mode of expression which is peculiar to Vedic Saṁhitās is now shed, and conceptual mode of expression is resorted to. Nevertheless, the Upaniṣads are known more for their *ādhyātmika* interpretation of the Divine. Although speculative understanding regarding the nature of the Divine in itself is present in the Saṁhitās it generally tended towards scepticism. Apart from these differences which do not concern us here directly, both the Saṁhitās and the Upaniṣads belong to the same genre of literature; both form Śruti tradition.

With the emergence of Smṛti tradition we find different schools of thought evolving their own methods of Vedic interpretation. What is, however, common to all these schools, which are from within tradition and are orthodox in character, is that they all have ungrudgingly accepted the revealed character of the Veda and its infallibility.

The major concern of the school of grammarians *vis-à-vis* the Veda is to show or establish the general validity and eternality of the Veda (*śabda*) by means of explaining the nature and origin of words or speech, and the relation between words and meaning; and in that they made a significant contribution towards understanding the Vedic concept of *vāk*, and its revelatory function. Beyond this they have not gone in explaining the meaning of the Saṁhitās, or the basic vision of the seers expressed through the hymns of the Veda.

The method developed by the school of etymologists (*nirukta*) in interpreting the Vedic Saṁhitās is that of analysing the meaning of individual Vedic words, especially those that are peculiarly Vedic in usage, in terms of their basic roots. They have also tried to formulate the rules that govern such etymological derivations. This method, which later on has been adopted by most of the Vedic interpreters, has its limitations. Although the Sanskrit language is older than the Veda, the Veda is the first known literature in Sanskrit language. Therefore, what the words as used in the Veda may mean can best be known only by referring to the Veda. It is the first known record of their usage. What the various words may mean in the context of Vedic usage, or the Vedic intention of their usage is not easy to determine independently of their Vedic usage; whereas the rules about the Sanskrit language, or the regulative principles that govern its usage are formulated much later. In this process the current usage of the language must have been the main guiding principle. Therefore, these rules which are generally helpful in defining the words cannot, strictily speaking, help us in determining their meaning in the context of their Vedic usage.

For instance, some of the key Vedic words like, *deva, kavi, kāvya, kratu, ṛṣi, vāk, go, dhenu,* etc. the proper grasp of whose meaning will be of invaluable help in comprehending the meaning of the Saṁhitās do not carry with them the same meaning in their Vedic and non-Vedic usages. Much of their Vedic connotation is lost in later day usage, and new meanings or shades of meaning are acquired by these words. This is not, however, to deny the help the etymological definition of words can render in understanding the meaning of the Saṁhitās, as the language in its growth retains to a large extent its basic meaning structure. Only the later day usage of the words need not be a determining factor in understanding their Vedic usage. Further, all the possible meanings a word can have cannot be derived from a single root, whereas the various meanings a word can have can best be known in the light of its usage in different contexts, as well as in the total context of the thought. Besides, how a word stands to mean different things cannot be explained satisfactorily in terms of a single root. As, according to *Bṛhaddevtā,* all the words indicate becoming, the same word can be used meaningfully to denote a particular function or quality to be found in more than one thing.[2] Likewise, the same thing can be known by many words as a thing may have several qualities and functions. To avoid these problems if we introduce different roots to derive different meanings out of the same word, the attempt to explain the meaning of words etymologically will not be of much significance and value. All the meanings which a word can have or the several words by which a thing is known cannot be explained in terms of or derived from the same root. This difficulty has been recognised by the etymologists themselves, and therein lies their significant contribution. The *Nighaṇṭu,* which is a very valuable guide to understanding the meaning of the Veda, contains lists of words used synonymously in the Veda, and all those synonymous words cannot be explained etymologically to mean the same. For instance, it contains fifty-

---

2. *Bṛhaddevatā* I.31.

seven synonyms for speech (*vāk*), and all of them cannot be analysed etymologically to mean speech. But almost all of them are actually used in the Veda to mean speech; and in most of the cases their usage is either symbolic or figurative or even analogical. Yāska, who is known for etymological approach to Vedic interpretation, has tried to explain the meaning of certain Vedic hymns in his *Nirukta* to exemplify his approach, or to show the validity of his approach. Although his work is supposed to be a commentary on *Nighaṇṭu*, he has not tried to explain or justify, in terms of his etymological analysis, how the various synonyms as contained in the *Nighaṇṭu* can mean the same thing. Therefore, the science of etymology may not be of much help in knowing the meaning of several Vedic words.

Moreover, the etymologists cannot be regarded as free from their own doctrinal or metaphysical presuppositions in defining the meaning of Vedic terms etymologically. Most of the key Vedic words are used symbolically, and even analogically to communicate the revealed truths, whereas in their ordinary usage they are meant to convey their plain sense. Therefore, in both the cases the intention of their usage and their referent need not be the same. Most of the words are used in the Veda to convey a sense which they do not do so ordinarily, or in their post-Vedic usage. In most contexts the words of ordinary usage are employed in the Veda, not with the intention of communicating ordinary experiences of mankind, but with their help to communicate divinely inspired speech or wisdom of the Vedic seers. Therefore, the Vedic usage of most of the words is either symbolic or analogical. For instance, the words *go* and *dhenu*, which are used in the Veda to mean divinely inspired speech, do not mean so in their ordinary usage. They cannot also be defined etymologically to mean speech. On the other hand, the significance of their Vedic usage becomes clear if we try to understand their meanings either symbolically or analogically. Therefore, the attempts either at paraphrasing the Saṁhitās into current idiom of Sanskrit, or in translating them into a foreign language involve interpretation, which is practically unavoidable, as the Veda is not simply a piece of Sanskrit literature in which some empirically known and verifiable reality is described poetically.

Different interpreters of the Veda have often tried to derive the meaning of a word from different roots thereby giving rise to the impression that the process of such an analysis is predetermined in terms of what one is trying to derive. Likewise, thinkers with distinct standpoints of their own have often tried to derive different meaning from the same word by means of tracing it to different roots. Thus the method of etymological definition of Vedic words has often been used conveniently by different thinkers in imposing their own views on the Veda. These make the problems more complicated, and at times confused, and show how far we can rely on the method of etymological analysis to understand the meaning of the Saṁhitās. Therefore, instead of trying to determine the meaning of a word solely in terms of uncertain roots, or in the light of the later day usage, its Vedic meaning can be grasped by observing how it behaves in all the contexts of its Vedic usage, as well as in the light of total Vedic thought or vision. The meaning of the words or concepts cannot be comprehended individually or in isolation of total thought. This was recognised by Yāska also, who, after attempting to explain etymologically the meaning of various difficult terms of the Veda, admits that reason (*tarka*) and context (*prakaraṇa*) are of value in understanding the meaning of Vedic hymns.[3]

Words help us in comprehending the thought, and equally the thought is of help in determining the meaning of words. Although the words retain their basic meaning structure despite changes in their usage, which can be known either by looking into their actual usage, or in terms of their root definitions, they also acquire a special sense, especially when they are employed

---

3. *Nirukta* 13.12.

to communicate non-empirical truths, and that can be known by understanding them in the total context of thought. Understanding a language is not the same as comprehending the thought expressed through that language, though understanding of language is a necessary condition for comprehending the thought. Of course, it is true that only with the help of the meaning of individual words we can arrive at the total picture of thought; but the latter when it is comprehended, which involves more than knowing the meaning of individual words, also helps in understanding the meaning of individual words. This is more true when the language is used poetically. Thus with the help of the same words different thinkers with distinct perspectives of their own try to communicate their thought, and in doing so they give their own meanings or senses to the words or concepts. This is true with every philosophical thinker. And this is more so when the language is used to communicate revealed truths or divinely inspired experiences.

In determining the meaning of some of the Vedic words, some of the Western interpreters of the Veda sought to find help in the cognate languages of Sanskrit. How far can these cognate languages of Sanskrit shed light on the meaning of the Vedic words? There are words common to these languages, but as their number is so insignificant their value in illumining the meaning of Vedic language is negligible. The presence of common words in more than one language need not necessarily imply their common origin. Moreover, the general orientation of the thought, and the direction it has taken in the course of its development of which Sanskrit language is the vehicle of expression are not the same elsewhere, or with those who think and express themselves in terms of cognate languages. For instance, what is there either in the root meaning of the word "Agni", or in its ordinary Sanskrit usage, or as it is used in other cognate languages to indicate its divine nature? Here we cannot say that the divinity of Agni is a matter of poetic imagination or interpretation on the part of the Vedic seers, as, when they describe Agni as a deity, they refer to what is seen or experienced due to divine inspiration. And also they are aware of the distinction between Agni, the deity, and Agni an element of nature or a natural phenomenon. How are we to explain on the basis of these principles of interpretation the various epithets that are used in the Veda to describe Agni, such as, *kavi, vipra, ṛṣi, pracetasa, jātavedasa, Īśvara* or *Ina*, etc. and which stand to reveal his divine nature? Only the phenomenal aspect of Agni, as the principle of heat and light, or an element of nature is all that can be known by this process, but not the divine nature of Agni which is the primary concern of the Vedic seers.

The ritualistic or rather religious (*yājñika*) approach to Vedic interpretation, or interpretation of the Vedic Saṁhitās to serve the practical religious needs of man which was originally initiated in the Brāhmaṇas was later developed systematically and fully by the Pūrva-Mīmāṁsā School. Basic to this approach is the view that the primary object of the Veda is religious action. Accordingly, the meaning of the Saṁhitās is viewed and explained by the Pūrva-Mīmāṁsā School in relation to the performance of various religious rites and duties. Even though a distinction is made by the school of Pūrva-Mīmāṁsā between descriptive and injunctive type of statements — the Saṁhitās comprising the former type of statements — the descriptive statements are, however, meaningful, according to it, only in so far as they lead to or inspire action directly or indirectly. This is based on its general understanding of the nature of language, according to which, a statement to be meaningful should intend some action. Thus according to this school of interpretation the meaning of the Saṁhitās is secondary to or dependent upon religious action. Now the problem whether the object of the Vedic hymns is primarily to inspire the performance of various religious rites and duties, or to communicate the nature of the Divine as revealed to the Vedic seers is of basic importance in understanding the problem whether the meaning of the hymns is secondary to or tied up with the performance of religious rites, or do they have a meaning which can be known independently of their relevance to the performance of religious action. It is one thing to adapt the Vedic hymns to ritualistic or religious purposes, and quite another to think that they are intended primarily for that purpose. Man's awareness of the Divine and his response to it are two distinct things though they are closely related, and go together. Now, if we view the object of the Veda as primarily to communicate the nature of the Divine as revealed to the Vedic seers, then in comprehending its meaning we need not necessarily view it in relation to the practical religious needs of man. In other words, religious action need not necessarily be the primary object of the Veda. Then instead of the Saṁhitās gaining their significance in terms of the religious life of a people it is the latter that obtains its meaning and value in the light of Vedic revelation. Thus how man responds to divine revelation, and organises his religious life in the light of it is a different problem, and has no logical relation to the understanding of the meaning of divine revelation. While religious action is a means to an end, apprehension of truth is an end in itself. Thus when faced with the problem of explaining the divine nature of the deities, or why the diverse phenomena of nature are seen as the dwelling places of the deities, the school of Pūrva-Mīmāṁsā has no satisfactory explanation; it instead resorted to a sort of naturalistic interpretation guided by pragmatic considerations.

Sāyaṇa who mostly followed this method of interpretation in his commentaries on the Vedic Saṁhitās has, however, made an attempt to understand the meaning of certain Vedic hymns independently of their ritualistic significance and relevance. He has tried to understand the meaning of those hymns in the light of the Upaniṣads, and given them a spiritual interpretation. But thereby he has not achieved much, for interpretation of some of the hymns, according to the Upaniṣadic thought and vision, does not fit in well with the general trend or tone of his interpretation. And he has not done anything to reconcile and integrate the thought of those exceptional hymns with the general philosophy of the Veda as interpreted by him. Such an approach would naturally give rise to the view that the Veda has no unity of thought or vision; and to which he himself would not have subscribed.

The historical method of Vedic interpretation which is the one that has been followed in modern times by Tilak and some other scholars, both Indian and Western, and which in its wake has given rise to the Āryan-Draviḍian controversy, is an attempt to interpret the Veda as an historical account of a struggle, either between primitive people and their hostile environment over which they had no means of control or mastery, or a racial or national hostility and conflict between powerful migrating invaders and the natives. Although there are some historical elements here and there in the Veda, especially in the *Ṛgveda*, they cannot be construed as the primary object and meaning of the Veda. Its spiritual significance and philosophical worth are totally overlooked by this school of interpretation. This method of interpretation which is present within the Brāhmaṇas was later developed fully, or made use of in the Purāṇic literature. Much of the Indian understanding of the Veda, at least at the popular level, is influenced by the Purāṇic explanation of the Vedic thought and myths. The anthropomorphic view of the Vedic deities, which is fully developed in the Purāṇas, has led to their complete individualisation, and is primarily responsible for the view that the Vedic deities are independent in their existence. However, the Purāṇas have not lost sight of the symbolic character of the events described in the Veda, most of which do not occur in empirical space and time, or in concrete historical situations.

These traditional schools of Vedic interpretation have, however, kept in view, though partly, the tradition developed subsequent to that of the Veda while understanding the meaning of the Veda. They have not completely overlooked the help and guidance the later Hindu tradition, especially the Upaniṣads, can provide in understanding the meaning of the Saṁhitās. However, they made no systematic and significant attempts to see and appreciate clearly the unity of spirit and logical continuity between the Saṁhitās and the later tradition, in respect of both content and direction. The failure to recognise the spiritual unity and logical continuity of the Hindu tradition, which has its foundational beginning in the Saṁhitās, had given rise to antagonism between the two schools of Mīmāṁsā, and has continued to influence the Hindu tradition.

Most of the modern approaches to Vedic interpretation are laden heavily with the basic presuppositions of the modern thought, and are influenced by modern world views. In India, Dayananda Saraswati is the only person who made an attempt to interpret the Vedic Saṁhitās in the proper sense of the term. But his approach to Vedic interpretation was influenced and guided by the religious demands of the day, as well as by certain other considerations and even prejudices which would not allow one to be really free and objective in his approach. Among other things he has adopted a rigid fundamentalist position with regard to the Veda, and hence dogmatically denied any value to tradition in understanding the meaning of the Veda. According to him, tradition instead of being a source of elucidation of the sense of the Veda is a positive distortion of Vedic thought. In all this he was guided by certain extraneous considerations.

The other creative thinker who took keen interest in interpreting the Veda is Srī Aurobindo. However, his approach too has its limitations. In the first place his is not a systematic approach. But in the modern times he has provided certain insights which are very valuable in understanding the possible meanings of Vedic symbolism. Instead of relying much on the root definitions of key Vedic terms, he tried to understand their meaning at a higher or spiritual level, or how they express symbolically the divinely inspired wisdom of the Vedic seers. Above all, he offered a perspective as well as a direction for understanding the meaning of Vedic symbolism. He is also the first one to see and appreciate the continuity and integral unity of Hindu tradition of which the Veda is the foundational beginning. According to him, in understanding the meaning of the Veda subsequent Hindu tradition is of much help and value. Likewise a proper grasp of the meaning of the Veda will provide a perspective in understanding the later Hindu tradition. On the other hand, attempts to understand the Veda by itself or in isolation of tradition, and likewise to understand the tradition independently of the Veda will not be meaningful and fruitful. Also thereby the real significance of both may be lost. Nevertheless, because of his excessive emphasis on psychological or rather mystical approach to the Veda his interpretation of it tended to be one sided. His approach may not therefore be of much help in understanding the meaning of most of the Vedic hymns.

The other Indian scholars who have worked on the Veda have either accepted *in toto* the Western interpretation of it, and followed the methods developed by them, or generally interested themselves in some highly scholastic or technical problems which are of interest mainly to the students of Sanskrit language and literature. In either case they have not concerned themselves with the problem of comprehending the general philosophy or the basic vision of the Veda. As the Vedic studies are mainly carried out in the departments of Sanskrit language and literature in the Indian universities which have little or no interest in grappling with the problem of general thought or philosophy of the Veda, and as there are no separate schools to study and interpret the Veda, the Vedic studies have received very scant attention from the Indian academic community in modern times.

In modern times, the work done on the Veda in the West is more thoroughgoing and sustained than what has been done in India. But in general the Western scholars in pursuing their studies on the Veda are not able to rise above or free themselves from the presuppositions which are basic and peculiar to their own tradition. One such presupposition is that the Veda as the earliest known literature of mankind reflects primitive man's problems and aspirations, as well as the basic structure of his thought. And also as reflecting primitive man's understanding of himself and of the world, the Veda when properly interpreted will be immensely helpful in knowing the workings of primitive mind, especially in the realm of religion. Thus their concern for the Veda is primarily for its historical importance and value. Also they tried to find out in it a direct literary evidence or rather confirmation of some of the pet theories of modern man about the origin and development of religious beliefs and philosophic speculation. The presence of philosophical insights of a higher order in the Veda, which they have recognised, are however, according to them an exception in a literature which is otherwise primitive.

In general the Western scholars have failed to see any continuity and unity between the Veda and highly evolved later Hindu tradition, and hence tried to understand and interpret the Veda in isolation of the tradition. They viewed the Veda by itself. To study and interpret the Veda independently of tradition means that the Hindu tradition developed subsequent to the Saṁhitās, which is a continuous and living one, has not much to do with the Saṁhitās either in thought content or in general direction. This line of thinking has led some to think in terms of borrowing to explain the supposed gap between the Veda and the later Hindu tradition. Although the Indian thinkers in general have not committed this error, yet they have not tried to explain how the Upaniṣads and the tradition later to them are a continuation of Vedic thought and vision.

Now with regard to the general meaning of the Saṁhitās we find two broad views. According to one, the Vedic deities are but a deification of the natural forces or phenomena done by the poetic imagination of the Vedic seers. Therefore, the various Vedic deities when stripped off of their divine attributes poetically superimposed on them can be identified as standing for the different aspects of nature. This has been the general conclusion about the meaning of the Saṁhitās according to one view both in the past and in the present. This naturalistic interpretation of the Vedic thought also fits in well with the modern theories about the origin of religious beliefs and concepts.

The other view aims at giving a wholly mystical or spiritual meaning to the Vedic deities. The spiritual or *ādhyātmika* interpretation which was meant originally to seeing the divine within a particular realm of human experience, that is within the reality of man, which is equally revealed in the reality other than that of man and is equally mystical and spiritually fulfilling is now reduced to mean seeing the Divine solely within the inner being of man. This as stated earlier is due to the antagonism developed between the Veda and the Vedānta, and the general preference or bias of later Hinduism for the Upaniṣadic vision of reality which it has come to regard as the highest possible attainment of man's spirituality. Thus as the Divine life has been taken to mean the spiritual unfoldment of man, attempts have been made constantly in later Hindu tradition to interpret every significant experience of man spiritually or from the *ādhyātmika* standpoint, so as to make it more meaningful or to give a higher value to it. The meaning of Divine is thus reduced to inner spiritual life of man. Consequently, every significant experience of man is sought to be reduced to spiritual level, or is interpreted spiritually to have any higher significance and value for man, or else is ignored. Hence the attempts at explaining the Vedic thought in terms of inner or spiritual reality of man.

Thus in both the schools of interpretation those Vedic hymns and the epithets of the deities which are not favourable to either type of interpretation are either conveniently overlooked, or are distorted to mean and support the respective interpretations. While the naturalistic interpreters have laid exclusive emphasis on the phenomenal description of the deities, the mystical interpreters have completely ignored the phenomenal character of the deities; whereas in the Saṁhitās no deity is described exclusively in terms of either divine or phenomenal attributes or qualities. Every Vedic deity is an abode or centre equally of both the types of attributes. We do not find a hymn concerning a deity in which it is described either exclusively in terms of its phenomenal character or in terms of its divine nature. Both the aspects or natures are intrinsic to the nature of a deity, and are hence integrally related in the nature of a deity. By ignoring, therefore, either of the two aspects or natures of a deity we will not be able to comprehend the true nature and meaning of a deity, as well as the true significance of Vedic revelation. Every deity is both phenomenal and divine, and the divine nature of a deity reveals itself in and through the phenomenal manifestations of a deity. The Divine is not revealed to the seers of the Veda independently of its manifestation in phenomenal reality. No deity is purely phenomenal or exclusively divine. One more peculiarity of the Vedic Saṁhitās is the general absence of concern for speculative understanding about the nature of the Divine in itself, or in its abstract nature. The Divine in itself, is an abstraction arrived at on the basis of the Divine experienced in and through its varied manifestations. And in all the contexts in which the nature of the Divine in itself is speculated upon, it tended towards scepticism. This is generally the tone of speculative hymns present in the Saṁhitās; whereas when the Divine is addressed and prayed in the form of various deities, either individually or collectively, utmost reverence and devotion are shown, and the felt certainty of the Divine is never doubted. Such descriptions of the divine are vivid, spontaneous and stirring, and their tone is highly devotional, and the felt certainty of the poet is fully reflected in the hymns. How to explain this, as well as the double nature of a deity? To explain these satisfactorily and adequately, keeping in view at the same time the general spirit of the Veda, as well as that of Hindu tradition, we have to adopt a philosophical position distinct from the above two positions with regard to the meaning of the Veda, and accordingly develop a method of interpretation. Here we have to ponder over a basic problem. How is the divine revealed to the Vedic seers, or what is the mode of its revelation to them? Is it revealed to them as it is in itself, or in its abstract nature directly, as if in a vacuum, so that they arrived at the notion of the Divine independently of their experiences either of their own reality or that of the world? Or is it known to them as it reveals itself in and through its varied forms of self-manifestation or self-expression? Is it the case that man abstracts the nature of the Divine from what it is revealed to him in and through his lived experiences, and thus forms a general and abstract concept of the Divine? The mode of divine revelation determines the nature of the Divine, or the manner in which man apprehends the Divine, or the mode of its revelation to him determines his understanding of the nature of the Divine. Now, the basic approach of the Veda in this regard, as of Hindu tradition in general, which is wonderfully expressed in the tenth chapter (*Vibhūti Yoga*) of the *Bhagavad-Gītā*, is to know the divine through its presence in nature of which man is a self-conscious expression. And accordingly the various phenomena of nature are seen as varied forms of self-manifestation or expression of the Divine. Thus revelation of the Divine is not limited to the inner reality of man alone. It reveals itself in and through all that a man experiences at all levels, as all are equally the manifestations of the Divine, though the mode of divine revelation and its meaning to man may vary from realm to realm. On the other hand, those who talk of the Divine in itself, which is more a matter of speculative understanding or intellectual abstraction than of direct seeing, do not see its presence anywhere. It is like seeing humanity without man.

It is thus each Vedic deity, as a form of self-expression of the Divine, has a twofold nature. That which is peculiar to each deity, and in terms of which its individual identity is known and is seen as distinct from other deities; and that which it has in common with all other deities. In the Saṁhitās, the divine qualities are attributed commonly to all the deities, while the phenomenal attributes which distinguish a deity from other deities, are peculiar to each deity. The phenomenal attributes of a deity give it its individual identity, while the divine attributes, which are common to all of deities, tend to negate their individuality. In other words, in terms of its divine attributes, the individual identity of each deity tends to merge itself in that of other deities. Hence the Vedic concept of Viśvadeva, according to which a deity is conceived as being one with all other deities. In the Saṁhitās, as well as in the Brāhmaṇas, almost all the deities are identified with all other deities, and to each deity the attributes proper to the Divine are attributed. Now, the identification of each individual deity with all other deities is meaningful and justified only when the same divine reality is seen as being manifested in all the deities. Therefore to explain satisfactorily the significance of the twofold nature of a deity and the identification of each deity with all other deities, we have to adopt the position that the deities in their phenomenal aspect represent and reveal the different forms of self-manifestation of the Divine. And as in all the forms of its self-manifestation the nature of the Divine is revealed, all the deities, in so far as they reveal the presence of the Divine within themselves, share in common the attributes of the Divine. As each form of self-expression of the divine is distinct from its other forms, a deity representing a particular form of expression, is distinct in its phenomenal character from other deities. Thus while there is difference in forms of self-expression, what is expressed or revealed through them all is same. Therefore, a deity as a revelation of the Divine, as well as on form of its self-expression, is known as the abode of both the natures. In other words, a deity as a self-expression of the Divine reveals the nature of the Divine, as well as those qualities that are peculiar to an individual expression of the Divine. Now, since the double nature of a deity, as well as other problems raised here, cannot be explained adequately either in terms of naturalistic interpretation in which the divine nature of the deities is completely overlooked, or is explained away, or in terms of spiritual or mystical interpretation in which the phenomenal character of the deities is not taken into serious consideration, they are to be rejected. Moreover, according to these interpretations the divine reality remains a mere idea or notion having no basis or support in human experience.

The mode of divine revelation to the Vedic seers also helps us in understanding the nature and meaning of the Divine as presented in the hymns of the Veda. The Vedic seers do not talk in terms of mystical experience in which they are transported away from nature to commune with a reality that is above and beyond what is given to man's experience. The Divine is revealed to them through its presence in nature, or divine revelation is mediated to them through the deities, who as the primary self-manifestations of the Divine dwell in nature, and manifest themselves in and through its varied workings. It is nature in all its phenomena, or the deities that dwell in them that are the immediate sources of divine inspiration to the seers. They often speak of being inspired divinely by the deities, and most of the Vedic hymns are prayers addressed to the deities seeking Divine inspiration as a gift from them. Divine inspiration, the source of Vedic wisdom or hymns is regarded by the seers as a divine gift to them by the deities. It gives birth to devotion and worship in man and fulfils his life supremely, and those who receive it are known as seers and seer-poets. It is in the light of divine inspiration the Vedic seers see the presence of the Divine in Nature, and as Nature is the immediate source of divine inspiration to the seers, it is not devoid of divine presence. The Vedic manner of expressing this vision is to identify each phenomenon of nature as the abode of a deity, or seeing a deity as dwelling within a phenomenon of nature and governing it.

Finally, since the Veda is the fundamental source of Hindu spiritual tradition, which is continuous and living, its interpretation should be consistent with the basic spirit of Hindu tradition which has been expressed more clearly and coherently in the post-Saṁhitā tradition. Here again we have no valid reasons to assume the position that the Veda as the beginning of the Hindu tradition need not necessarily contain within itself what has been developed and formulated more clearly in later Hindu tradition. Some scholars are of the view that as the starting point of the Hindu tradition, the Vedic Saṁhitās contain, if at all, only the rudimentary beginnings of Hindu tradition waiting for development and even fulfilment. Some even think that the later Hindu tradition is a radical departure from the Veda and its vision. According to this line of thinking, there is a gap doctrinally between the Saṁhitās and the later Hindu tradition, which cannot be explained without looking for other sources. Is it then meaningful to think of the *Bhagavad-Gītā* as a development or fulfilment of the Upaniṣads, and the latter as the fulfilment of the Vedic Saṁhitās and Brāhmaṇas? If we admit this then we not only have to compromise with the revealed character of the Veda as traditionally held, but will also have to explain the traditional view that the Upaniṣads belong to the Veda (Śruti) integrally. Moreover, the Upaniṣads themselves proclaim that they continue to represent the same Vedic revelation, though expressed differently. Unless we have strong reasons against the validity of the traditional standpoint in this regard, and whatever reasons that are offered against it are in the final analysis rest on a particular type of interpretation of the Veda, we have to accept the validity of the traditional position. The Veda is, therefore, to be viewed and interpreted in relation to or in confirmity with the total Hindu tradition, as the same vision and spirit permeate the whole of the Hindu tradition of which the Veda is the fountainhead. As the Veda is to be viewed in relation to tradition to understand its meaning, so also the tradition is to be viewed in relation to the Veda to understand its meaning comprehensively. The true meaning and value of both can be obtained by understanding each in relation to the other. On the other hand, by trying to understand them in isolation, or independently of each other, we may not be able to comprehend and appreciate the meaning of either.

A systematic attempt is made in the following pages to understand and interpret coherently the basic vision or the central philosophy of the Vedic seers as presented in the hymns of the *Ṛgveda*. Although the work is based solely on the text of the *Ṛgveda*, the other Vedic literature is consulted in understanding the meaning of the *Ṛgveda*. Among the Vedic Saṁhitās, the *Ṛgveda Saṁhitā* occupies a pre-eminent position, as it reflects fully and comprehensively the basic vision of the Vedic seers. Apart from the fact that most of the Ṛgvedic hymns are incorporated into the other Vedic Saṁhitās, they have not much to add to the thought content of the *Ṛgveda*. To systematise the vision of the Vedic seers is to miss it. The *Ṛgveda Saṁhitā*, as the name suggests, is primarily a collection of prayers and songs of glory addressed to various deities. Almost all the hymns of the *Ṛgveda* are prayers and songs of glory addressed to the Divine as revealed to the Vedic seers in and through the varied forms of its self-manifestation, or the deities. They express the devotion and reverence of the seers to the deities which are inspired in them by the deities themselves. They are a gift from the deities, and are offered back to them in reverence and worship. More significantly the meaning of the Divine is revealed to the Vedic seers in devotion itself. Phenomenologically, devotion is the meaning of Divine. Devotion is Divine, and it makes one bow down spontaneously in reverence to the Divine or the deities, and finds its expression in prayer. And the poetic form of language is best suited to express the heart-felt devotion of man. It is, therefore, not an easy task to systematise and conceptualise the vision of the Vedic seers, or to organise it into a rigid conceptual framework. It may not be desirable also. The meaning of devotion and worship cannot be conveyed adequately through concepts. However, as the hymns also express the nature of the Divine by way of glorifying it, and its meaning to the seers, the attempt to understand systematically the thought content of the *Ṛgveda* is not altogether insignificant. What is, therefore, done in this work is to present, organise and interpret coherently the insights of the Vedic seers regarding the nature of the Divine, and the mode of its revelation to them.

The concept of Divine is central to *Ṛgveda*, and all its hymns are an attempt on the part of the post-seers of the *Ṛgveda* to give expression to the nature and meaning of the Divine as it is revealed to them in and through the varied forms of its self-manifestation. And as the presence of the Divine is experienced in nature, the various phenomena of nature are seen by the seers of the Veda as the dwelling places of the deities, the primary and universal manifestations of the Divine. Nature in all its phenomena is the means of self-manifestation or self-expression of the Divine, as well as the immediate source of its revelation. Since nature is the source of divine revelation to the Vedic seers, the nature of the divine is not described by them in abstract terms. The various deities dwell in nature and reveal themselves in and through its diverse workings. The Divine is not known to them independently of its presence in Nature. Therefore, the nature of the Divine is described by the seers conjointly with the attributes of Nature. Nature as a self-manifestation of the Divine reveals, besides its own qualities, the presence of the Divine to an inspired poet or seer. The Divine is the ultimate source and ground of the phenomenal reality, and the latter is a self-manifestation of the former. Both are, therefore, integrally related, and reveal themselves together.

In the first chapter we tried to present the nature and meaning of the Divine, the common source and ground of all the deities, as described in the hymns of the *Ṛgveda*, addressed to various deities either individually or collectively. The Divine is the inner unity and common essence of all the deities, who as self-manifestations of the Divine, reveal in themselves the nature of the Divine in all its aspects according to their own measure. So the attributes common to all the deities reveal their inner unity, common source and essence, or the nature of the Divine.

In the *Ṛgveda* the divine unity of the deities is clearly asserted while no attempt is made to understand speculatively the nature of the Divine in itself in abstract terms. This is beyond the scope of the *Ṛgveda,* which as a collection of prayers, is intended primarily for worshipping the Divine.

In the second and third chapters the nature and meaning of two individual deities, Agni and Indra, are discussed mainly with a view to elucidating and substantiating the position or thesis maintained in the first chapter. The chapter on Agni is intended to show how Agni as seen by the seers of the *Ṛgveda* or as revealed to them, is both a phenomenal reality and a deity at the same time. It reveals the Divine besides its own phenomenal qualities. Agni the deity, the object of several Agni-hymns of the *Ṛgveda,* is truly divine and at the same time a phenomenon of Nature. He reveals himself in Nature and at the same time reveals the Divine, his supreme Father or the source. In him both are related integrally as essence and manifestation. Therefore, the nature of Agni cannot be conceived without his phenomenal qualities, and at the same time our understanding of him will be incomplete without seeing him as a deity, as a self-manifestation of the Divine. The prayers and worship of the seers are due to him as a deity, and in and through him the Divine is addressed, prayed and worshipped.

The third chapter discusses the nature of Indra, and the object of it is to show how the vision of the Divine of the Vedic seers is more fully expressed in Indra-hymns. He is both a phenomenal reality and a deity, and in him the nature of the Divine is more fully revealed.

The third chapter is devoted to a discussion on the mode of divine revelation to the Vedic seers. The main object of it is to understand the nature and meaning of divine inspiration, the source of Vedic wisdom or hymns. The nature of divine inspiration, its immediate sources, and the manner in which it affects the seers or acts on their creativity and helps them in seeing the divine presence in Nature are some of the problems discussed in it. The nature of the Divine as known to man is determined by the manner of its revelation to man. To the Vedic seers nature in all its aspects is the immediate source of Divine inspiration, or the seers see the presence of the Divine in Nature, which in the language of the Veda is to see the deities as dwelling in Nature and governing it. Nature acts on the finer sensibilities of man, inspires in him the sense of Divine and evokes in him devotion and reverence.

In the fifth chapter, the discussion on the nature of divine inspiration is continued. However, the main purpose of it is to discuss how the creative flow of divine inspiration within man transforms him into a seer or seer-poet and finds its expression through the hymns of the Veda. In the Vedic symbolism, the deity Soma represents divine inspiration and its creative flow within man. It is the supreme or Divine Rasa, or divinely inspired state of man's existence, the source of Vedic hymns. It finds its expression through the hymns of the Veda, and gives birth to devotion and worship in man.

The final chapter is devoted to a discussion of various symbols associated with the nature, meaning and expression of divine inspiration. The Vṛtra myth, which is central to *Ṛgveda* and runs throughout it, and the various components of it are interpreted to show how the recovery or discovery of "cows" (*go* or *dhenu*) and the release of creativity "water" (*āpaḥ*) and the winning of light stand to mean symbolically the fact of Divine inspiration and its spontaneous and creative expression in the form of Vedic hymns.

2

The Nature and Meaning of the Divine

WITH the exception of a few hymns containing deep and even critical reflections of Vedic seers on problems related to ontology and cosmology, the *Ṛgveda Saṁhitā* is primarily a collection of prayers and songs of praise addressed to various deities (*deva* or *devatā*) either individually or collectively. Even the speculative hymns are in intent prayers, and are full of devotion and reverence which are characteristic of Ṛgvedic hymns. However, they are not addressed to deities who can be identified in terms of their phenomenal description. They do not, like other deities, partake of the attributes of Nature, nor do they represent any aspect of it. The general tone of these hymns is one of scepticism, as doubts are often expressed about man's ability to know that which is the ultimate source and ground of all that is, including the deities. On the other hand, the hymns addressed to various deities, either individually or collectively, do not betray any trace of scepticism. They are full of devotion, which is spontaneous, deep and stirring, and reflect fully the faith of the seers in the existence of the deities addressed to in them. Only once a doubt is entertained regarding the existence of Indra, and that too not by the seer of the hymn but by others, and the seer adduces evidence or gives reasons for the existence of Indra. As the presence of the deities is experienced in Nature, or as dwelling in it, their reality is not a matter of speculation, but refers to something that is revealed or experienced.

Some of the Ṛgvedic hymns are addressed to different ritual objects, mostly connected with *yajña*, and they derive their divine significance and value by virtue of their association with *yajña* which is divine. There are a few hymns in which the deities addressed to are certain human emotions and virtues like anger (*manyu*), charity (*dakṣiṇā*) and faith (*śraddhā*). A few of the hymns are addressed to knowledge (*jñānam*) in its abstract nature, and to *vāk*, the divine speech or wisdom. Thus though most of the hymns are addressed to various deities, either individually or collectively, the quality of being divine (*divya*) is not limited to them only. As a quality divine is attributed to some of the human experiences and faculties, and also to various other objects; or as a presence it is experienced within the reality of man also. Likewise, certain experiences and emotions or passions of man, and even certain types of persons are regarded as undivine (*adevam*). This indicates that the presence of the divine is experienced by the Vedic seers not only in Nature but also within the reality of man. Further the various priests associated with the conduct of *yajña* are seen as divine which is due to their association with *yajña*. Ṛbhus, the sons of Śudhanvan, had attained divinity or the status of the deities (*devatvam*) by their wisdom and deeds. The ancient seers (Aṅgīrasas), the first discoverers of divine speech and *yajña*, or who had first received Divine revelation are also divine, and their divinity consists in their knowledge and wisdom. And it is the common aspiration of the Ṛgvedic seers that they also attain divine wisdom and become divine (*devavantam syāma*). Divinely inspired or illumined intellect (*dhī*) is also divine, and it is by means of it the divine is apprehended. The hymns or prayers that are born of such an intellect are also divine, and the seers earnestly pray to the deities to inspire and illumine their hearts and intellect divinely. While the human powers and facilities can be both divine and undivine, the powers of the deities are always divine. Divinely inspired devotion, and the hymns or prayers which express it are also Divine, and above all the inspiration because of which human intellect is able to apprehend the divine is divine. It is a divine gift to man, and the Ṛgvedic prayers are primarily intended to awaken the deities and win their favour and benevolence, or to receive the gift of divine inspiration from them, and one who has received such a gift is a *ṛṣi* (seer) or a *kavi* (seer-poet).

The sceptical attitude of the Vedic seers is generally reflected in those hymns which contain the speculations on the nature of ultimate reality or the divine in itself, and the precise nature of its relation to the phenomenal reality. The knowledge of the Divine in itself cannot be attained even by the deities, as in the order of existence they are later to it (*arvāk devāḥ*).[1] * Being born of the Divine, or as its manifestations, their existence is logically later to that of it, and therefore, they cannot know that which as the source of their existence is prior to their coming into being. The Ṛgvedic seers speak about the beginning when the deities did not exist (*devānām pūrva yuga*).[2] They come into existence in the process of self-manifestation or self-expression of the Divine, and so belong to the realm of manifestation or becoming. Moreover, to know the ultimate source and ground of all that is there is to transcend time, or all that has come into existence in time; and that is something beyond the reach of man. Man's experiences and knowledge are limited to the realm of manifestation or becoming and anything that is not revealed within it cannot be known by him. Therefore, if the Divine is known to man it is known to him through its revelation in Nature, the realm of its manifestation and revelation. On the other hand, if the Divine is not revealed to man either in Nature or within his own reality, then the knowledge of it is denied to him. Speculative knowledge of it, even if it is considered possible, cannot evoke in man devotion and reverence,

---

* In this work the *Ṛgveda Saṁhitā* with the commentary of Sāyaṇācārya published in five volumes by Vaidic Samsodhana Mandal (Vedic Research Institute), Poona, is followed. And in translating the hymns into English the translations of the *Ṛgveda* by Ralph T.H. Griffith, and published by Motilal Banarsidass, Varanasi, and by H.H. Wilson, and published in seven volumes by Cosmos Publications, New Delhi, are consulted. On occasions the translations of Griffith are quoted either partly or fully.

1. 10.129.6.

2. 10.72.2 and 3.

and fulfil his life. To be prayed and worshipped the Divine is to be seen or experienced, and Nature is the immediate source of such an experience to man, or man sees the presence of the Divine in Nature.

According to the vision of the Vedic seers, as presented in the hymns of the *Ṛgveda,* Nature is the immediate source of divine revelation to man, or the Divine is known to man through its revelation in Nature. Nature is, therefore, seen as the abode of the deities who as the primary and universal self-manifestations of the Divine dwell in Nature and reveal themselves in and through its diverse workings. Each deity is accordingly described as dwelling in and presiding over a phenomenon of Nature which reveals it. However, Nature as Nature, or in its phenomenal or physical aspect is not Divine. It acquires Divine significance and value, or is seen as a manifestation of the Divine because of its inherent capacity to reveal the Divine which it does by inspiring or illumining the heart and intellect of man divinely. The attitude of the Ṛgvedic seers to nature is not, therefore, to seek a theological or metaphysical explanation of it. Although such attempts are made in the *Ṛgveda* they are of secondary importance to the seers. The various deities like Indra and Agni are not, therefore, conceived to explain Nature. They are not explanatory or interpretative categories or concepts of Nature, but refer to or describe the Divine as revealed to or as seen by the seers in and through its manifestations in Nature. And a *ṛṣi* is one who can apprehend the hidden presence of the Divine in Nature, as the primary meaning of the term *ṛṣi* is one who sees the object of a hymn, or to whom the object of a hymn is revealed. The seers often claim that they have seen (*paśya*) or known directly (*vedāhametam*) the object of their hymns with the sight or vision that is granted to them by the deities themselves, or due to divine inspiration. And the hymns are an expression in language of the divinely inspired wisdom of the seers. In revealing the Divine as being immanent within itself, Nature does not cease to be in the vision of a seer. It only acquires divine significance, or is divinely transformed. Nature is then seen by the Vedic seers as the abode or centre equally of both phenomenal and divine attributes. As the Divine is known through its revelation in Nature, or as Nature is the immediate source of Divine revelation to the seers, the Divine and the phenomenal are seen by the seers as inherently related, and are, therefore, described together in all the hymns. While the deities in their divine aspect refer to the Divine as it reveals itself in and through nature, in their phenomenal character they represent nature in its various phenomena. Thus a deity which dwells in and presides over a phenomenon of Nature possesses inherently divine and phenomenal attributes which are integral to its nature. We do not, therefore, find a hymn addressed to a deity in which it is described either exclusively in terms of its phenomenal character or in terms of its divine nature. Both the aspects are intrinsic to the nature of a deity, and are hence related integrally in the nature of a deity. While a deity in its phenomenal description represents a phenomenon of Nature, it is divine because of its capacity to reveal the Divine, or to inspire man divinely. While a deity acquires its individuality and is identified in terms of its phenomenal attributes, it tends to lose its individual identity in terms of its divine attributes which belong to all the deities commonly. While the phenomenal attributes of a deity distinguish it from the rest of the deities, the divine attributes which are common to all the deities reveal their inner unity and common source of origin. And no distinction is made among the deities in attributing various divine qualities to them.

The Divine is identified by the seers as that which inspires in man devotion and worship which make him bow down in reverence to the deities. It acts on his creativity, and unfolds to him the inner depths of his own being, or reveals to him the "precious treasure" hidden within himself. It generates within man the sense of holiness and sanctifies his existence. It is the source of all bliss, and man sees in its realisation the ultimate fulfilment of his life. Thus man's awareness of the Divine and the birth in him of devotion and reverence go together. They are experienced simultaneously, and refer to the same experience. As man's spontaneous response to his awareness of the Divine, either in Nature or within his own reality, devotion expresses in human terms the meaning of Divine. We can thus understand the tendency of the seers to identify divine with devotion or reverence. Reverence (*namaḥ*) or bowing down to the Divine or the deities is described in the *Ṛgveda* as divine and all comprehensive; it holds within itself all the deities and rules over them.[3] Similarly, devotion (Brahma) which is experienced inwardly, or the state of being divinely inspired is seen as the matrix of the deities who are known because of it, and are sustained by it as well.[4] They also grow or increase in terms of it or along with it. Devotion is divine, and anything that inspires it in man is divine. To experience Divine is the same as to experience devotion within.

As nature is the immediate source of inspiration to man of devotion and reverence, or as man experiences them in relation to Nature, it is seen as a manifestation of the Divine and its glory, or as an abode of the deities. Nature is divine or the deities dwell in it as it is the source of man's awareness of the Divine, or because of its capacity to awaken in man the sense of divine. How otherwise can it inspire man divinely, and evoke in him devotion and reverence? The Divine in Nature acts on the Divine within man, and awakens him to the presence of the

3. 6.51.8.

4. The term *brahma* is used in several contexts of its usage in the *Ṛgveda* to mean devotion; and that seems to be its primary meaning. In this sense *brahma* means that which grows or increases and devotion is also described in the *Ṛgveda* as growing or increasing, within the hearts of seers. However, it is also used to mean prayer or hymn, as prayers or hymns express devotion. In the *Ṛgveda* the same word is used to indicate a thing and its manifestation, as for instance, the term *manīṣā* is used to mean both wisdom and its expression or hymn, and the word *mati* to mean both mind or understanding and its creation or hymns.

Divine. This explains the Vedic vision of nature as a self-manifestation of the Divine, or seeing it as the abode of the deities. Nevertheless, the peculiar manner in which different phenomena of Nature act on man's creativity and affect his finer sensibilities are not the same. Although Nature is Divine, as every phenomenon of it is capable of inspiring in man the sense of divine, yet the nature of the Divine so revealed differs from phenomenon to phenomenon depending upon the way in which each phenomenon of nature acts on man or inspires him. The way lightning acts on man's creativity is distinct from the way in which the phenomenon of dawn inspires him. Thus depending upon the way in which each phenomenon of Nature acts on man or inspires him the different facets of the divine glory are revealed to him. The various epithets employed in the *Ṛgveda* to describe the Divine convey the different facets of its glory and splendour as revealed to the seers. And to the extent the Divine is experienced as a quality or presence either in Nature or within man, its revelation allows degrees. In certain phenomena of Nature, or in certain persons the presence of the Divine is experienced more clearly and fully. Their capacity to reveal the Divine is more striking. This is indicated by describing certain deities as more or most divine (*devatama* or *devattama*). Although the entire Nature is divine, yet the different phenomena of Nature differ in their capacity to reveal the Divine.

In the *Ṛgveda* most of the deities are identified with all other deities, and all the deities are often identified with a particular individual deity. Some of the deities, especially Agni, Indra, Brahmaṇaspati and Soma, are viewed as comprehending all other deities within themselves. For instance, Agni is identified with all other deities, or all the deities abide in him.

All the deities are in Agni, and he is in all. The same vision is expressed differently when the deities like Agni, Indra and Soma are addressed as *viśvadevaḥ*. The epithet *viśvadeva* means that the deity who is so addressed is the soul or essence of all the deities. He is one with all the deities, or he is all the deities. Agni is all the deities; he encompasses or has become all the deities (*paribhū*). The epithet *viśvadeva* in relation to a deity can be meaningful only at the divine level, as each deity in its phenomenal aspect is distinct from all other deities. Phenomenally each deity has its own individuality which cannot be merged in that of another. For instance, Agni as manifesting himself in such natural phenomena as fire and lightning cannot be identical with Indra who manifests himself as power in all the phenomena of nature. The Ṛgvedic description of each deity in its phenomenal aspect is lucid, though expressed in poetic language, and the distinction among the different phenomena of Nature, which the various deities represent, is never blurred and confused. Agni as the principle of heat in all the forms of its manifestation has its own characteristics, and hence it cannot be identified with other deities who manifest themselves in and through other phenomena of Nature and have their own characteristics. This is true about all the deities in so far as their phenomenal natures are concerned. They represent different phenomena of Nature which do not allow identification with each other. But the Divine which is seen as dwelling within them all, or as manifesting itself in and through them all is recognised as one, though the mode and meaning of its revelation differ from deity to deity.

The Ṛgvedic seers while describing the Divine as revealed through Nature usually employ symbols and metaphors, but they have not made any distinction among the deities when they describe them in their divine aspect. All the divine attributes are attributed commonly to all the deities, or the deities possess in common all the divine attributes. However, the epithet *viśvadeva* is not applied to all the deities, and those to whom it is applied are also described as more or most divine. The reason for this may be the following. Agni, in his phenomenal aspect as the principle of heat is all-pervasive, and is present inherently in almost all the phenomena of Nature.

He is present within the Sun, in the Lightning, in the Waters, in the Plants and in all living beings, including man. Likewise, Indra as the phenomenon of power is also present inherently in varying degrees in all things. They do not belong exclusively to any one phenomenon of Nature. Moreover, there is no phenomenon of Nature which can be identified exclusively in terms of any one single characteristic. No single phenomenon of Nature possesses certain qualities exclusively. Several qualities are found together in the same phenomenon of Nature. Nevertheless, a particular quality is to be found predominantly in a phenomenon of Nature, and in terms of such predominance a phenomenon is identified. In this sense Agni is Sūrya (the Sun) or Sūrya is Agni as heat and light are inherent in both. Both are expressions of the same reality. However, Fire as Fire is distinct from the Sun as Sun, though in both of them heat and light find their manifestation. Thus heat and light are more pervasive, and are present in almost all the phenomena of Nature, and thus comprehend them within themselves.

Although all the deities are divine, and manifest within themselves the divineness (*devatvam*), no individual deity is identified with the Divine in itself. All the deities are divine as they are the self-manifestations of the Divine which is more than and beyond all the deities. This idea which is clearly expressed in the Puruṣa-Sūkta wherein it is stated that one-fourth of the Divine being has become all this, including the deities, while three-fourths of His being remain in the highest, is present throughout the *Ṛgveda* though not stated explicitly and clearly as in the Puruṣa-Sūkta. A particular individual deity is described as more or most divine according to its comprehensive nature, or depending upon the pervasive character of the natural phenomenon it represents. Thus though some of the deities like Agni, Indra and Soma are addressed as most divine among the deities (*deveṣu devatama*), they are not regarded and addressed as the Divine in itself. The expression "most divine" in the general context of the *Ṛgveda* does not in any sense mean the supremacy of a deity over other deities. The various epithets indicating the supremacy and lordly character of a deity such as lord (Īśa, Rāja and Prabhu), upholder (*dhārtā* or *vidhārtā*) and creator (*vedhase* or *vidhātā*), etc. and which may appear to indicate that the deity so addressed is supreme over all other deities, are, however, attributed to almost all the deities. The various attributes which can belong properly to the Divine are attributed to all the deities commonly, as being its self-manifestations they partake of its nature in their own way and measure.

Now, the problems related to the existence and nature of the Divine in itself are mainly speculative. When the Divine is seen or experienced through its presence either in Nature or within the reality of man, the problem arises regarding the existence and nature of that which reveals itself in and through nature. It is a problem which man becomes aware of while reflecting upon his experiences in which he encounters the Divine. If the Divine is experienced through its revelation in Nature then it is a logical necessity that guides man to think in terms of the Divine as such or in itself. How can man understand divine revelation without assuming an independent existence to that which reveals itself through Nature? However, direct awareness of the Divine, according to the seers of the *Ṛgveda*, is not possible for man, as in itself the Divine is not an object of man's experience. The Divine in itself, or in its unmanifested state of existence is logically prior to all its manifestations, including the deities and man. So man who belongs to the realm of manifestation can know the Divine only through its manifestations, but not in itself. And whether the Divine in itself can remain unaffected by all its manifestations, so that it in itself can be known independently of its manifestations is purely a speculative problem with which the Vedic seers are not generally concerned. Even if such a possibility is admitted, man has to transcend the world of manifestation to apprehend it. The Ṛgvedic seers seldom indulge themselves in such speculative problems. The Divine is apprehended directly by them through its revealtion in nature, and at the same time it is not known or experienced independently of nature. The various deities, as the primary and universal manifestations of the Divine, are, therefore, seen as dwelling within or representing the diverse phenomena of Nature. This is a poetic way of expressing the truth that Nature in all its aspects is a creative self-manifestation of the Divine. Thus the Ṛgvedic hymns are addressed neither to the Divine in itself nor to Nature as Nature or in its phenomenal aspect. They are addressed to the Divine that reveals itself in and through the diverse phenomena of Nature. Accordingly, Nature is seen and worshipped as the dwelling place of the deities. Nevertheless, the Divine is recognised as the inner unity of all the deities, or as what is common to them all. The general tone of the hymns in which the nature of the Divine in itself is reflected upon is distinct from the one that is reflected in the hymns addressed to various deities either individually or collectively. The attitude of the seers generally reflected in the speculative hymns is also distinct from that which is reflected in the hymns addressed to the deities. Although the attitudes of reverence and worship are reflected commonly in all the hymns, the personal attachment to the deities and faith in their existence reflected in all the hymns addressed to them are not to be found in the speculative hymns. The latter shows an intellectual approach and all that is peculiar to it; whereas the other type of hymns, as prayers addressed to various deities, express spontaneously divinely inspired devotion of the seers to the deities.

As various manifestations of the same divine reality, the deities reveal within themselves all the qualities of the Divine; these are what they possess in common. But the way in which each individual deity reveals the nature of the Divine is distinct. On the other hand, the attributes peculiar to a deity belong to a phenomenon of Nature, which it represents, or through which it is revealed. While the attributes commonly attributed to all the deities are divine and have no representation in Nature, the attributes which distinguish each deity from the rest are phenomenal in nature, and belong to Nature. And in terms of the phenomenal attributes each deity gains its individual identity, and is distinguished from the rest of the deities. Thus every deity possesses inherently two types of attributes; one divine and the other phenomenal. The divine attributes which each deity has in common with all the deities, and on the basis of which each deity can be identified with all other deities, are applied to all the deities. They constitute the inner unity of the deities, and also reveal their common source and substance. On the other hand, the phenomenal attributes in terms of which each deity gains its individual identity, and is distinguished from the rest of the deities are peculiar to each deity.

Now it may be pointed out that if the same divine reality is recognised as manifesting itself in and through all the deities, why such an awareness is not expressed explicitly in the *Ṛgveda*? Why the oneness of the Divine, or the divine unity of the deities is not adequately expressed in the *Ṛgveda* if the seers are clearly aware of it? To understand this problem in the context of the *Ṛgveda* we have to consider a more basic problem. What is the basis or evidence for seeing in Nature the presence of the Divine, or for regarding nature as a manifestation of the Divine? Or what is the mode of divine revelation to the Vedic seers? Is it the case that the seers have first experienced the Divine through its presence in Nature and then arrived at the notion of the Divine, or is it the other way round, namely that they have arrived at the notion of the Divine either intuitively or through a process of rational understanding, and then tried to work out the process by which the Divine has become all? Do we first know the Divine independently of its manifestation in Nature, and then recognise its presence in Nature? How is the Divine known to the Vedic seers, or what is the mode of its revelation to them? Although direct evidence in this regard is scant in the *Ṛgveda*, still we can arrive at a significant understanding of the problem on the basis of the indirect evidence available, and also in the light of the general approach of the *Ṛgveda* to this problem. As this problem is discussed independently and comprehensively in another chapter,[5] we present it here in brief, and that too in a general way to the extent it is relevant in understanding the nature of the Divine. At the outset we have to state that the problem is not treated as an epistemological one, for the Veda does not consist of knowledge acquired through ordinary means of knowledge. It speaks of revealed or inspired knowledge or wisdom in attaining which human endeavour is almost insignificant. The human intellect (*dhī*) which plays an important role in attaining such knowledge, or rather it is the seat of it, is not, however, the ordinary or uninspired intellect. Only when it is divinely inspired or illumined it is able to apprehend the Divine. Further, as the object of Vedic knowledge is not Nature in its empirical or phenomenal aspect, it is beyond the range of ordinary understanding of man. Thus our discussion precludes usual epistemological questions which are otherwise relevant in any discussion of this type. Therefore, instead of raising problems normally connected with an epistomological enquiry, we try to understand, for the sake of clear comprehension of the nature of the Divine, the mode of its revelation to the Vedic seers. An epistemological enquiry into the Vedic means of knowledge of the Divine is strictly a requirement for a systematic and intellectual understanding of the Veda, and will have no importance to those to whom the Divine is something that is experienced or revealed.

According to the seers of the *Ṛgveda,* Nature is a dwelling place of the Divine or the deities, and is, therefore, a source of its revelation. It reveals the Divine besides its empirically observable qualities. All the deities are, therefore, described in terms of phenomenal and divine attributes. The phenomenal nature of a deity is described more elaborately and vividly

5. See chapter IV.

though in a poetic language. A deity can, therefore, be easily identified as representing a particular phenomenon of Nature. But the epithets used to describe a deity do not always refer to its phenomenal aspect only. If what is represented by the various deities are simply the different phenomena of Nature, the various divine qualities attributed to them, which have no representation in observable Nature, will remain unexplained. And at the same time the deities are not known to exist independently of Nature, as they are revealed in and through it. In every hymn addressed to a deity both the types of attributes are applied together to a deity, and refer to the same reality. Each deity is a centre of both types of attributes. Now we cannot meaningfully reduce or explain one type of attributes in terms of the other. Though the phenomenal side of a deity is well presented in the hymns, the divine nature of it is not lost sight of. Therefore, by taking note of one aspect of a deity, to the neglect of the other, the true nature of a deity eludes us for ever. To comprehend the nature of a deity truly and fully we have, therefore, to take into consideration both types of attributes. How then to understand the nature of a deity in terms of both the types of attributes? Can a deity be both phenomenal and divine at the same time? To explain these problems satisfactorily and adequately, and also in consistence with the spirit of the Veda, we have to assume that the Vedic seers have experienced the presence of the Divine in Nature, or Nature is the immediate source of divine revelation to them. Accordingly, nature is viewed by them as a vehicle of self-expression of the Divine, its dwelling place or abode (*dhāma*), as well as the source of its revelation. To them the Divine is not simply an idea but a living presence that is experienced in Nature. Therefore, the hymns which are essentially prayers and praises addressed to various deities, and express the devotion of the seers, are in intention addressed to the Divine that is revealed in and through Nature. Nature becomes divine or gets divinely transformed to those who can see in it the presence of the Divine. Thus in the light of the *Ṛgveda* we can identify the Divine as that capacity or presence in Nature which inspires or illumines human heart and intellect divinely, and evokes in man devotion and reverence. Anything that is a source of divine inspiration is seen as a manifestation of the Divine, and is worshipped by the seers. And as Nature is the immediate source of divine inspiration to the seers, it is viewed as a manifestation of the Divine, or as the abode of the deities. To be able to inspire man divinely Nature must be Divine. Thus the Divine is known to man when it acts on him, and inspires or illumines his various faculties. The different etymological definitions of the term *deva* include the capacity to inspire (*dīpana*) and to illumine (*dyotana*). As Nature has the power or capacity to inspire in man the sense of divine, it is seen as Divine, and its diverse phenomena are identified with various deities, who as the varied self-manifestations of the Divine dwell within Nature and reveal themselves in and through its workings.

In the *Ṛgveda* the inner unity of the deities is clearly maintained while the Divine in itself, which is not known to man independently of its manifestations, is not spoken of. It is only indicated. What is directly revealed to man are the various deities, and the Divine is revealed through them as their essence and inner unity. It is their common source and ground (*nidānam*), and presides or rules over all the deities (*adhyakṣa*).[6] The inner unity of the deities is asserted by stating that the great wisdom or glory of the deities is one (*mahān asuratvam*).[7] "That wisdom which is present in all the deities is one" (*tat devānām samavartata asu ekaḥ*).[8] While, according to *Nighaṇṭu* (compilation of Vedic synonyms), the term *asu* is a synonym of wisdom (*prajñā*), Sāyaṇa explains it to mean divine splendour or glory (*aiśvaryam*). The divine splendour (*dīdhiti*) manifests or reveals itself among all the deities.[9] The supreme Divine Reality or lord of all the deities,

6. 10.114.2; 10.129.7.
7. 3.55.1, and Sāyaṇa's commentary thereon.
8. 10.121.7.
9. 1.186.11.

which is within and yet beyond all the deities, is one (*deveṣu adhidevaḥ ekaḥ āsīt*).[10] The awareness of the transcendental unity of the deities is expressed when the seers enquire about the matrix of all the deities, which at the same time transcends them, and by abiding in which all the deities witness all (*kimsvit garbham paraḥ devebhiḥ yatra devāḥ sama paśyanti viśve*).[11] "He is the creator, lord and destiny of all, and he knows the abodes of all the deities."[12] He who is the definition of all the deities is One (*yaḥ devānām nāmadhā ekaḥ*).[13] The Divine Reality is one; and the wise and the poet-seers fashion or conceive it severally in terms of their speech or praises (*suparṇam viprāḥ kavayaḥ ekam san tam bahudhā kalpayanti*).[14] What is One the wise speak of differently (*ekam sat viprāḥ bahudhā vadanti*).[15] All the deities are born of the One who is in the highest realm (*parama vyoman*). They are prayed to attend and accept the worship of the seers with one awareness (*sacetasā*) or with one mind (*samanasā*) and with one intention or accord (*sajośasā*). Besides these different direct expressions, the transcendental unity of the deities is maintained throughout the *Ṛgveda* by commonly attributing to them all the divine attributes. This is appropriate and meaningful only when one and the same reality is seen as manifesting itself in and through the deities.

The inner unity of the deities is indicated by relating them all to *ṛta* and *satya*. Born of *ṛta* and *satya* the deities manifest them within themselves. They are also the means of extension and revelation of *ṛta* and *satya*. While the deities in their phenomenal aspect are known to all, as they manifest themselves in and

10. 10.121.8.
11. 10.82.5.
12. 10.82.3.
13. 10.82.3. Generally, in Sanskrit language things are named according to their essential qualities, and, therefore, giving a name to a thing is also to define it.
14. 10.114.5.
15. 1.164.46.

through the phenomena of Nature, their real or divine nature, which is hidden to our empirical understanding, proceeds from the highest. As to be born (*janma*) means to become manifest, or to come within the range of human perception, the birth of the deities from the highest means self-manifestation of the Divine in and through them. Therefore, to know the deities in their hidden or higher natures is to know them as the manifestations of the Highest or the Divine. And to be able to apprehend the hidden nature of the deities is to recognise at the same time their inner divine unity. Thus the deities have two births. As varied self-manifestations of the Divine they are born of the Highest, and in manifesting themselves within Nature they are born again. To see a deity, therefore, as a deification of a phenomenon of Nature, or as simply representing it is not to know it truly and completely. To know the deities truly and completely they are to be known as manifestations of the Divine. The Divine and the phenomenal, or the higher and the lower, or the immortal and the mortal are integrally united as essence and manifestation; and one who sees the unity of both is a *r̥ṣi*. Or to see the two as integrally related requires the wisdom of a *r̥ṣi*. We only see the one, the phenomenal reality, and fail to see the other, the Divine reality, and also think that the divine is different from and beyond the phenomenal reality; whereas a seer is one who sees them as integrally united or in their inseparable unity. "He who knows the Father in the highest as the inferior associated with the superior, and the superior associated with the inferior, is as it were a seer."[16]

The highest or the Divine reality, which is indicated by such terms as "That", "the Highest", "the One", "Imperishable" and the "Supreme Father" is often described as great light (*mahān jyoti*), and the deities are those who shine with it, and reveal it to man. The Highest or the Divine is that which shines through the deities (*devebhyo ātapati*).[17] The supreme form of the Divine

16. 1.164.18.

17. Puruṣa-Sūkta according to *Kr̥ṣṇa Yajurveda* and Sāyaṇa's commentary thereon.

as revealed to man is *ṛta*, which being co-extensive with the Divine comprehends all, including the deities, within itself. A deity is also comprehensive, but it holds together only a phenomenon of Nature, and is revealed within it, whereas *ṛta* is all comprehensive and holds together all that is, including the deities. It is the dynamic side of the Divine, within and by which all that is there, including the deities, is held together and sustained. The term *ṛta* stands to mean, according to the context of its usage, truth, the principle of Cosmic order, Sacrifice and also Water. However, in most of the context of the *Ṛgveda*, it is employed to mean the dynamic Divine Principle pervading and sustaining all. It holds everything together (*dhārayanti*). "All that is there shine with *ṛta* or manifest it (*ṛtana viśvam bhuvanam virājadha*)."[18] Moral order is comprehended within the Cosmic order, that is *ṛta*. *Ṛta* which is inherently present within all creation is revealed within man as moral order. It unites all by holding together all, and finds its expression in various ways; and moral order is one such expression. At the same time it is something more than universal order as it becomes clear in our discussion. *Ṛta* as *satya* is the same as the Divine though viewed in its dynamic or creative aspect. All the deities are born of *ṛta* (*ṛtajāta* or *ṛtaprajāta*), and are sustained by it. They grow or increase in it, and also because of it. In turn each individual deity in its own individual manner manifests and upholds *ṛta*. Thus it is a mutual process in which the deities are sustained by *ṛta*, and in their turn the deities uphold and extend *ṛta*. However, *ṛta* is described as self-sustaining, and extends itself by itself by means of manifesting itself through the deities. *Ṛta* and *satya* are not governed and controlled by any; they are self-governed, and at the same time everything is governed by them. In other words, by means of the same *ṛta* which manifests itself within the deities each deity is able to sustain the Cosmic order. It is the indwelling principle of all the deities, as well as their supreme form (*śreṣṭham vapu*).[19] It is revealed

18. 5.63.7.

19. 5.62.1; see also 4.7.7 (*ṛtasya dhāman raṇayanta devāḥ*).

to man as the law that sustains and governs the deities. "It is the law of the deities as man knows it."[20] All the deities are great, and are able to unite and sustain different phenomena of Nature because of *ṛta* that dwells within them. They all reveal it, and extend it to all the regions of the world. They are its protectors, and help in its increase or extension. They all possess it and love it. They are the charioteers of *ṛta*, or the means of its expression and extension. Even Varuṇa, who judges man in terms of their good and evil deeds, is only an embodied form of *ṛta* (*ṛtapeśa*).[21]

Ṛta is also the source of prayer. Prayer is born out of *ṛta*.[22] It is only when human intellect or heart is informed and illumined by the light of *ṛta* it can give birth to prayer. When the wisdom of man fully participates in *ṛta*, or is informed by its light, it becomes effective in destroying the sins of man. This aspect of *ṛta* is discussed later.

Ṛta as truth (*satya*) is sacred as well as sanctifying. Man becomes holy, or his existence is sanctified by possessing *ṛta*. The deities are holy because they possess *ṛta*. It constitutes the auspiciousness (*bhadra*) of the deities which they bestow on man. By virtue of being born of *ṛta* and dwelling in it, the deities are often identified with it. For instance, Agni is *ṛta*, Soma is *ṛta*. However, as being common to all the deities, *ṛta* is not identical with any one individual deity. It is something more than and beyond all the deities though it is inherent within them all. It is inherent within the whole creation as that which binds, upholds, regulates and governs it. It contains all within itself, and is not contained by anything. The deities only manifest it, and help in its extension. *Ṛta*'s infinite splendour finds its expression through the diverse functions of the deities, and thus reveals itself in varied forms. For instance, though *ṛta* as expressed in and through the deity Soma, who is regarded as

20. 10.35.8. (*bhajanta viśve devatvam nāma ṛtam*); see also 1.68.2.

21. 5.66.1.

22. 7.36.1; 10.139.2.

the tongue of *ṛta*, is the same as that which is expressed in and through the deity Agni, yet the mode of its expression is distinct in both.

Ṛta being the source and ground of all the deities is the truth of all the deities. It is by being the self-manifestations of *ṛta*, the deities are true and divine. And as revealed within man *ṛta* is moral order or truthfulness, and in being truthful man also in his own way upholds and spreads it. He is also a source of its manifestation and revelation. Now, in being related to *ṛta* the deities are related to truth. In the substantive sense of the term or in itself *ṛta* is the same as the divine (*ṛtam bṛhat*), and in several contexts of their usage in the *Ṛgveda* the terms *ṛta* and *satya* are used synonymously. *Ṛta* is *satya*; and *satya* is *ṛta*. They are also used adjectively to mean what is righteous and truthful. Adjectively *satya* means the opposite of what is false, as when we say a statement is true. *Satya* in this sense is a quality of human or divine actions, intentions and speech. It is also used to mean the reality of a thing, as for instance, the various deeds of the deities are true or real. But when used substantively the term, *satya* stands for what is ultimately and unconditionally true or real. In this ontological sense of the term *satya* is used in relation to the deities, and often the deities are identified with truth. In relation to the deities like Agni, Indra and Soma the term *satya* is used substantively. They are addressed as truth, or are identified with it. Nevertheless, identification of truth with any of the deities is not done. Every deity is identified with truth, but truth is not identified with any deity. They only manifest and reveal truth being born of it.

Truth is the nature of the deities which they reveal within themselves (*satyadharmāṇaḥ*).[23] It sustains them by being their reality or substance. This idea is conveyed by addressing the deities as *satyārādhaḥ* or those whose substance or wealth is truth. Truth is their strength, and they are known by it (*satyaśrutāḥ*). It is their glory (*mahimā*). They are known and characterised by

23. 5.51.2; see also 1.12.7; 10.121.9; 10.139.3.

satya as it is inherent within them all. They are addressed as *satyasya patayaḥ*, literally protectors of truth, which, however, can be interpreted to mean, according to Sāyaṇa, as those having truth as their character or nature (*śīla*).[24] The epithet *satyayoni* (born of truth) which is applied to Indra expresses the relation between deities and truth. The deities are the progeny of *satya*, or *satya* is their matrix, the poetic way of saying that the deities derive their existence from truth. The deities are addressed as the children of truth (*satyasya sūnum*). Being the self-manifestations of the Divine, the deities embody truth, and reveal it to man.

As self-manifestations of the Divine the deities are objects of man's devotion and worship. They are worshippable (*yajñīya* or *yajiṣṭha*), and the supreme form of worshipping them is to bow down to them in reverence. All the prayers and praises addressed to different deities are in reality addressed to the Divine that is revealed through them. The term *yajña* which in its primary sense means worship, or a means of expressing man's devotion to the Divine, however, is employed in most of the contexts of its usage to mean symbolically the creative process involved in the creation, sustenance and fulfilment of the universe. In observing it not only man participates in the cosmic process, but also helps in its extension. In observing it the divine purpose of creation is promoted by man at various levels. *Yajña* is thus primarily a form of Vedic worship of the Divine by which the divine purpose that is involved in creation is extended by man to all the spheres of his life. However, the deities are not its object, as they are not above it. They are also involved in the process of *yajña*, and are born out of it. It is observed or extended even by them. In the *Ṛgveda*, the terms *namaḥ* and *brahma* are frequently used to mean reverence and devotion respectively. The latter can also mean prayer in the sense that prayer is an expression of devotion. Generally *brahma* means devotion, or the inner state of being devoted to the Divine

24. 7.35.12 and Sāyaṇa's commentary thereon.

or the deities, and the primary means of expressing one's devotion to the deities is to bow down to them in reverence. Reverence expresses the sense of surrender to the deities, and it is devotion that makes one bow down. "I bend down with devotion to you Indra."[25] "We yoke our devotion (*brahma*) with reverence"[26] (*yuja vām brahma pūrvyam namobhiḥ*). Thus devotion and reverence are the spontaneous expression of man's response to the Divine, and are born of man's awareness of the Divine, or spring from a heart that is divinely inspired. "The praise that is born from the heart, and is sung by the reciters of hymns proceeds to the presence of Lord, and is his awakener."[27] The deities are to be approached with a heart full of devotion and prayer. Prayer is born when man is awakened to the divine presence, and is intended to awaken the deities. Devotion is love that binds the devotees to the deities. Apart from the ontological unity (*sajātīya*) that exists between the deities and their worshippers, prayer is the bond that binds them together in love at the level of manifestation. The deities are seen as kin (*āpyam*) of the devotees. They are the ultimate refuge of the worshippers, who seek through prayer and worship the innermost benevolence and blessings of the deities, and hope to become divine (*devavantam*) by the gracious help of the deities. "Like a hawk to its nest I fly to thee O Indra."[28] The Divine is attained by devotion (*brahmavāha*). The deities are pleased with prayer which is meant to enter their hearts and awaken them. It is asserted by the seers that the deities are not pleased either by works or by libations, but by devotion and prayer.[29] Anything that is offered to them without prayer is not acceptable and pleasing to them. And when man is fully awakened to the divine, or the divine within him is fully awakened, his life is divinely transformed, and then every act of

---

25. 7.32.20.
26. 10.13.1.
27. 3.39.1.
28. 1.33.2.
29. 7.26.1.

his will be an act of worship. Then all that a man does will be an invocation to the deities (*yoge yoge tava staram vāje vāje havāmahe*).[30] Even such mundane acts like harvesting become a means of expressing ones devotion to the deities.

Devotion, reverence and prayer, which have divine inspiration as their common source, are divine and sacred. They refer to the same experience, and fulfil man's life supremely. Phenomenologically birth of devotion in man is the same as his experience of the Divine. When the sense of divine is awakened in man, devotion springs up within him spontaneously, and finds its expression through prayer and worship. The hymns are an expression in language of the devotion experienced inwardly, and the Veda as a collection of them is, therefore, sacred. Prayer is both spontaneous and creative. As a spontaneous expression of devotion prayer depends for its inspiration on the Divine. It is born in man due to divine influence. "I restore to thee praises derived from thee as a shepherd returns to the master the sheep.[31] Thus the deities are prayed with the prayer that is inspired by them. Devotion is a divine gift (*devattam brahma*),[32] and seeks the divine as its object. Prayer is born in man when his intellect is made divine, or is inspired or illumined divinely (*daivyā dhiyā*). "Devotion stirs the pious as wind the forest."[33] Divine inspiration stirs the heart and mind of man and makes him attached to the deities. When devotion springs up within man he spontaneously bows down in reverence to the deities (*svayameva namante*). Thus one way of identifying the nature of the Divine is its power to evoke in man devotion and worship, or it is that presence in Nature which inspires man divinely and evokes in him devotion and worship. Therefore, Nature as Nature which is an object of experience to all is not an object of worship for all. It becomes an object of

30. 1.30.7; see also 1.100.7; 3.31.13.
31. 1.114.9.
32. 8.32.27; see also 1.37.4.
33. 10.23.4.

worship for those who see in it something more than what is phenomenal, or the presence of the Divine. It is to the Divine that is revealed in nature reverence and worship are due.

The sense of certainty felt about the existence of the Divine known through inspiration is *śraddhā* (faith). It is to hold on firmly to truth (*śrat*) when it is intuitively grasped.[34] Therefore, devotion and faith are two aspects of the same experience. While *śraddhā* is more on the cognitive side, devotion as an inner response of man to his awareness of the Divine is more emotional in character. However, the seat of both *śraddhā* and devotion is the heart of man.[35] It is also the seat of prayer. Prayer springs from within the heart of man, and is addressed to the deities from there. It is within the heart of man, faith, devotion and reverence are experienced. "The human heart, mind and wisdom are the sources of prayer.[36] Although heart and mind or intellect are distinguished by the seers, often both are regarded as the seats of devotion and prayer. Similarly, prayers are intended to enter the hearts of the deities and please them. The deities are awakened by prayers and praises (*jaḍābodha*) which also help their growth or increase as rivers the sea. Prayer is a divine gift, for the Divine, the ultimate source of devotion and prayer is not known to man by his own efforts (*na tasya vidma puruṣatvatā vayaṁ*).[37] When the heart and intellect of man are divinely inspired man is able to apprehend the Divine, and, therefore, the deities are known by an intellect that is divinely illumined. And such an intellect is also the source of the Vedic hymns.

Devotion as an inspired state of human heart makes man attached to the deities as spontaneously as water seeking

---

34. *Śrat* is a synonym of truth, and *dha* means to hold on. Thus the term *śraddhā* has been defined by Śaṅkara and Sāyaṇa as holding on to truth when it is intuitively grasped.

35. 10.151.4.

36. 1.61.2; see also 1.171.2.

37. 5.48.5.

declivity.[38] It is like the passionate attachment of a loving wife to her loving husband.[39] It makes man approach the deities with reverence on bended knees with raised hands. Devotion and prayer are irresistible when man is awakened to the presence of the Divine, or when the sense of divine is awakened in him, for "who is there in the world that does not solicit and pray to his lord."[40] Prayer is thus the means of expressing man's sense of attachment to and dependence upon the Divine. Devotion or prayer is viewed by the seers as a debt to the deities.[41] Even creation bows down to the Divine as if in a state of reverence, for it is also indebted to the Divine for its existence. Prayers are the messengers of man to the deities who love them, and are pleased by them. The deities also dwell among the prayers (*viśveṣu gīrṣu āyatam*). The Divine is the source as well as the object of all prayers. Devotion or prayer is even regarded as the matrix of the deities, for man comes to know the meaning of divine through devotion, or the Divine is revealed to him directly within the state of devotion. The various deities are prayed with the prayer that is inspired by them, and in their turn the prayers are effective in the growth of divine in man. As man's awareness of the Divine is the same as to experience devotion, with the growth and maturity of devotion, man's awareness of the Divine also increases, and becomes clear and comprehensive. In the absence of devotion the sense of divine is also absent. Without prayer no offering to the deities is meaningful, and even the meaning of the Veda cannot be comprehended without grasping the meaning of devotion and prayer. "Through devotion we have fashioned the hymns."[42] Thus the meaning of divine to man consists primarily in its power to inspire in him devotion and prayer. They spring from man's experience of the

38. 8.32.23; 8.6.34.
39. 1.62.11.
40. 8.1.20.
41. 8.61.12.
42. 8.6.33; see also 3.32.2; 5.39.5.

Divine and seek it as their object. When this circle is completed the nature of the Divine is revealed to man more fully, or the Divine within him is fully awakened. Now, the capacity to inspire in man devotion and reverence is common to all the deities, and to them, either individually or collectively, the hymns are addressed. All the deities are worshippable (*yajñīya*), and to whom worship is due as repayment of debt. They are to be approached with a heart full of devotion and with great reverence (*haviṣmatā manasā* or *mahānamasā*).[43] The seers pray even for those who are the enemies of prayer, so that they may also be filled with devotion, and are awakened to the divine presence. When the divine is experienced, which is possible for man in and through its varied manifestations, his attitude to Nature will be changed radically, and the usual distinction between divine and phenomenal will not be meaningful to him. The whole of Nature will then be seen as radiating the splendour of the Divine and revealing its glory. Nothing in Nature is wholly divine nor wholly phenomenal. The Divine is what lies hidden within Nature. "Men filled with understanding find him there when they have sung prayers formed within their hearts."[44] The Divine and the phenomenal are integrally related, and hence no deity is completely divine nor completely phenomenal. There are no hymns in the *Ṛgveda* addressed to the deities in which both the aspects are not viewed and presented together. Nature is the visible manifestation of the Divine, which in itself is not an object of man's experience, and no phenomenon of Nature is devoid of divine presence and significance.

Prayer is not only a devotional response of man to the deities, but also expresses his love for them. A seer is attached or devoted more passionately to the deities than to his parents, and prayer expresses that devotion. "The will and thoughts within my heart exert their power or strive to offer worship,

43. 7.67.1; see also 7.12.2; 8.23.12; 3.14.5.

44. 1.67.2.

they yearn with love and fly to all religions around."[45] "None other comforter is found save only these (*viśvedevas*)."[46] "My longings and my hopes are fixed upon the deities."[47] The love to the deities is often compared to the love of a wife to her husband. The deities are invited to worship as sons invite their father.[48] "The ties by which His (Indra) devotees are bound to Him are ties of love."[49] "We invoke Aśvinīs by a name as venerable as that of a father."[50] "You are more to me than my father, you and my mother appear alike to me."[51]

We now discuss some of the important epithets such as *kavi, ṛṣi, vipra, kratu, kāvya,* etc., which are commonly applied to all the deities, and reveal their divine nature. These epithets which constitute the divinity of the deities are pre-eminently spiritual in character, in the sense that all of them are expressions of man's higher or spiritual nature. These the deities have in common with man, and, therefore, help us not only in understanding the nature of the Divine, but more importantly the point of unity between the Divine and man. As they are applied to enlightened human beings or seers also, they point to what is common between man and the Divine. Although to understand and appreciate their meaning we look to man, as in him they find their conscious expression, yet he is not regarded as their ultimate source. They constitute the nature of the Divine, and belong to it primarily; and the deities and man possess them derivatively. When wisdom, creativity, etc., which flow ultimately from the Divine, are attained more fully by man he too becomes entitled to these epithets. But how to understand the significance of these epithets in relation to the

45. 4.64.2.
46. 4.64.2.
47. 4.64.2.
48. 1.130.1; 7.26.2.
49. 6.24.4.
50. 10.39.1.
51. 8.1.6.

deities who dwell in Nature? It is in man, a self-conscious being, that wisdom, knowledge, discernment, discrimination and poetic creativity are revealed. And it may be pointed out that the attribution of these qualities to nature may be due to poetic imagination, or when attributed can have only figurative or even animistic significance.

But, according to the vision of the seers, though the divine qualities manifest themselves within man and the deities, none of them are their ultimate source. They are only sources of manifestation and revelation of these qualities. The Divine manifests itself not only in Nature, but within man also who is not radically different from Nature. He is an integral part of Nature, and Nature in all its aspects is present in him. Nature is a unity of diverse phenomena, and the ground of that unity is the Divine whose glory Nature manifests. So what is present in Nature is also present within man, and vice versa, though the mode of its manifestation is not the same in both. Man also in his own way stands to reveal the unity of Nature in the sense that the whole of Nature is present in him in an integrated way. In him all the aspects of Nature are present integrated, or in him nature finds its conscious unity. It is only by assuming a radical difference between man and Nature on the one hand, and Nature and the Divine on the other, we may regard man in his higher nature as the source of revelation of the Divine. This approach, which is alien to the Veda, regards Nature as something other than the Divine, and is consequently relegated to a position inferior to both man and the Divine. But within the Vedic tradition in general, and in the *Ṛgveda* in particular, no gaps are seen between man and Nature, and Nature and the Divine. All is a whole, and both man and Nature manifest the same reality though in their own unique ways. Therefore, what is not in Nature is not to be found in man, and what is revealed within man is also there in Nature though in a different form. The same reality is present inherently within both, and is revealed through them. Thus Nature and man in their own ways, but in harmony, represent the same process of the divine self-manifestation, and fulfil the same divine purpose.

This idea which is present in the *R̥gveda*, though not explicitly stated and developed, is later developed in the Brāhmaṇa and post-Brāhmaṇa literature. According to the Vedic scheme of classification of all that is there into three realms of *ādhidevatā* (the realm of deities), *ādhibhautika* (the phenomenal or physical realm) and *adhyātma* (human or spiritual realm) the same Divine Reality manifests itself in and through these realms, though it is known and interpreted differently. What is present in one realm is equally present in the other two realms, and, therefore, each realm is a source of divine revelation. Only the mode of revelation will be distinct at each level. For instance, to see Agni as the principle of heat or fire is to know Agni at the physical level, and to see him as a self-manifestation of the Divine is to know him as a deity, and to realise Agni as present within man (*vaiśvānara*) either as speech or as the principle of growth is to see him at the *adhyātma* level. It is thus the same Divine reality manifests itself, though in different forms, in all the realms. What we therefore find in man is essentially the same as that which manifests itself in the other two realms also, though the manner in which each realm affects man, or the way in which he understands the significance of each is distinct. Therefore, to realise integrally the nature of the Divine is to see it in all its manifestations at different levels of human experience, in different realms.

Although we look to man to understand and appreciate the meaning of divine qualities, he is not, however, their measure and standard. They are not revealed in man perfectly. These are human, and at the same time more than human; they are divine. The full and perfect meaning of these qualities cannot, therefore, be known and determined in terms of their manifestation in man. This may be the reason why man's understanding of these qualities is not complete and perfect. Their full significance eludes him. The deities are also not their ultimate source. Compared to man the deities are the perfect revealers of these qualities, or in them they are revealed more fully, or in full measure (*pratimānam*). Their revelation or manifestation in the deities is more perfect. The deities are, therefore, described as best of seers and seer-poets, and their knowledge is all-comprehensive and perfect and they are supremely wise. This is indicated by suffixing the superlative term *tama* to the epithets when they are used in relation to the deities. But no deity is absolutely divine, absolutely immortal and absolutely wise, and hence these qualities are not attributed to them in an absolute sense. The deities also participate in the nature of the Divine and partake of its qualities, as man does. They are not identical with the Divine, but as the signs of it (*ketavaḥ*) they reveal its splendour and glory more fully.

Now, Nature in its physical aspect, or as it is known empirically is not divine, and hence the various divine qualities do not belong to Nature viewed as Nature. But when the Divine is seen as manifesting itself in and through nature, Nature becomes the source of revelation of these qualities. The Divine presence in Nature is not a matter of poetic imagination but real. It is something that is seen or experienced. In being awakened to the sense of divine man is inspired by Nature, or it is Nature that awakens in man the sense of divine by inspiring his higher faculties. It is only when man is inspired divinely he becomes aware of the Divine, and as Nature is the immediate source of such an inspiration it is divine, or the Divine is present inherently within Nature. Seeing the presence of the Divine in Nature may, therefore, mean its capacity to inspire man divinely, and man experiences the divine qualities or realises them within himself when he is awakened to his higher or spiritual nature. Thus the Divine in Nature acts on the Divine within man, and that moment is the moment of divine revelation to man.

The epithets commonly applied to both the deities and man do not always have the same connotation in relation to both. However, their essential meaning remains the same. This difference in connotation of the epithets also helps us in understanding the source of these qualities. The deities are often described as if they are the sources of these qualities. This is evident from the fact that these qualities when attributed to the deities are not only used substantively, but often the deities are identified with them. For instance, *kratu* besides being an attribute of the deities is also seen as identical with them. Thus a deity is known not only as possessing these qualities, but often they are identified with the deity. They describe the very nature of the deities; whereas in relation to man these qualities are always used adjectively and moreover he has to attain or realise them. Thus while a deity stands for wisdom, man can only be wise. This distinction throws light on the meaning of the epithets, as well as on the nature of the deities and their relation to man. Another purpose in pointing out the distinction is to make clear that the meaning of the attributes cannot be known fully by understanding them in relation to man.. However, man is the key to understand the meaning of these qualities, though not to determine fully their meaning. Only those in whom these are more fully realised are able to know their meaning clearly, and to that extent they are also divine. While the deities are the universal manifestations of Divine, man as an individual is a concrete manifestation of it. The deities are more pervasive, and are universally present. What is universal belongs to the deities. Therefore the divine qualities belong primarily to the deities, the primary and universal manifestations of the Divine. However, their essential meaning, whether understood in relation to man or the deities, remains the same. The difference in their meaning is not so much due to degree of manifestation, as to the source and its concrete manifestation. While man can hope to attain perfection in respect of these qualities, the deities are perfect by nature. Because of the fulness of these qualities in them, the deities can inspire man to realise them within himself.

Almost all the deities are addressed as seer-poets (*kavi*) in the *Ṛgveda*. While the term *kavi* in relation to man may mean a thinker, an inspired poet and a seer, in most of the contexts of its usage in relation to the deities, it stands to mean their creative intelligence by means of which the deities manifest the divine glory and splendour. It is also used to mean the omniscience of the deities, as in most cases it is used synonymously with the terms *viśvavidam* (all-knowing), *vipaścita* (discerning) *vipra* (inspired), *madhira* or *dhīra* (intelligent), *manīṣā* (wise) and *pracetasam* or *cetiṣṭha* (of perfect knowledge). These various terms reveal the different creative aspects of divine intelligence. The deities are *kavi* as they are perfectly wise and omniscient. Some of them are addressed as great (*mahān*) or supreme among the seer-poets (*kavitama*).

The primary characteristic of a *kavi* as a creative and all-knowing seer is *kāvya* (wisdom), and *kratu* also to an extent characterises a *kavi*. Therefore, an analysis of the meaning of the term *kāvya* can throw light on the meaning of the term *kavi*. Though *kāvya* and *kratu* are the characteristics of a *kavi*, and are often used to mean the wisdom of the deities, *kāvya* chiefly indicates the creative side of divine wisdom, and reveals itself variously through all the forms in which the various deities manifest themselves in Nature, while *kratu* stands for the volitional or intentional aspect of divine wisdom. In other words, *kāvya* and *kratu* represent knowledge or cognitive and volitional aspects of divine wisdom respectively. And every act of a deity reveals both the aspects of a *kavi*, his creative intelligence as well as his will. They proceed together, and are revealed together in the case of the deities.

A deity is known as a *kavi* for being omniscient or all-knowing (*viśvavit*) and knows all by being within all. For instance, Agni who is full of knowledge and wisdom, dwells within mortals and knows thereby the intentions, thoughts and actions of man. Omniscience of the deities in the above sense is indicated further by means of other epithets. They are often described as *nṛcakṣasā* (observers of man). They witness man in all his intentions, thoughts and actions by being within him. A deity is a *kavi* because he observes all men (*nṛcakṣah kavi*).[52] The deities distinguish the wise from the unwise (*cittam* and *acittam*), and also discern between good and evil in man. The epithet *jātavedasa* which is applied to other deities besides Agni also shows the deities know all that is born, or by being born within all they know all. The same idea is conveyed when it is stated that the deities Mitra and Varuṇa know all that is born (*bhūtasya pracatasā*). The whole of creation in and through which the various deities manifest themselves represents their wisdom (*kāvya*). Nature is an integrated whole of different phenomena, and in each phenomenon of nature the other phenomena are present, though, a phenomenon is identified and distinguished from the rest in terms of a dominant characteristic. There is thus nothing in Nature which is not interwoven by all the aspects of Nature and this explains the capacity of the deities to know all. The deities know all that is there by their wisdom (*kavi kāvyena asi viśvavit*).[53] The epithets like *sahasracatasa* (of infinite knowledge or wisdom), *cetiṣṭha* (supreme among knowers) and *viśvavedasa* (all-knowing) show the boundless and comprehensive character of the knowledge of the deities. The idea of *antaryāmī* (internal ruler) is present in the *Ṛgveda,* though not stated explicitly aș in the Vedānta texts. For instance, Agni is described as controller of human thoughts or intellect (*dhīnām yantāram*).[54] Also the epithets *dhartā* and *vidhartā* commonly applied to all the deities show that they hold together and sustain all by being within all. They hold together and sustain all not only in the natural sense of being the constituent element of the whole creation, but in spiritual and moral senses also. They know the good and evil intentions and deeds of man. They inspire divine wisdom in man, and save him from sin. They know all that a man intends, thinks and does by witnessing them from within man (*antariti paśyanti*).[55]

52. 3.54.6; 9.92.2.
53. 10.91.3; see also 3.19.1; 1.128.8; 10.4.5.
54. 3.3.8.
55. 2.27.3.

Similarly, they not only receive and are pleased by the prayers and praises of man, but also know them and respond to them. They are perfect knowers (*viduṣṭhāram*).

The deities are omniscient and know all by becoming all. All that is there is their manifestation. By wisdom Indra creates heaven and earth, and Varuṇa is able to assume several forms at will. Creative intelligence enables its possessor to reveal his glory in varied forms. The varied richness of the world, and the varied forms of creative expression of human intelligence point to divine intelligence, their source. The creativity of divine intelligence is boundless. The deities manifest and reveal it in and through their various creative acts, and the whole creation stands to reveal their creative intelligence and wisdom.

Man as a *kavi*, either in the sense of an inspired poet or a seer, is one to whom is revealed the hidden wisdom of the Divine, while the deities are *kavi*s naturally, for they are the manifestations of divine wisdom. While a human *kavi* is able to know the hidden truths about the divine because of his inspired wisdom, the deities are known as *kavi*s as they are the embodied forms of divine wisdom. As the universal self-manifestations of the divine, the deities reveal within themselves divine wisdom and intelligence. Because of creative intelligence one creates, and sees oneself in all that he creates. A *kavi* is one who creates, or without being creative one is not a *kavi*. His understanding or knowledge is profound (*gambhīra cetasa*),[56] because of which he knows truly and comprehensively. *Kavi*s are known for their ability to apprehend the truth, or they are known by truth (*satya śrutayaḥ kavayaḥ*).[57] They are knowers of truth, and are righteous (*ṛtajñaḥ* and *ṛtavānaḥ*). They shine with divine splendour, and reveal divine glory.

By being present within all the intelligent beings, the deities hold in themselves all the forms of creativity, and by being the sources of inspiration, they also release the forms of creativity

---

56. 8.8.2.

57. 6.49.6; 5.57.8; 5.5.88; *kavim satya dharmānam* 1.12.7.

latent in man (*viśvā rūpāṇi pratimuñcate kavi*).[58] They are supreme among *kavis*, and the wisest among the wise. While man can become a *kavi* by being inspired by the deities, the deities are by nature *kavis*. Nature reveals their creative intelligence and wisdom, or it is a creative expression of their wisdom. It is the *kāvya* of the deities. It is said of Varuṇa that he is the abode of all wisdom. All the worlds are in the glory of Soma, and they also express it. Heaven and earth, the abodes of the deities, are self-refulgent *kavis* because of their wisdom. All the forms of the world are creative manifestations of heaven and earth, who weave newer and newer forms. In this context Sāyaṇa interprets the term *kavi* to mean one who is conscious of his creative functions.[59] Thus *kavi* is known for his creative intelligence and wisdom, and the deities manifest themselves in varied forms of Nature because of their creative intelligence and wisdom. This sense of *kavi* is common to both deities and man. While all that man creates expresses his wisdom, the whole of creation stands to reveal the wisdom of the deities. In its greatness the world reveals the *kāvya* of Indra (*devasya paśya kāvyam mahatva*).[60] Varuṇa manifests himself in diverse forms by his *kāvya*.[61]

Wisdom of man is a gift of the deities. They are the inspirers of wisdom in man. It is because of the inspiration which man receives from the deities he is raised to the status of a *kavi* and a *ṛṣi*. In this sense the deities are known as the makers of *kavis* and *ṛṣis* among men. The creative intelligence and wisdom of the deities are perfect, and ever manifest themselves. All wisdom is centred in Varuṇa. From Agni proceed all wisdom, and none can excel Agni in wisdom.[62] His wisdom is ineffable. The majesty of the deities consists in their wisdom, and they are worshippable because of their wisdom. Nobody can hinder or

58. 5.81.2.
59. 1.159.4.
60. 10.55.5; see also 10.29.6.
61. 8.41.5 and 6.
62. 5.3.5, see also 10.91.3; 3.1.16 and 18.

resist the wisdom of Varuṇa, the most wise. Soma can fill man with divine wisdom and glory by his *kāvya*. Thus the deities not only reveal the Divine to man, but by inspiring in him divine wisdom they can make him divine. It is by their wonderful wisdom (*kāvya*) Ṛbhus, the sons of Sudhanvan, attained the status of the deities.[63] And man can become a *kavi* or a *ṛṣi* because of his creative intelligence and wisdom. And unless one is divinely inspired one cannot attain divine wisdom or speech, and become a *kavi*. Although man is inherently intelligent, unless his intelligence is divinely inspired it cannot apprehend the divine, and make him a *kavi*.

In the *Ṛgveda* the deities are prayed to help man in overcoming sin in all its forms. In this context it is significant to note that the deities save man from sin by virtue of their *kāvya*, showing thereby the moral dimension of divine wisdom.[64] Wisdom and righteousness go together. The wise are also righteous or truthful (*ṛtavānāḥ kavayaḥ*).[65] To know the divine is to know it in and through *ṛta*. *Ṛta* is the revelation of the Divine within Nature.

The following discussion of the epithets *kratu* and *ṛṣi* which are applied to both deities and man, and are in most cases used synonymously with the terms *kavi* and *kāvya* will help us further in knowing the meaning of divine wisdom. *Kavi*, *vipra*, *ṛṣi* and *dhīra* are related concepts, and are used on several occasions synonymously. *Kavi* is of inspired knowledge (*viprasya dhārayā kavi*).[66] The term *dhāra*, according to *Nighaṇṭu*, is a synonym of knowledge or wisdom. Consider the following expressions : *ṛṣihi vipraḥ vicakṣanaḥ; vipratаman kavīnam; sukratuḥ kaviḥ*.[67] All the deities are addressed as *kratu* or *sukratu* while Indra is more often addressed as *śatakratu*, *amitakratu* or *tuvikratu*. The deities are

63. 4.35.4.
64. 10.87.2.
65. 7.76.4.
66. 9.12.8.
67. 9.107.7; 10.112.9; 9.12.4; see also 8.79.1; 9.73.7; 10.91.3.

known as *sukratu* as they possess *kratu* (*kratunā sukratu*), and in most of the contexts it is used to mean will or intention (*saṁkalpa*). It also means wisdom. Though in general *kāvya* and *kratu* mean wisdom, there is a subtle distinction in the nature of wisdom which they signify. They express two distinct aspects of divine wisdom. While *kāvya* signifies knowledge aspect of wisdom, *kratu* refers to the volitional aspect of it. However, both are integral aspects of divine wisdom. They are further distinguished, though not clearly, in terms of intellect and heart, their respective seats of manifestation. While *kāvya* is intellectual in character, *kratu* is related to heart. In the *Ṛgveda* heart is distinguished from intellect or mind, the seat of knowledge, discrimination and discernment. It is also related to *medhā* (intelligence). Heart is also a seat of knowledge and wisdom, but the way it knows is distinct from the manner in which knowledge is attained by intellect. Heart knows more by identity. While *kāvya* is a spontaneous expression of divine intelligence, *kratu* is something that is to be invoked in the deities. All the saving and benevolent deeds of the deities, for which they are prayed — and most of the hymns are a grateful acknowledgement of the help received from the deities — are attributed to their *kratu*. Indra is *śatakratu*, as infinite are his benevolent and auspicious deeds. Aśvinīs are known for their saving deeds (*kratu*). All the deities are known for their benevolent, saving and auspicious *kratu* which is wonderful (*adbhuta*) or incomparable and victorious (*jaitram*).[68] A further distinction can be made between *kāvya* by which one is known as a *kavi*, and *kratu* by which one is known as *sukratu*. While man can become a *kavi* because of his *kāvya*, he is not regarded as *sukratu* or having good *kratu*. He is known as only an observer of *kratu*. Agni is kindled, and Soma is shed by means of *kratu*, and the deities are prayed to grant *kratu* to man.

Man observes or follows *kratu* to attain the deities, or the deities are attained by *kratu* (*kratuvid*). Man has to observe or

68. 5.10.2; 10.36.10.

follow *kratu* to win their benevolence. In the post-Vedic (*saṁhitā*) literature *kratu* generally means *yajña* (sacrifice as performed by man). He performs *yajña* in imitation as well as to continue the process initiated by the Divine, and being perpetuated by the deities. Man's observance of *kratu* is intended to continue and extend by way of participation the process of creation. In continuing and extending the cosmic process man is only doing the will of the Divine as revealed to him in and through creation. Creation reveals the *kāvya* as well as the *kratu* of the Divine, and in doing the will of the Divine man is known to observe *kratu*. *Kratu* does not, therefore, mean ordinary intentions and deeds of man, but refers to divinely inspired will of man. Any act of man cannot be known as *kratu*. Only those acts of man which are divinely inspired and have cosmic significance are indicated by it. *Kratu* in this sense means the dynamic side of divine wisdom or *kāvya*, or the volitional side of it, and is reflected in the divine act of creation. "The Aṅgīrasa seers attaining divine held in themselves the divine will" (*aṅgirasaḥ devatvam prāpta deveṣu kratum dhārayantaḥ*).[69] Also in most of the cases, whether in relation to the deities or in relation to man, the term *kratu* and *dakṣa* (ability, dexterity, or competence) are employed together. In some cases *dakṣa* is used as a qualifying characteristic of *kratu*. "Inspire me for *kratu* and *dakṣa*."[70] "Soma flows granting man *kratu* and *dakṣa*."[71] However the term *dakṣa* is not used in relation to *kāvya* which simply means knowledge or the cognitive aspect of divine wisdom. The use of the terms *kratu* and *dakṣa* in association is significant and appropriate as they express the relation between the will and its resolve or competence. Simple will without resolution and ability to execute it competently is unfruitful. Therefore, the firmness of human will to do the will of the Divine or the deities by means of continuing and extending divine *yajña* is due to the favour of the deities. The

69. 10.56.4 and Sāyaṇa's commentary thereon.

70. 10.36.3.

71. 9.109.2; 9.100.5.

deities are worshipped with the will that is made firm by the deities (*tava kratvā saneyam*).[72] On the other hand, man's failure or inability to do the will of the deities is due to the weakness (*dīnatā*) of his *kratu*.[73] The religious acts of kindling Agni and shedding of Soma are due to *kratu* granted to man by the deities. The deities inspire the will of man and make it resolute to do the will of the Divine. In one context even the birth of devotion (*brahma*) is regarded as due to *kratu*.[74]

The deities posses inherently *kāvya* and *kratu*, the two chief characteristics of divine wisdom. Both the aspects of divine wisdom are revealed together in all the acts of the deities. However, in some of the contexts of its usage the term *kratu* signifies wisdom of the deities. "Indra witnesses people by his wisdom (*kratu*)."[75] Agni helps people to discern by his *kratu*.[76] Even it is stated clearly that one who discerns is *sukratu* (*yaḥ ciketa saḥ sukratuḥ*).[77] Agni holds together all by his *kratu*. In one expression *kratu* is related to head or intellect (*śīrṣāṇi kratum*).[78] In the expression *kavi kratu* (*kratu* or wisdom of a *kavi*), *kratu* is characterised as belonging to a *kavi*. Here it means the same as *kāvya*. However, it is not seen as a defining characteristic of a *kavi*; only *kāvya* characterises a *kavi*. Thus in the expression *kavi kratu*, *kratu* does not define a *kavi*, but it is qualified by *kavi*. We may, therefore, explain the expression *kavi kratu* to mean those deeds of a deity which are informed by the wisdom of a *kavi*. Thus *kratu* (will or intention) of the deities is fully informed by their wisdom. The divine acts are fully informed by the wisdom of the Divine, or in the case of the deities their intelligence and will are in perfect harmony, and are revealed together. The divine

72. 8.19.29.

73. 7.89.3.

74. 10.61.1.

75. 1.132.5.

76. 1.65.5; 4.12.1.

77. 5.65.1.

78. 2.16.2.

wisdom reveals itself in and through the operations of divine will. *Kratu* of the deities is qualified further by such terms as *bhadram* (good or suspicious), *dyumantam* (resplendent), *dakṣa* (able or competent), *jaitram* (victorious), and once by the term *ghoram* (terrible).[79] The deities save their worshippers from sin and affliction by their *kratu*. Its moral aspect is revealed when the seers pray to receive good or noble intentions from everywhere (*bhadraḥ kratavaḥ yantu viśvataḥ*).[80] Uṣas is prayed to bless the seers with noble or good intentions, or with *kratu* that is both good and competent (*krato bhadrasya dakṣasya*).[81] In such expressions in which *kratu* is qualified as good, able, victorious and terrible, which are not used in relation to *kāvya*, the meaning of *kratu* as will, and its distinction from *kāvya* as knowledge, are made clear.

Kratu is related to *ṛta*. It is good or auspicious when it is in accordance with *ṛta*. As the deities are full of *ṛta* their *kratu* shines with the splendour of *ṛta*. It is by *ṛta* that Mitra and Varuṇa have attained their mighty or great *kratu*. As pointed out earlier, *kratu* is more a matter of heart than that of intellect. The deities desire the *kratu* that is in the hearts of man. Heart is the seat of *kratu*, or from within heart good and noble intentions proceed (*kratu yanti kratavaḥ hṛtsu dhītayaḥ*).[82] Indra's heart is full of *kratu* (*hṛdi kratumān*), and it is victorious (*jaitram kratu*).[83] Moreover, the deities are fulfillers of man's *kratu* (*kratuprā*). Ṛbhus had attained the status of the deities by doing the will of the deities, or by holding it in themselves (*deveṣu kratu ādadhuḥ*).[84] The deities witness the righteous deeds of man (*kratu*), and men are saved by their *kratu*. When pleased with man's *kratu*, the deities help him in overcoming sin. All these expressions show clearly that *kratu* primarily means the will, either of the deities or of man

79. 7.28.2.
80. 1.89.1.
81. 4.10.2; see also 1.123.13.
82. 10.64.2; see also 4.41.1.
83. 4.41.1.
84. 10.56.4.

that is in accordance with, or is informed by wisdom. When divine wisdom inspires all the faculties of man he becomes divine, or attains the status of the deities. The wisdom that cannot inspire will, or the will that is not inspired by wisdom, are not divine. The deities hold together and sustain the universe not only by their wisdom, but also by their will, that is by willing good and by fulfilling it whenever it is willed by man. In and through the *kratu* either of the deities or of man the Divine will, which no one, including the deities, can resist and overcome, is expressed and fulfilled. It is by ruling over the will of man the deities hold men together, and in this sense they are known as *vibhu* and *paribhū*.

Another important epithet which expresses the divine nature of the deities is *ṛṣi*, and it is applied to man also. Here again the meaning of the term *ṛṣi* when used in relation to man is not the same as in relation to the deities. Essentially the terms *kavi*, *vipra* and *ṛṣi* stand to reveal the different dimensions of divine wisdom. Without being divinely inspired one cannot be a *kavi*, or a *vipra* or a *ṛṣi*. All these terms are used to describe a divinely inspired person and his wisdom. *Kāvya* and *kratu* are equally the characteristics of a *ṛṣi* and *vipra*. And in the human context a *ṛṣi* is one who knows or sees the Divine in all its diverse manifestations, or sees the divine unity of all that is there. This cannot be true in the case of the deities as the divine constitutes their reality. There is no meaning in their being *ṛṣi*s by knowing the divine in and through its varied manifestations, as they are divine by being the self-manifestations of the Divine. It is not by virtue of their knowledge of something that they are *ṛṣi*s; they are so by their very nature; whereas man is not by nature a *ṛṣi*, he can become one by attaining divine wisdom or knowledge.

Although divine inspiration is common to *ṛṣi*, *vipra* and *kavi*, their significance is not the same. *Vipra* in relation to man can mean either one who is divinely moved, stirred or who can discern (*vipaścita*). While *kavi* is one in whom the creative aspect of wisdom is prominent, *ṛṣi* is one who sees the creation in its divine unity. While a *kavi* is one who creates or is known for his creativity, a *ṛṣi* is one who sees the divine unity of all that is there. Although all these terms indicate divine wisdom, the Vedic seers are selective in using them, as the wisdom of a *ṛṣi* is not the same as the wisdom of a *kavi*. The creative aspect of divine wisdom is more manifest in a *kavi*, and finds its expression in all that he creates; whereas the wisdom of a *ṛṣi* is unifying; he sees the creation in its divine unity. Now, a deity is a *kavi* not only because he is an individualised self-expression of the Divine, but as he in turn manifests himself in different forms of Nature. The creativity involved in the process of self-manifestation of the Divine is revealed in all the deities, as Nature in all its diversity is their self-manifestation, and that constitutes the definition of *kavi* in their case. It is in terms of that wisdom whereby a deity creatively manifests itself in diverse forms of nature, a deity is known as a *kavi*. Likewise it is the primary function of a human *kavi* to visualise and express the Divine in different forms. Wisdom in its creative aspect finds its expression in a *kavi*. On the other hand, the wisdom of a *ṛṣi* may be defined as that by which the unity of all creative manifestation is apprehended. One who sees the divine unity of all is a *ṛṣi*, or he sees all that is in its divine unity. To apprehend the unity of Nature is to see it as a creative self-manifestation of the Divine; and the *ṛṣi* is one to whom such a unity is revealed. While a deity constitutes the unity of a particular phenomenon of Nature, the Divine constitutes the unity of all the deities. In the case of the deities, the creative and unifying aspects of divine wisdom are revealed together. It is not by any effort that the deities create all and know themselves as their unity. A deity expresses itself through the varied forms of Nature, and also constitutes their unity. It sees itself in all, and all in itself. Thus a deity is revealed in and through all its manifestations, and also as their unity. This idea is presented in the *Ṛgveda* poetically when it is asserted that the purpose of Vedic metres or Vedic wisdom is to restore the divine unity of that which is diversified in the process of creation, and the *ṛṣis* are those to whom the metres are revealed.[85] The various deities have entered into various metres; and man becomes a *ṛṣi* by knowing this truth.[86]

The Veda is thus a revelation of both the aspects of divine wisdom. It contains knowledge about the process of creation or self-manifestation by which the Divine has become all, and also the knowledge of the Divine as the inner unity of all that is there. While a man becomes a *ṛṣi* by seeing the divine unity of all, the deities constitute that unity. Although no individual deity is the unity of all that is there, as it constitutes the unity of a particular phenomenon of Nature, yet by revealing the Divine, their common source and inner unity, the deities reveal the unity of all that is there. Thus the deities represent the various phenomena of Nature as well as their underlying unity. While in their phenomenal aspect, the deities represent the diversity of nature, in their divine aspect they constitute the divine unity of Nature. And while that aspect of wisdom by which the Divine manifests itself and becomes all is indicated by the term *kāvya*, the characteristic of a *kavi*, that aspect of wisdom by which the Divine is seen or realised as the unity of all characterises a *ṛṣi*. And *kratu* is the dynamic side of divine wisdom by which the creation is willed, brought into existence and sustained.

The purpose of our earlier discussion on the nature of *ṛta* was to show how it constitutes the essential unity of the deities, and our present discussion of it is intended to show how it constitutes the divinity of the deities. All the deities are related to *ṛta*, and that reveals their common divine nature and unity. To understand the nature and meaning of *ṛta* we have to follow its usage in different contexts. In several contexts of its usage it is used to mean the highest reality or truth (*ṛtam bṛhat*). It is the dynamic side of the divine, and reveals itself in different forms at different levels of its manifestation. It is revealed within Nature as that which holds it together, sustains it and governs

85. 10.130.5; *ṛṣisu praviṣṭhām jñānam* 10.71.3.

86. 10.130.6.

it. If Nature has a revelatory function and reveals something more than its phenomenal aspect, it is the *ṛta* that it reveals. All the phenomena of Nature reveal it as that which sustains and governs them. Each deity in its own characteristic way expresses *ṛta*, and upholds it as well. It is the dwelling place of the deities, as well as their indwelling principle. Both heaven and earth from the beginning bear it and express it (*sanāt ṛtam vahadha*).[87] The ultimate reality or the divine is not only revealed by means of *ṛta*, but it is also identified with the divine (*ṛta sat* and *ṛtam bṛhat*).[88] As the dynamic side of the divine, *ṛta* is co-eternal and co-extensive with the Divine. Thus *ṛta* means the highest reality as well as the truth that is revealed in and through Nature. Truth is its own revelation, or truth is known by truth only. In the *Ṛgveda* both these senses are given to the term *ṛta*. Though the terms *ṛtam* and *satyam* are used synonymously in the *Ṛgveda*, the former as the dynamic side of the Divine reveals it to man. It is the Divine as revealed in and through its varied manifestations. It also constitutes the divinity of the deities (*viśve devatvam nāma ṛtam*[89]). The deities are its forms of expression. It upholds, regulates and governs all, and is not upheld and governed by any. The deities only help its revelation by manifesting it within themselves. Knowledge of it saves man from sin, and for that reason it cannot be identified with moral order operative within man. Moral order is only a mode of its manifestation. Thus moral law and the order inherent within nature do not contain *ṛta*; they only manifest and reveal it.

It is by means of knowledge born out of *ṛta* or as inspired by it, man is able to apprehend truth. It is the divine light illumined by which man sees the divine. It opens up even the deaf ears of man to receive truth.[90] To those who are inspired by *ṛta*, or whose understanding is illumined by it, Nature is the revelation of the

87. 4.5.6.

88. 4.40.5; 8.25.4.

89. 10.35.8.

90. 4.23.8.

divine. *Ṛta* is enveloped by *ṛta*, or the Divine is hidden or enveloped by its own manifestations. Therefore, the latter may either reveal the Divine as their source and ground or conceal it. The phenomenal reality stands to reveal or point to that which is its ultimate source and ground to those whose intellect is illumined by *ṛta*; whereas to those who cannot see beyond manifestations, they act as a cover and conceal the divine.

The deities are addressed as the forms (*peśa*) of *ṛta*. They are the supreme forms of its manifestation and revelation (*tadekam devānām śreṣṭham vapuṣām apaśyāma*).[91] In this sense it is the same as the divinity of the deities. It constitutes their glory and greatness. By possessing *ṛtam* they reveal it (*ṛtam āghoṣata*).[92] All the deities are born of *ṛta* (*ṛta jāta* or *ṛta prajāta*) and, therefore, the truth of them consists in their being the manifestation of *ṛta* (*ṛta jāta satyā*).[93] Agni is addressed as shedding truth (*ṛtasya varṣṇe*).[94] The deities are lovers of *ṛta*. They extend or increase it, and also are increased by it (*ṛta vṛdhā*).[95] They are sustained by *ṛta*, and in turn they sustain it. Thus the description of the deities as *ṛtavānāḥ*, *ṛtājātāḥ*, *ṛtāvṛdhā* and *ṛtasya gopā* intend to express the truth that the deities are the manifestations of truth, possess it and spread it. They are addressed as *ṛtasya radhyāḥ* or leaders or charioteers of truth.[96] They follow the laws of *ṛta* which they can never violate. The sun toils because of *ṛta*, and what he spreads far and wide is the splendour of *ṛta*.[97] Thus as the common source of origin as well as the common dwelling place of the deities *ṛta* is the truth of the deities, or the various deities are its individual expressions. Because of this the deities can

91. 5.62.1.

92. 8.25.4.

93. 6.50.14; see also 4.51.7; 3.6.10, 6.50.14

94. 5.12.1.

95. 1.2.8; see also 1.23.5; 1.159.1.

96. 7.66.12.

97. 8.75.5; see also 10.8.51; 2.27.8.

reveal truth to man, or can inspire in him the knowledge of the divine. They shine with *ṛta* and reveal it to man (*ṛtadyumna* and *ṛtasya bodhi*).[98]

The relation between *kavi* and *ṛta* is also worth considering. The first seers (*sapta viprāḥ*) who are also addressed as *kavis*, are those who have discovered the ways of manifestation of *ṛta* (*ṛtasya paddhām*).[99] One is a *kavi* or a *vipra* by knowing *ṛta* and the diverse ways of its manifestation. They are full of *ṛta* (*ṛtavānaḥ*), and are its knowers (*ṛtajñāḥ*).

As pointed out earlier the problem of the Divine in itself is speculative or metaphysical with which the Vedic seers are not generally concerned. The Divine that is described in the hymns of the *Ṛgveda* refers to what is experienced or revealed in Nature as a presence. It is that presence in Nature which inspires man divinely, evokes in him devotion and reverence and fulfils his life. And the various deities are the names given to it according to its revelation in different phenomena of Nature. As the primary and universal manifestations of the Divine, the various deities represent and reveal the Divine within the phenomenal world; they are its signs (*ketu*); and point to it as their ultimate source and inner unity. Thus all the deities being of one mind and of one wisdom proceed respectfully to the presence of the one, the source of all wisdom, or the agent of all creation (*viśve devāḥ samanasaḥ saketāḥ ekam kratum abhi vi yanti sādhu*).[100]

98. 9.113.4; 4.3.4.

99. 3.10.2.

100. 6.9.5.

3

Agni

THE main object of this and the next chapters is to elucidate further the nature and meaning of the Divine with the help of two individual deities, Agni and Indra, or to understand the nature of the Divine as it reveals itself in and through those phenomena of Nature which Agni and Indra represent. While discussing the Nature and meaning of the Divine in the previous chapter, we have not taken into consideration any particular individual deity, but have discussed some of those attributes which are attributed to all the deities commonly, and reveal their divine nature and inner unity. Now, we intend to elucidate and substantiate some of the observations made in the previous chapter regarding the nature of the deities and their relation to the Divine. The purpose of these two chapters is also to substantiate the thesis maintained in the previous chapter that a deity is neither wholly divine nor wholly phenomenal, but represents both, and, therefore, the deities are described in the hymns of the *Ṛgveda* in terms of both divine and phenomenal qualities, and that while the phenomenal attributes of a deity constitute its individuality and distinguish it from the rest of the deities, the divine attributes which are applied commonly to all the deities reveal their divine essence and inner unity. In this chapter we discuss the nature of the deity Agni with a view to understanding the nature and meaning of the Divine as it reveals itself in and through the phenomenon of Nature which Agni represents.

The choice of the deities for discussion in these two chapters does not involve any special consideration, nor is it purely arbitrary. Any deity would have served the purpose. However, the choice is based on the fact that the deities Agni and Indra are described in the *Ṛgveda* more comprehensively in terms of both the aspects, which is mostly due to pervasive and striking character of the natural phenomena which they represent. As the Divine is experienced by the seers as the ultimate source and unity of all the deities, no one deity in its divine aspect is greater or superior to other deities. However, some of the deities because of their striking phenomenal character stand to reveal the nature of the Divine more prominently and clearly. The splendour and glory of the Divine, though not limited to any one phenomenon of Nature, are experienced in their richness more clearly and prominently in relation to certain phenomena of Nature. As Agni and Indra represent two pervasive aspects of Nature they are of supreme significance to man as sources of divine revelation.

In all the hymns addressed to Agni he is described as representing a phenomenon of Nature, and at the same time as a manifestation of the Divine. There are no hymns addressed to him in which he is described exclusively in terms of either of the aspects. As every Vedic hymn is either a prayer or a praise, all the hymns addressed to Agni are prayers and praises addressed to Agni as a deity. It is Agni in his divine aspect that deserves worship and prayer, and such that even in those hymns in which the phenomenal character of Agni is well presented, his divine side is not lost sight of. It is the divine nature of Agni which has attracted the attention of the Vedic seers most, and forms the central theme of most of the Agni-hyms. There is a further dimension of Agni which we may identify as mystical, and this aspect is also clearly presented in the hymns. The mystical side of Agni is not unrelated to his other two aspects. All the three aspects are integral to the nature of Agni, and therefore to comprehend his nature truly and fully we have to take into consideration all the aspects. And all are equally significant in comprehending the nature of Agni. Thus Agni as revealed to the Vedic seers is both phenomenal and divine, and at the same time something more than these, a divine mystery. In this chapter whenever we refer to Agni in his phenomenal aspect, we use the impersonal pronoun *it*, and the personal pronoun *he* is used in relation to Agni as a deity.

Even in its phenomenal aspect Agni is nowhere in the *Ṛgveda* identified exclusively with the natural element of fire. Fire as an element of Nature is only a form of manifestation of the phenomenal Agni. As a universal principle Agni manifests itself in every fire that is kindled, and its manifestation in every fire that is kindled is only a form of manifestation of its phenomenal nature. "Whatever other fires there may be, they are but manifestations of the Agni."[1] Agni the universal principle manifests itself whenever a fire is kindled. "Agni shines throughout the world with all fires kindled" (*viśvebhiḥ agnibhiḥ sarvam jagat bhāṣyata*).[2] Fires are many, but Agni as the principle that manifests itself in all the fires is one. Agni the deity is kindled in all fires. It is often stated in the *Ṛgveda* that Agni the deity is enkindled by Agni or fire, and the enkindled fire is only a form of Agni, or one of its several forms of manifestation at the phenomenal level. All the fires depend upon Agni for their existence like branches on a tree (*yasya te agne anye agnayaḥ upakṣitāḥ*).[3] Agni is often described in the *Ṛgveda* as having two births (*dvijanma*) and having three regions as its abode (*triśadaṣṭha*), or as having three types of existence (*trīṇi āyūṁśi*). It has either two or three types of existence depending upon the way in which the universe is divided and classified. If we prefer the classification of all that is there into celestial and terrestrial spheres, then Agni which is present in both the spheres will have two places for its existence, and is born twice. Agni that is born and present within the celestial sphere is of one form, and manifests itself there in celestial ways, while Agni that is born and present within the terrestrial realm is of another form, and the ways of its terrestrial manifestation are distinct. On the other

1. 1.59.1.
2. 6.12.1; see also 6.11.6.
3. 8.19.33; see also 2.35.8.

hand, if we prefer the more detailed classification of the universe into celestial, terrestrial and mid-regions, then Agni will have, according to its distinct forms of manifestation within these three regions, three types of existence. But through all these modes of existence and forms of manifestation the same Agni reveals itself. It exists in all the three regions as one and the same reality, though the modes of its existence or the forms of its manifestation differ from region to region. As there is no evidence in the *Ṛgveda* to show that the celestial and the mid-regions are extra-empirical as compared to the terrestrial region, we have to regard all the three regions as constituting the phenomenal reality. These refer to the limits of the phenomenal world. Therefore, all the forms in which Agni manifests itself in all the regions constitute the phenomenal nature of Agni. They constitute the observable form, or phenomenal aspect of Agni (*darśatam vapuḥ*). Thus when we talk of Agni in its phenomenal aspect we refer to all the manifestations of it in all the three regions. He has several forms in his womb, and manifests himself in all the worlds (*purupeśāsu garbha* or *pratikṣiyantam bhuvanāni viśvā*).[4] "Filling heaven, earth and the mid-region with thy radiance, the protector of the world."[5] "Thou by thine might rulest over all that is in heaven and on earth."[6]

As presented in one of the Brāhmaṇas, all that is warm is Agni, or wherever and in whatever form the principle of heat is present that is all Agni.[7] In the *Ṛgveda* also the conception of Agni is so comprehensive that it is difficult to determine its nature adequately, or to set limits to its manifestation. It is present everywhere or in all things in which the element of heat is present. It is present within all the fires, within plants and trees, within all living beings, including man, and within waters. Most commonly observable characteristics of Agni are its capacity to burn, to shed light, to give warmth and to consume all things that enter into it

4. 2.10.3 and 4.
5. 1.73.8; see also 8.39.9.
6. 1.144.6; see also 10.88.9.
7. *Śatapatha Brāhmaṇa* 1.6.3.23.

with flames going always upward (*viśva ādam puruvepasam*).[8] Agni that is inherently present within the plants, animals and men manifests itself in more than one form. In all these the principle of heat is present. Besides being the bodily heat within animals and men, Agni is the principle responsible for the growth of plants and trees, as well as for the ripening of fruits. "He matures the standing corn by his potency."[9] He is the embryo of plants, and ripens trees of every form and nature. By being the source of their growth, Agni is born anew every time a plant is born, and helps it to grow and mature. As the source of their growth and maturity, Agni is poetically described as the lord of plants and trees (*vanaspati*), and also as their child. "The forest trees and plants bear him within them, and produce him ever more."[10] Agni is present in the wombs (*jaṭhara*) of all living beings as the principle that is responsible for the digestion of food on which process depends the sustenance and growth of the bodies. "He stirs with life in the wombs dissimilar in kind."[11] He is the vital principle in all living beings, and in this mode of his existence, Agni helps all the vital functions of the body. Although the concept of Vaiśvānara is more comprehensive and has mystical overtones, it is identified primarily as the vital principle within all living beings. When the vital principle is weakened bodily growth is hampered, and with its extinction the body perishes. Thus Agni is the source of growth and sustenance, as well as destruction of all beings.

Within the living beings Agni is present as the principle of strength and vigour. As the source of growth and sustenance, he is the source of strength and vigour in all living beings. He is the lord of strength or vigour (*ūrjāmpati*).[12] Agni also dwells within waters, or they are also the source of its manifestation. He is present within floods, rivers and oceans. However, the sense in

8. *Ṛgveda* 8.44.26.
9. 1.127.4.
10. 8.43.9; see also 1.67.5; 3.1.13; 7.4.5.
11. 3.2.11.
12. 8.23.12.

which Agni is said to dwell or manifest himself within waters is not made clear. To our observation water and fire are the opposites, as water extinguishes fire. But as water stands for all forms of moisture, or it is the moistening principle, water in the form of vital sap in all living beings contains Agni. Vital sap is one instance wherein we find the inherence of Agni in water. Other commentators have pointed out to the presence of lightening within the clouds which bear water. According to the *Ṛgveda*, Agni helps in producing rain by agitating the clouds. However, the terms *samudra* and *āpaḥ* are often used symbolically in the *Ṛgveda* to mean human psyche in its primordial condition, and the creative flow of divine inspiration is frequently compared to the flow of waters. Similarly, the "seven rivers", which are described as the mothers of Agni, are used symbolically to mean the seven principal Vedic metres at various places in the *Ṛgveda*, as well as in other Vedic literature. Even in the *Ṛgveda*, the term *āpaḥ* is used to mean something other than water, and in relation to Agni it is described as a witness or observer of man. Whenever Agni is talked in relation to *āpaḥ*, his relation to man is also indicated. It is sufficient to point out for the present that the word *āpaḥ* is not on all occasions used to mean water. We come to the symbolic significance of the terms *āpaḥ* and *samudra* when we discuss the mystical aspect of Agni.

Agni in its phenomenal aspect manifests itself not only on earth, but also in the other two regions of the world, namely the mid-region and heaven. He fills heaven, earth and the mid-region with his might and light. In the mid-region Agni is identified with lightning (*vidyut*). "Ten quarters produce Agni as lightning (*vidyut*), who is inherent in all beings as *jaṭhara*."[13] "He is willing to be seen in ten quarters."[14]

The primary and pre-eminent form of Agni in heaven is the Sun. The Sun as the source of all light and energy represents

---

13. 1.95.2.
14. 1.146.5.

Agni in the celestial sphere. The Sun is the chief form of manifestation of Agni. "Thy moving radiance is the chief of all luminous bodies."[15] Agni is the centre of all light. Because of their poetic form of expression the Ṛgvedic statements are not always to be taken in their literary sense. While in several hymns Agni is identified with the Sun, there are hymns in which the sun is seen as only a manifestation, though the pre-eminent one, of Agni. In his manifestation as the Sun, Agni is described as the sign of the days (*ketum ahnam*), and the revealer of heaven (*ketum divaḥ*).[16] He is the head of heaven, and fills it with his radiance. As will be evident from the following discussion wherein Agni's divine aspect is dicussed, Agni cannot be identified with the Sun. All the phenomena in which Agni is inherent can be identified in a sense with Agni. But thereby his omnipresent character should not be lost sight of. He is present on earth, in the mid-region and in heaven, but at the same time his existence is not limited to any of these regions. All that is known about him through all the forms of his manifestation refers to his manifested state of existence, and he is more than all the forms of his manifestation. He cannot, therefore, be identified exclusively with any or all of his manifestations, however pre-eminent they may be. Thus Agni's identification with the Sun is meaningful only in the sense that the Sun, as the chief of all luminous bodies is a supreme form of manifestation of Agni. He is described as, "established above the light of the Sun."[17] The idea of Agni's transcendence is indicated when it is stated that he abiding on the top or head of the universe (*bhuvanasya mūrdhan*) shines along with the radiance of the Sun (*saharocanena*).[18] Again in the expression that Agni is born first in heaven as the Sun, or reveals himself in the form of the Sun in heaven, he is regarded as the source of Sun's light (*sūrye jyotiḥ ādadhuḥ*).[19] He is the light of all lights, or the source of all

15. 4.7.9; see also 3.55.9.
16. 3.2.14; 10.88.12.
17. 10.88.5.
18. 10.88.5 and 6.
19. 10.12.7.

light, and all the luminous bodies in heaven manifest his light. They represent him in the celestial sphere, and he is present on earth and in the mid-region in the two other modes of his existence. Thus Agni manifests himself equally in all the regions of the world, and by being present in all the regions, he constitutes their unity, or in him all the regions are united.

Thus even in his phenomenal aspect Agni is all-pervasive, and is present in both the worlds, or the three regions. Being present in all the worlds (*bhuvanāni viśva*) he manifests himself in diverse forms (*puru rūpa*), and none of them can reveal him fully. He is present everywhere in his manifested condition. Although he is of many forms, and is present everywhere, as a deity Agni is one. In his wholeness (*anūnam*) Agni is more than and beyond all his manifestations. He is limitless, and even the heavenly bodies like the Sun do not attain his true greatness (*animān*).[20] The Sun and the Moon are only his eyes through whom he observes all that is there. They are only his phenomenal forms (*darśatam vapaḥ*), and reflect his glory and splendour (*mahimā* or *śrī*). In other words, Agni is known at the phenomenal level by his most powerful and mighty acts, and the varied manifestations of his greatness, like the Sun and the Moon, serve to reveal his glory. The Ṛgvedic seers are clear in their vision that what is known about Agni at the phenomenal level does not reveal his nature completely. He is divine or a deity, and his divine nature reveals itself in and through his manifestations. In all the hymns addressed to Agni his divine nature is given prominence. Every hymn that is addressed to him is a praise of his greatness as a divine being. He is an object of worship and prayer. However, a complete understanding of his nature and greatness requires that he is viewed in his divine and phenomenal aspects. Therefore in no hymn addressed to him, he is viewed and described exclusively either in terms of his divine or phenomenal attributes. At the same time, Agni as a deity is not known independently of his empirical manifestations. His divine nature

20. 1.27.11.

reveals itself to a man of inspiration in and through his varied manifestations at the phenomenal level, and therefore, there is no strict division and conflict between his divine and phenomenal natures. While his phenomenal nature is known directly to man through his senses, his divine nature reveals itself in and through his visible forms of manifestation to an inspired person. Thus what is phenomenal is an expression of the Divine, or the Divine is what manifests or reveals itself through the phenomenal. There is, therefore, no separation or gulf between the phenomenal and the Divine. And both the aspects belong to a deity, and are integrated in him. Keeping this in view we now proceed to present and discuss the nature of Agni as a deity or as a divine being. The fact that Agni is seen as more than and beyond what is known about him through his several phenomenal manifestations in all the regions of his existence is a point of departure for us to understand his divine nature.

In his true nature or in his wholeness (*anūna*), which is indivisible and one (*aditi*), Agni is more than and beyond all his manifestations in all the regions of the world. He is known indirectly through his manifestations, which are like his footprints, and point to him as their source. "He plants his footprints on the lofty ridges of broad earth."[21] While Agni is nothing more than what is known about him empirically for those who cannot discern, all that is empirically known about him only serves the purpose of revealing his undivided divine existence for those who are wise (dhīrā). His real or divine nature is hidden to our ordinary or uninspired understanding. And while his various manifestations point to his reality as a divine being, he himself points to something more than himself which is his ultimate source and ground, and of which he is only an indication or sign. The divineness of Agni lies in his capacity to reveal the Divine. His existence is of the nature of a manifestation, and as a manifestation of the Divine he reveals the Divine. He is a great sign (*bṛhat ketu*) of Divine, and is known

21. 1.146.2.

for his revelatory function or form (*sañjnata rūpa*).[22] He is an embodied form of the Divine, or a phenomenal mode of divine existence. In knowing his true nature as a divine being through his several acts of self-manifestation, wise can trace the source of his existence to the highest or the divine (*pade parame*). Agni exists within the phenomenal realm, as in the highest. He is known to all in his phenomenal existence, but his relation to the divine, the ultimate source of his existence, is not open to ordinary or uninspired understanding of man. His birth in the highest is a mystery for our ordinary understanding, while his birth in the phenomenal realm is known to all. He truly exists in the highest, which is his real abode (*asmin pade*), and is therefore described as the first born of truth (*pradhamajā ṛtasya*).[23] He comes to us in a visible or embodied form as a revelation of the Divine, or he comes to us from the Supreme Father (*pituḥ paramāt*), and reveals himself in a form which all can see (*darśatasya vapuḥ virājati*).[24] His real abode is the highest, which is the source of all the deities as well, and also of *ṛta* (*ṛtasya yone devasya sadane*).[25] He holds within himself the embryo of the Father and Generator, and thus reveals the source of his origin. "From birth he knew his Father's bosom and set his father's streams and speech in motion (*pituḥ ca garbham janituḥ bibhre*). With his birth his Father stayed not hidden."[26] Being born of *ṛta* (truth) he reveals it to us, or he manifests in himself the knowledge of *ṛta*. He knows the truth, and can therefore reveal it to us. Knowing the *ṛta* he sends forth the streams of it to us, or comes to us with the knowledge of *ṛta*, as the term *dhāra* is a synonym of knowledge, according to *Nighaṇṭu*. Being born of truth he knows the truth, and, therefore, judges mortals in terms of their truthfulness and untruthfulness. He shines as a manifestation of *ṛta*. He is the eye of *ṛta*.[27] The

22. 1.69.5.
23. 10.5.7; *asmin pade parame tastivāmeam* 2.35.14.
24. 10.140.4; see also 1.141.4.
25. 1.144.2.
26. 3.1.9.
27. 10.8.5; 5.7.6.

same idea is expressed differently when it is said that Agni is the first born among immortals (*pradhmajā amṛtānām*). Representing the Divine on earth he reveals it to us in the form of immortality. The Divine is often characterised in terms of light and immortality, and Agni reveals both the aspects of the Divine. He is a sign of immortality (*amṛtasya ketu*) as well as its centre (*amṛtasya nābhi*).[28] He is the likeness of divine light (*svandriśām*), the light of all lights, or the ultimate source of all light. And as the Divine is known by its own light, Agni is addressed as *svavidam* or one who is known by divine light, or who makes us attain it. He upholds and reveals it within himself (*svapati*). As the source of all light within the phenomenal world, he is the centre of all light (*rocanasya nābhi*). In his identity with all that is brilliant and shining, Agni is the centre and source of all light within the phenomenal world. He is the lord of light as well as its revelation. But light also means symbolically the light of divine wisdom, as darkness stands for ignorance. In this sense Agni reveals divine wisdom to man. He is, therefore, prayed to destroy with his divine light (*jyotiṣā daiyena*)[29] the forces of untruth and spiritual darkness which obstruct the full manifestation and revelation of the light of truth. In this sense he is seen and described as the awakening of divine in man (*devasya cetanam*).[30] Or he represents the Divine consciousness in man. He spreads and discloses the truth of the Father and Creator (*pitā janitā satyam ukṣan*), and hence he is addressed as truth (*satya*).[31] He is truth though in a derived sense. He is worshipped and prayed as if he is the highest reality. And as a manifestation of the Divine within the phenomenal realm, he unites and integrates the phenomenal and the Divine. He is a bridge between the two realms which is of course true with all the deities. "He brings together mortals and immortals by sacred rite for the sake of obtaining mutual

28. 3.17.4.

29. 10.87.12; *jyotiṣā bṛhat* 5.2.9; *rājantam divyene śocisā* 3.2.4.

30. 4.7.2.

31. 4.1.10; 3.14.1.

sustenance."[32] He brings down to the realm of mortals the light of the Divine, and reveals it to them. He is the presence of the Divine within the phenomenal realm.

As a primary and universal manifestation of the Divine, Agni reveals in himself all the qualities of the Divine. The epithets which Agni bears in common with all the deities are appropriate to him as a manifestation of the Divine. If Agni is nothing more than what is known of him empirically, the various divine qualities attributed to him will have no meaning. We will now discuss Agni as a divine being whose nature is revealed through his diverse manifestations either in Nature or within man. In his divine aspect he is an object of man's devotion and worship, and all the hymns addressed to him describe him as a divine being or a deity.

As a deity Agni is seen and described as a bridge between the Divine and the phenomenal, or the immortal and the mortal. He is described as the immortal principle abiding within the realm of mortals.[33] Not only he reveals the Divine to the mortals, but by being within them he also helps them to rise higher and become divine or attain immortality. He helps man in attaining what is great and excellent. Because of his twofold function of revealing to man the nature of the Divine, and helping him to become divine, Agni alone is described as *dūta* (messenger) in the *Ṛgveda*. He is a bridge between the Divine and man. He is a principle of unity, as all deities are, between the Divine and the phenomenal, or the immortal and the mortal.

Agni accomplishes his twofold function by being the prime factor of *yajña*, the Vedic form of worship. He is the primary means of accomplishing *yajña* (*yajña sādham* or *sādhanam*). He is the sign of *yajña* (*ketu*), as well as the source of its knowledge to man (*adhvarāṇām cetanam*).[34] It is only when man is divinely inspired he realises the significance of *yajña*, and is impelled to

---

32. 1.141.6.
33. 4.2.1; 4.1.1.
34. 3.3.8; 3.3.3; 3.10.4.

extend it to all the spheres of his life. Agni is described as the face or expression of *yajña* (*anīkam*).[35] He is also the generator and leader of *yajña* (*pita* and *neta*). *Yajña* is not something that is to be done or performed as an act. It is to be spread or extended (*tan*), that is to say, man has to participate in and extend the divine process involved in creation. Everything in creation, including the deities and man, are involved in the process of divine *yajña*, and therefore to observe it is to realise its meaning in one's life and to extend the process involved in *yajña* to all the spheres of one's life. Without *yajña* man has no existence. To perform it is therefore to continue the process by realising the involvement of one's existence in it. Thus *yajña* as observed by man at various levels of his existence is only a continuation and extension of the *yajña* originally enacted by the Divine, its real agent, and because of which everything has come into existence, including the deities. It is not by standing out of the process but by being involved within it *yajña* is performed by man.

As the supreme form of man's worship of the Divine, as conceived in the Veda, *yajña* is centred around Agni. By offering oblations into Agni, man not only worships Agni, but through him all other deities, for in his divine nature Agni represents or includes all the deities. *Yajña* as conceived in the Vedic literature is the means by which the Divine has become all, or created the worlds. It indicates the process of self-manifestation of the Divine. It is also the means by which the creation is sustained. Thus *yajña* is not an act accomplished in time once and for all, but indicates the process of self-manifestation of the Divine. And in knowing the meaning of *yajña* as an act of self-expression on the part of the divine, man comes to know the meaning of the Divine. What is an act of self-expression for the Divine is for man the source of divine revelation. It is through the acts of self-manifestation of the Divine man comes to know the nature and meaning of the Divine. The divine act of creation is for man the divine act of self-revelation. The creation which has come

35. 10.2.6.

into existence through the act of self-sacrifice on the part of the Divine, reflects within itself the process of *yajña*. Therefore, to observe or perform *yajña* is to continue it, and extend it to all the spheres of human life by participating in the process of creation. By realising his involvement in the process of *yajña*, man can become an agent of furthering the process of *yajña* or extending it. Thus the primary object of *yajña* in relation to man is to help him to overcome the sense of his separation from the process, and to make him realise his involvement in the divine process of creation and sustenance of the world.

Now, while the Divine is identified, both in the *Ṛgveda* and in the later tradition, with *yajña*, the deities are regarded only as means of accomplishing it. They are born out of the process of *yajña* and are its agents or extend it at the cosmic level. In all this process the Divine is the object of *yajña*, as well as its real agent. Therefore, *yajña*, which is divine, is also a revelation of the Divine (*amṛtasya cetanam yajñam*).[36]

As pointed out earlier, Agni has a special place in the divine scheme of *yajña*. He awakens in man the sense of *yajña*, and inspires him to realise his involvement in the process of divine *yajña*. And through man as an agent of *yajña* at the phenomenal level Agni helps to integrate the phenomenal and the Divine, so that their original unity is restored. What was accomplished originally in the timeless beginning by the Divine, and what is being accomplished by the deities at the cosmic level is to be accomplished by man at the human level. The deities, and specially Agni, reveal within themselves the principle of *yajña*. *Yajña* which stands for the process of creation through self-sacrifice is reflected fully in the nature of Agni who destroys and creates as well. As the divine principle of both destruction and creation, Agni extends the meaning of *yajña* to all the realms. He reveals its meaning to man. "Deities established him (on earth) for the accomplishment of *yajña*."[37]

---

36. 1.170.4.

37. 1.48.1.

Worship is a spontaneous response of man to the divine experienced in and through the deities. All the deities, as universal manifestations of the divine, are objects of man's devotion and worship (*yajiṣṭha* or *yajñīya*). Divinely inspired devotion finds its expression in prayer, or prayer is a spontaneous expression in language of the devotion inwardly experienced. Besides giving expression to devotion, prayer also expresses by way of praise the nature of the Divine. The nature of the Divine which is experienced by the seers in and through the deities is what is sought to be communicated through the hymns. Thus all the hymns speak the glory of the Divine.

In the *Ṛgveda,* the Divine is identified as that which inspires in man devotion, reverence and worship, and as the various deities are the immediate sources of such inspiration, they are the objects of man's devotion, reverence and worship. Although devotion and divine refer to the same experience, from the standpoint of man the birth of devotion is more significant. It confers on man blessedness and joy. He sees in its experience the supreme fulfilment of his life, or it is the highest to be desired and attained by man. Now, Agni is an object of worship, as well as a means of expressing it. He is an object of worship as he is a manifestation of the Divine, and as in worshipping him all the deities are worshipped he is also means of worship. He inspires in man devotion and prayer. "Grant us devotion and understand our prayer."[38] "I offer to Agni, as if to the Divine (*vedhase*) the great praise of old, for the sake of animating the energies of the pious."[39]

Devotion is an experience that springs up within the heart of man, and flows from there, and is intended to touch and stir the hearts of the deities. "Within my heart I bring forth a hymn for Agni."[40] "Praising thee with devout heart, I, a mortal, earnestly invoke you, an immortal."[41] Prayers are addressed to

38. 1.94.8; see also 2.6.4; 3.13.6; 6.16.30.

39. 3.10.5; see also 8.43.11.

40. 10.91.14; 6.16.47.

41. 5.4.10.

Agni with great reverence (*mahā namasā*), so as to touch the "centre of his heart", like a loving and well- attired wife her husband.[42] It is Agni who can make devotion shine with love. He inspires devotion even within ordinary men, and quickens even the wisdom of the wise. Stirred by devotion and love people approach him on their bended knees with upraised hands.[43] "He is like a well of water in a desert to the man desirous of worship."[44] "We adore thee in the place of devotion or heart (*namasaḥ pade*)."[45] The place of devotion mentioned here can mean the inspired heart of man as it is the seat of reverence and devotion. Man experiences the sense of fulfilment of his understanding when engaged in Agni's worship. Agni is addressed as father, mother and saviour (*trātā*). He is the centre of all devotion, in whose presence men sit like sons in the house of their father.[46] Men of devotion approach him like a servant going to the dwelling of his master.[47]

Like all other deities, Agni not only inspires in man devotion and prayer, but he is also increased by them. The presence of the Divine in nature, though is an objective fact to an inspired person, it is not objective in the sense that all can see it like any object. Only those who are divinely inspired can see the presence of the Divine in Nature, and to them it is real and objective. When it is not experienced it is not real for man. Thus those who have experienced the Divine through its presence in Nature, and are devoted to it can inspire devotion in others, and become a source of its revelation to others. When man's awareness of the divine increases and becomes more comprehensive the devotion within him also grows and matures. The Divine reveals itself within the state of devotion, or devotion is a source of

42. 10.91.13; 7.12.1.
43. 3.14.5.
44. 10.4.1.
45. 8.23.9; see also 1.53.5, 1.158.2.
46. 1.73.3.
47. 1.150.1.

manifestation of the divine at the human level. In this sense devotion and prayer help the growth or increase of the deities, as with the growth and maturity of devotion within man, his awareness of the divine increases, or becomes more and more comprehensive. Now, Agni is known to all in his phenomenal aspect, but in his divine aspect he is known to the seers. It is by means of devotion, which Agni inspires in man, man sees the divine nature of Agni. Agni in his divine aspect, or as a divine being, is revealed to man in the state of devotion. He is increased by devotion or grows in it; and he is also a source of its inspiration to man (*agni vardhantu naḥ giraḥ yataḥ jāyate uktyaḥ*).[48] He is attained by *brahma* or devotion. The terms *brahma, namaḥ* and *giraḥ* which indicate the various aspects of devotion are the increasers of Agni, the deity. He is awakened by prayer, and is increased by devotion. "He is present within the devotion of man, and is revealed in their hearts."[49] Devotion is divine, and all the deities are revealed to man in the state of devotion. Agni is described as born of prayer (*mānasya sūnuḥ*).[50]

Although devotion finds its expression through prayers or hymns, they are not adequate to express it. The state of devotion is ineffable; and the hymns only try to express it, although they are not always adequate to express it. Even the sacred speech in the form of hymns is to be granted and perfected by the same source which inspires devotion in man, to be able to express devotion adequately. Thus the seers have realised the inadequacy of their hymns to comprehend and express fully the divine nature of Agni.[51] And not only man is devoted to Agni and worships him, but the whole creation, of which he is the lord and controller, bows down to him as it were in reverence (*tubhyam namantaḥ pradiśaḥ catasraḥ*).[52]

---

48. 3.10.6.
49. 3.16.4.
50. 1.189.8, 2.6.2.
51. 1.76.1, 1.77.1, 8.73.2.
52. 10.51.9.

In being a self-manifestation of the divine, Agni is identified with the divine, but not exclusively, for all other deities are equally the self-expressions of the divine. In this sense Agni is addressed as or identified with truth. He is born of truth, as well as the truth, and all the attributes which are appropriate to the Divine are attributed to him also. He is the creator (*cakrī*), as well as the life of all (*viśva āyu*).[53] "He is the creator or generator of all men, heaven and earth, and creation has imbibed life from him."[54] This is true of him even in his phenomenal aspect, for without him as the universal principle of heat nothing can be sustained. He is addressed as if he is the highest reality, and accordingly described as the creator, knower and upholder of all. He is the martix of all (*viśvasya ketu bhuvanasya garbha*), and lives in all (*pratikṣiyantam bhuvanāni viśvā*).[55] He knows all that has come into existence, including the deities, or in being born within all he knows all (*jātavedasa*). He is described as one who sees all (*viśvacarṣani*), and knows all (*viśva vedasam*). He has infinite eyes (*sahasrākṣa*), or sees all with the eyes of all. As Vaiśvānara he is within all the living beings, and knows them all. He is the lord of all that was, all that is, and all that shall be.

He is the strength and vigour of all the deities, and knows their generation. He is most wise, and none, including the deities, can excel him in wisdom. In his divine nature he is one with all the deities. He is *Viśvadevam* which epithet is applied to other deities also. It means the deity so addressed is one with all the deities, or he is the self of all the deities (*sarvadevātmaka*, according to Sāyaṇa). Agni is all the deities as he in his divine nature comprehends or includes within himself all the deities, like the spokes of a wheel in the hub.[56] Therefore, all the prayers addressed to various deities are at the same time addressed to him also. He is of many forms and names, and all the divine

53. 6.4.2; see also 8.43.25.

54. 1.149.2, 3.16.4.

55. 2.10.4.

56. 5.13.6.

names refer to him and belong to him. He is Brahmaṇaspati, he is Rudra, he is Viṣṇu, he is Indra, or he is all the deities.[57] Being present inherently within all the deities he knows them all. He is one with or represents every deity by his might and glory (*pratyardhim devasya devasya*).[58]

Agni hears and knows the prayers of his worshippers, and accepts their worship. In his wisdom he discerns between those who are devoted to him and those who are not, but protects them both. He discerns between the wise and the unwise, and protects even the weak and unwise. He is earnestly prayed to save the worshippers from all types of sin and evil. He is *trātā* or the saviour of man from sin.[59] Because of his gracious help man can overcome his evil and sinful thoughts (*amati*). He is prayed to save man from sins committed either against him or any other deity, and is begged for his forgiveness.[60] As saviour of man from sin he is compared to a boat, who can ferry people across their sins.[61] He is also prayed to dispel the spiritual darkness (*tiraḥ tamāṁsi*) from his worshippers.[62] Man's righteousness and wisdom are his gifts. He bestows on man what is auspicious, supreme and excellent, and helps him to attain immortality, or realise his divine nature. "Save us by thy wisdom from sins or chase our sins away."[63] "Since the victorious rays (*bhānavaḥ*) of Agni penetrate universally may our sins be repented of."[64] And all the divine attributes which were discussed in the previous chapter are attributed to Agni. He is described as *kavi, ṛṣi, vipra, manīṣā* and *dhīra*.

We now try to understand the mystical aspect of Agni without which our understanding or knowledge of Agni will not be

57. 2.1.3 to 6.

58. 10.1.5.

59. 5.24.1, 6.1.5.

60. 5.4.9.

61. 1.99.1, 1.97.8.

62. 8.63.5; see also 3.27.13.

63. 1.97.1; see also 1.189.1.

64. 1.97.5.

complete. When we talk of mystical aspect of Agni we mean by it the spiritual (*adhyātma*) dimension of Agni, or Agni as revealed within the spiritual life of man. According to the method of interpretation of the Vedic Saṁhitās adopted by the Brāhmaṇas, which was discussed in the previous chapter, each deity can have three distinct types of meaning according to its nature as manifested in the three distinct realms of the world. These three types of interpretation of the nature of a deity are not mutually exclusive, as they are not three different ways of understanding the nature of a deity. It is not the case that if one interpretation of a deity is accepted, the other two are to be rejected. Each interpretation is valid and meaningful at its own level, and together they reveal the nature of a deity. The scope for such an interpretation lies in the nature of the deities who manifest themselves distinctly in different realms. However, in all the three realms the same divine reality manifests itself, though distinctly, or that is how man apprehends the nature of the Divine in relation to each realm. The Vedic seers in their attempt to grasp the meaning of the world have divided it into three realms, and have tried to comprehend the nature and meaning of the Divine as it reveals itself in each realm. As explained in the post-Saṁhitā tradition, the chief purpose of the Vedic wisdom is to restore the original unity of the Divine which has become many in the process of creation.[65] It is to realise the divine unity of all that is there, or to see Nature in its divine unity without at the same time denying validity and meaningfulness to the diversity of Nature. Therefore, the nature of the Divine and the meaning of its revelation are known differently according to its different forms of manifestation in different realms. Thus though each deity manifests itself within all the three realms the manner of its manifestation and revelation differs from realm to realm. But the essential nature of a deity remains the same in all its manifestations; only the nature and function of its manifestations will not be the same. A deity is at the same time more than and beyond what is known about it in

---

65. *Śatapatha Brāhmaṇa* 10.4.2.2, 21 and 22; *Aitareya Āraṇyaka* 3.2.6.

and through all its varied manifestations. Therefore, in trying to understand the mystical nature of Agni our purpose is to identify it within the reality of man, especially within his spiritual life, as well as to point out how the real nature of Agni as a divine being is more than and beyond his threefold manifestation.

The attempts made in the Brāhmaṇas to identify the various deities with the different faculties and powers of man which culminated in the total identification of man's reality with the ultimate reality in the Upaniṣads, are a development of the vision expressed in the Vedic hymns. The fact that the Saṁhitās have not expressed this idea as explicitly and clearly as in later tradition is no indication that it is totally alien to the hymns of the *Ṛgveda*. They contain the vision or truth as revealed to the seers, and the Brāhmaṇas are the first to interpret it, or explain its meaning systematically. It is by way of interpreting the hymns the Brāhmaṇas have tried to understand the meaning of divine revelation in terms of the varied forms of manifestation of the Divine in all the spheres, or as it reveals itself at different levels of human experience. In thus trying to understand the meaning of divine revelation within the reality of man, they have identified the various deities with the different faculties and powers of man. And in the post-Saṁhitā literature the term *deva* is used to mean the senses of man.[66] Thus when we talk of the spiritual significance of the deities we are not deviating from the spirit of the Vedic Saṁhitās of which the *Ṛgveda Saṁhitā* is the most important. In the *Ṛgveda* the various deities are seen as dwelling within man, though the sense in which they live in man is not clarified.

The deities manifest themselves in and through Nature, and man is not viewed by the Vedic seers as standing outside of Nature. What is present in Nature is present within man also, though the mode of its manifestation is not the same in both the cases. In other words, the way in which the deities manifest and operate in man is distinct from the mode of their

66. *Śāṅkhāyana Āraṇyaka* 4.3 and 14.

manifestation in Nature. Man also manifests the same reality, which manifests itself in Nature or as Nature, and, therefore, man is not alien to Nature, and Nature is not something other than and different from man. Nature and man manifest and reveal the same reality. However, the Divine as it reveals itself within the reality of man will have a different significance, as the mode of its revelation in man is spiritual. So in understanding the nature of the deities at the *adhyātma* level or as revealed within the reality of man, we come to know the spiritual or divine nature of the deities more fully.

As pointed out earlier the Ṛgvedic knowledge of Agni is not limited to what is known about him through his varied manifestations in Nature. His divine nature is what has attracted the attention of the seers most, and in knowing which his revelation within man is of supreme significance. Agni has a transcendental dimension is evident from his birth in the highest. Over and above his presence in the phenomenal realm Agni in his true nature exists in the highest, and what is revealed of him at the phenomenal level is only his glory. And he transcends his glory. "Not Being, Being in the highest heaven, in Aditi's bosom and in Dakṣa's birthplace, is Agni our first-born of *ṛta*, the Milk-cow and the Bull in life's beginning."[67] Or being both manifest and unmanifest, the birth of Agni, the first manifestation of truth (*ṛta*), is in the bosom of Aditi (undivided). He exists before the creation (*asat ca sat ca parame vyoman dakṣasya janman aditeḥ upasthe agniḥ ha naḥ pradhamajā ṛtasya pūrve āyūni vṛṣabhaḥ ca dhenuḥ*). His real or divine nature is hidden to our ordinary understanding. "Who indeed art thou, where dost thou abide? Which of you discern the hidden (*niṇya*) nature of Agni."[68] In his transcendental aspect Agni is identified with the highest, and the seers have realised the inadequacy of their understanding to know him truly and fully in his transcendental aspect. What they know about him is according to their intuitive abilites, and their prayers fully indicate

67. 10.5.7.

68. 1.75.3.

the limitations of human understanding in grasping the true nature of Agni. They have realised that Agni in his transcendental dimension is more than their understanding of him. "He (Agni) in whom all the deities abide in the form of self-effulgent knowledge, that true nature of Agni we do not know" (*yasmin devāḥ manmani saṁcaranti apīcyena vayam asya na vidma*).[69] They are drawn to Agni in devotion and worship because of their awareness of Agni as a divine being, though their understanding of him in his divine nature is not complete. The sages express their wonder about him and his glory. "My mind hastens towards him. What shall I declare about him? How shall I comprehend him?"[70] Agni's wisdom is unbounded. He excels in wisdom all the deities and mortals. Nothing that is created can contain his wisdom. He knows all, but in his true nature and glory he is not known to us perfectly (*mūrāḥ amūra na vayam cikitvaḥ mahitvam agee*). Only Agni the wisest knows himself truly and fully.[71] "Being a mortal with limited capacities to know, I cannot know the perfect and true nature Agni, the Divine. If at all anyone knows him truly, it is himself."[72] Agni himself declares: "Who has beheld me, which of the deities has fully seen my manifold forms?"[73] Agni Vaiśvānara verily knows the origin and process of creation. He comprehends all that is there within himself. All the deities shine with the splendour of Agni. He is the source of all creation, as well as the source of all light and knowledge. Thus the real nature of Agni is beyond the comprehension of man; he is a divine mystery. "Which of you discern the hidden Agni, the great *kavi*, and the germ of all and sustainer of all."[74] "With what mind shall we bring oblation, and what oblation may we offer to Agni."[75]

---

69. 10.12.8.
70. 6.9.6.
71. 10.4.4.
72. 10.4.4; see also 10.79.4.
73. 10.51.2.
74. 1.95.4.
75. 8.73.5.

The real nature of Agni which is hidden to the understanding of man constitutes the mystical aspect of Agni. The hymns in which this aspect of Agni is presented are the most difficult to understand and interpret. They are enigmatic. The difficulty in understanding them lies in the highly symbolic character of the language used. Almost all the terms used in such hymns are symbolic in their meaning. And unless they are taken so their meaning may be totally lost to us. In their plain sense they do not convey any intelligible meaning. Therefore, while interpreting these symbolic expressions one inevitably brings in or falls back on his presuppositions and world view, as well as on what the Veda generally means to him. If one takes a completely naturalistic view of the deities the problem of interpreting such hymns becomes all the more difficult, for they are least amenable to a naturalistic interpretation, or, are highly unintelligible from a naturalistic standpoint. On the other hand, if we adopt a standpoint or perspectice which, in the first place, is consistent with the Veda as a whole and then with the Hindu tradition in general, we have to understand and interpret the significance of the deities spiritually; only then the symbols reveal their real meaning. This approach is valid and meaningful, and is not against the spirit of the Veda, as the various Vedic words reveal their symbolic meaning if we follow their actual usage in different contexts of the Veda. Although we are not spiritually as mature as the Ṛgvedic seers, so that we can really penetrate into the depths of their vision, at least by remaining open in our approach, and with the help of the traditional method of interpretation of the Veda as provided, for instance in the Brāhmaṇas, we can to a large extent appropriate the vision of the seers. This is more relevant and significant when we come to understand the mystical or spiritual meaning of the deities. Our naturalistic and even rational understanding are highly inadequate to comprehend the mystical depths of the vision of Nature as presented in the hymns of the *Ṛgveda*. To identify the spiritual powers or principles which the various deities represent within man is also a problem, and in this regard also it is better to accept and follow the account of the seers. What we can do to make their meaning intelligible, or to elucidate the mystical side of the Vedic vision, is to look to the possibilities of human experience.

As long as we are concerned with the visible manifestations of Agni, which are what our ordinary or unillumined understanding can know, the divine nature of Agni remains hidden from us. "We know only the outward forms and the real nature (of Agni) is concealed from us."[76] Husk is made known from husk. Though in his transcendental aspect Agni is hidden to man's ordinary understanding, he is revealed to one whose intellect is divinely illumined, or whose understanding is mature. "Men filled with understanding find him when they have sung prayers (to him) formed within their hearts."[77] He is to be approached with a pure and illumined mind, and is known in his true nature to one whose mind is free from all passions (*manīṣayā budhyā*), or to one who has achieved complete mastery over his mind.[78] The term *manīṣā* literally means lord of one's mind. To such an intellect the real or divine nature of Agni is revealed, and even then Agni is regarded as beyond its comprehension. A wise man (*manīṣī*) can only see Agni as something transcending his empirical manifestations, but cannot fully comprehend his nature. In himself he is beyond the reach of human understanding and wisdom (*paraḥ manīṣayā*).[79] However, to recognise Agni as a divine being, or as a manifestation of the divine is itself a spiritual discovery. It is one thing to know Agni as something more than and beyond what is known to our ordinary understanding, and quite another to know him in his real nature in which he is one with the Divine. To know Agni in all his manifestations at all levels is only to know him as a phenomenal reality, and to see in and through those manifestations the presence of Agni as a divine

76. 5.19.1.

77. 1.67.2.

78. 1.70.1.

79. 5.17.2; Agni is described as *agohyam* or inconceivable 10.64.3.

being requires the wisdom of a *r̥ṣi*. The fact that the Divine in itself is beyond the reach of human knowledge does not remove the possibility of its being known by man through its manifestations. So also is our knowledge of Agni, the deity. In his divine aspect he is both known and unknown.

Those who are spiritually immature or whose intellect is swayed by passions cannot see the real nature of Agni. "Though they know Agni (in his phenomenal nature) it is not known to them."[80] "Those who give no offerings, who practice untruth attain not the inconceivable deity whether abiding in nature or in perfect waters (*āpaḥ*)."[81] Agni is wise; and only wise can know him. While Agni as fire is kindled by fire, Agni the wise (*vipra*) is kindled by a *vipra*.[82] He is a seer (*kavi*) and only a *kavi* can know him. The spiritual aspect of Agni is revealed to those who are divinely inspired. The intellect of man is to be made divine to apprehend the divine nature of Agni. The first to discover the mystical or spiritual nature of Agni are the Aṅgīrasa seers. "Following a lost animal by its footprints, the wise Bhr̥gus desiring him and anxious to find him discovered him (*anvavindan*) by their reverence lurking in the cave (of heart)."[83]

Agni inspires devotion in man, and his divinity is revealed therein. When the understanding of man or his intellect is illumined by Agni, "it gets endowed with divine splendour (*tejīyasā manasā*)"[84] and is able to apprehend the divine nature of Agni. He gives an impulse to devotion, and his divine nature is revealed within the state of devotion, or one who has experienced devotion can see it as a gift of Agni. Thus what is revealed to a divinely inspired person or known by the wise is the true nature of Agni, while what is known otherwise is only his glory (*śreya*).[85]

80. 1.72.2.
81. 2.35.6.
82. 8.43.14.
83. 1.65.1.
84. 3.19.3.
85. 10.91.2.

In his divine nature Agni is identified with the highest reality or the divine. As a primary manifestation of the divine, he is divine, but at the same time as a mode of divine existence, or as its manifestation he is not the divine in itself. The manifestation of the divine is not limited to Agni only. The Ṛgvedic seers are clearly conscious of this distinction. While on occasions he is addressed as truth, and as the source of all that is there, on other occasions he is seen only as a deity born of truth, or as having his source of origin in the divine. Both the assertions are valid and meaningful if we view Agni as a divine being, or as a manifestation of the divine in which sense he is both the revealer and the revealed. He is the object of devotion and worship, as well as their source. He is the real priest, the real offering and also the object of worship.[86] In one of the hymns Agni is said to have disclosed his own identity as one who knows all that is born (*jātavedasa*), and whose mouth is immortality.[87] He is the life force of the threefold nature, measure of the regions and also the offering or oblation. He is the source of all that exists, and upholds it as well. He is present within all the deities and human beings (*viśveṣām hitaḥ devebhi mānuṣe jane*).[88] He is addressed as Brahma in the sense of the ultimate reality.[89] He comprehends within himself all the deities, or in him all the deities are included (*devāḥ tvam paribhūḥ asi*). By being in him all the deities are of one mind and of one wisdom. He is their oneness; and he is explicitly identified with all the deities. He is that divine splendour by which all the deities shine. He is the light of the divine which is sanctifying and auspicious. He is the centre as well as the revelation of the immortal principle. Shining with the light of the Great or the divine (*jyotiṣā bṛhat*) he reveals the true nature of things, and thereby helps man in overcoming undivine wisdom

86. Agni is often described as the real priest and real sacrificer 3.26.1; 6.15.14. He is the oblation as well as the object of it 3.4.10; 2.1.2; 2.6.7.

87. 3.26.7.

88. 6.16.1; see also 7.4.1.

89. 11.1.3.

(*adevī māyā*).[90] In his identity with the highest he bears a secret name which is revealed to the wise, or the wise know his name who is in the highest (*vidma te nāma paramam guhā yat*).[91] He is the lord of all lords, and is addressed as *prabhu* (lord), Father, Mother and Saviour. He is the bestower of happiness on all (*viśva śambhuvam*), and is its increaser as well. In his splendourous divine presence the wise experience the wonder of all wonders, and the divine that is revealed in and through Agni is both wonderful and awe inspiring (*ghora*).[92]

He is, however, a manifestation of the divine and the divine is more than what is revealed in and through Agni. He is the first-born of the divine, or self-revealing light of the divine. He is generated by the "Supreme Father" to reveal His glory. His birth place is the highest, the abode of all-pervasive reality, Viṣṇu. He is a visible form of the divine. The divine is the ultimate source and ground of all the deities, who are only its manifestations. The birth of the deities from the highest indicates their manifestive character. They are not unborn. In this sense none of the deities is exclusively identical with the divine, as it manifests itself equally in and through all the deities. Each deity represents a particular form of manifestation of the divine, and as the divine in itself is not known independently of its manifestations, the latter help to reveal its nature. What is directly known to man is the world of manifestation, and a wise man or a seer is one who sees in and through the manifestations the divine, their ultimate source and unity. Only in reflective understanding man faces the problem of ultimate reality or the divine in itself. Intellectual abstraction does not precede lived experience, but follows it, and the Upaniṣads generally stand in this relation to the Saṁhitās.

We now turn to the spiritual aspect of Agni, or Agni as revealed in the process of man's self-discovery and realisation.

---

90. 5.2.9; see also 5.16.1.

91. 10.45.2.

92. 4.6.6.

Agni as an all-pervasive principle of nature is within man also. The heat within man, without which he cannot live, and his body cannot perform its various vital functions represents Agni at the bodily level of man. "So apprehended by all that it may be for the support of the body for which it (Agni) has been created by bodily strength."[93] As Vaiśvānara, Agni is present within all human beings, or rather in all living beings. In this respect he is identified with the vital energy (*prāṇa-śakti*) which, according to Vedic understanding, is responsible for the vital functions of the body. He is the principle of life in all. Over and above his presence in man as Vaiśvānara, Agni is said to represent the immortal principle within the mortals. The deities reveal themselves to man not only in nature, but also by manifesting themselves within himself. It is expressed poetically in the *Ṛgveda* that the deities approach man by means of different vehicles (*ratha*). Each deity has its own vehicle to commune with man. In this connection it is stated significantly that the deities approach man not by means of any vehicle, but by being present within him. "They who approach man not by any conveyance being already present within man (*antariti samudre hṛdi*)."[94] Agni is described as the immortal principle dwelling within mortals, and because of his presence within man his greatness is beheld by man within himself.[95] The wise seers, Bhṛgus, desiring to know him truly discovered him as being within the cave of their hearts. He is the divine light within the hearts of men. Both in the Vedic and post-Vedic traditions, *guhā* (cave) generally stands as a symbol for the human heart, which is regarded as the centre of mystical or spiritual life of man, and also of its realisation. Likewise, the term *samudra* is used to signify symbolically the same, or more precisely the human psyche. The symbolism of the term *samudra* is discussed elsewhere.[96] We shall also discuss

93. 1.141.1.

94. 4.58.11; see also 2.6.7.

95. 3.1.18; 4.1.1; 4.2.1.

96. See chapter 4.

the distinction and relationship between the heart of man, the seat of divine inspiration, and mind or intellect the seat of divine knowledge. Both these are the centres of divine inspiration, and man comes to know the divine when they receive divine light. It is within the cave of one's heart one experiences the divine. It is within there the divine inspiration flows as it were, and floods the whole being of man. Divine Agni remains hidden within the cave of heart, and from there manifests himself through all the spiritual aspirations and achievements of man. Following these as if they are his footprints the seers have found out his presence within their hearts. Agni shines among the deities and enters the mortals. (*deveṣu rājati agni marteṣu āviśan*).[97] And if we take the meaning of the word *deva* in this context as the senses of man, then the expression will mean that Agni entering into mortals shines through his senses. He is the seer among non-seers or men, and the wisdom or consciousness among mortals (*ayam kavi akavīśu marteṣu pracetaḥ*).[98] Agni the revelation of *ṛta* in man is hidden in the cave of his heart. He reveals to man the divine by being within the cave of his heart. He who is within the cave is wonderful, and assumes various forms. "By being within the cave he is seen by all (*guhā santam viśva darśatam*)."[99] "Now hidden, now displayed, he spreads himself as if understanding the intentions of the sacrificer."[100] This can also refer to fire kindled in sacrifice.

Agni is clearly identified in the *Ṛgveda* as the divine light within man (*idam jyotiḥ amṛtam martyeṣu*),[101] or represents divinely illumined consciousness of man. He is the light placed within the heart of man (*jyotiḥ hṛdaye āhitam yat*).[102] While ordinary fire is kindled by ordinary people, the divine fire is kindled within

97. 5.25.4.
98. 7.4.4.
99. 5.8.3.
100. 1.140.7.
101. 6.9.4.
102. 6.9.6; see also 6.5.5.

their hearts by the wise and pious. Those who know him truly kindle him within themselves (*antaḥ hi agne īyase vidvān*).[103] The divine Agni is to be generated within the hearts of men. By being within the hearts of men he discerns between the wise and the unwise, between the devoted and undevoted (*bhaktam abhaktam*) and between the sinless and the sinful. He witnesses all the intentions and actions of man. He knows all the pious works done by man (*daivyāni vratāni cikitvān*). He knows and responds to the prayers of man, and the seers pray that their prayers touch his heart and awaken him to their prayers. "Mine ears are turned to hear him, mine eyes to behold him, this light that is placed within the hearts."[104] He is within the thoughts of men, or moves within them (*dhiyā samruṇvati*).[105] He knows all by being within the thoughts of all (*agniḥ dhiyā saḥ cetati*).[106] He is the regulator or controller of human intellect or thoughts (*dhīnām yantāram*), and shines with the wisdom of a seer (*kavi kratu*).[107] "He is the seer among seers and none can excel him in wisdom."[108] He is a *kavi*, and so he is to be kindled by a *kavi*. All these expressions show that Agni at the spiritual level, represents the illumined state of human intellect, or he is the divine spark within man. He is the supreme knower, and knows all by being a *kavi*. He is the eye of all living beings (*bhūta cakṣu*) or the light within all the eyes (*sahasrākṣa*). The knowledge of the highest is revealed by the rays of his light.

He is a source of divine inspiration to man, or divine inspiration flows from him. He is the inspiration of the inspirer (*āsavam savituḥ*).[109] As divine light, Agni is often identified with Uṣas, the dawn of divine wisdom. He inspires in man divine

103. 2.6.7.

104. 6.9.6.

105. 3.10.2.

106. 3.10.3.

107. 3.3.8; 3.2.4; 6.16.23.

108. 4.6.1; 5.3.5.

109. 8.9.6.

wisdom which finds its expression through hymns. By his wisdom he impels man to sacrifice (*māyayā vidhadāni procodayan*).[110] As divine light within man, Agni is associated with the creation of hymns. Being kindled by the wise within their hearts, he seeks *go* or hymns as his expression.[111] As "waters" (*āpaḥ*) symbolise the flow of inspiration within man, the expression that Agni the pure, divine and truthful shines always within "waters" can be explained to mean that Agni as divine light is experienced in the state of divine inspiration (*yaḥ apsu āśucinā daivyena ṛtavā ajasraḥ urviyā vibhāti*).[112] In the *Ṛgveda* the terms *go* and *dhenu* are used symbolically to mean divine speech, or its expression in Vedic hymns. In this sense Agni is connected with the creation of hymns, and this also strengthens our interpretation that Agni, at spiritual level, represents divinely illumined consciousness of man. "Him whom you inspire attains *go* (hymns)."[113] Brilliant flames of thine go swiftly to *go* (hymns)."[114] He shines along with or through the hymns (*gāvaḥ*). As Agni stands for divine light that is to be known by the heart, his flames or rays are holy and sanctifying. He is born out of devotion, and is awakened by it. "Inspirer of our devotion, hastens our prayers to fruition. He illumines our pure and pious religious observances."[115] He is the source of divine knowledge, hymns and prayers in man. "From you Agni wisdom (*kāvya*), from you *manīṣā* (wisdom) and hymns are born."[116] From him the seers are born, or he is the maker of seers (*tvāt viprāḥ jāyante*). He makes a man a *kavi* and a *ṛṣi*.

The divine Agni is to be kindled or awakened by man within himself. Agni the wise is known by the wise. He is a *vipra* and

110. 3.27.7.

111. 7.9.4; 8.60.3.

112. 2.35.8.

113. 8.60.3.

114. 6.56.7.

115. 1.143.6.

116. 4.11.3.

only a *vipra* can kindle him. The worshippers generate him by the strength of their prayers within their hearts. Divinely inspired or spiritually awakened persons (*jāgruvāṁsaḥ*) kindle him to existence.[117] The pious establish him in their hearts. Agni is to be urged to attend the worship by the wise (*manīṣiṇaḥ*), intelligent (*medhirāsaḥ*) and discerning (*vipaścitāḥ*) with their thoughts or hymns. Agni, who like the deity Savitā knows truly, is blissful like one's own self (*ātmā iva śevaḥ*).[118] Such Agni was kindled in the past by devout seers like Vāmadeva.

Identification of Agni, at the spiritual level, as divine illumination or divinely illumined consciousness of man is further evident from the following expressions. "Agni thoroughly comprehends the light that is to be known by the heart."[119] "He is the source of light that is to be comprehended by the heart."[120] "Mine ears are turned to hear him, mine eyes to behold him, this Agni that is placed in the heart."[121] Agni the divine light is so blessed in nature that it is the sole desire of the seers to behold him, and to be devoted to him. He is wonderful or incomparable (*adbhuta*), and is to be desired to be seen by all. "From inmost reservoirs in countless channels flow down these rivers which the foe does behold not. I look upon the streams of *ghṛta* (light) descending and, Lo the golden reed (Agni) is there among them."[122] He is the divine light or flame that is experienced within the state of inspiration which flows in countless forms of creative expression. He is the rouser and quickner of our thoughts, and thoughts inspired by truth (*ṛtasya dhenā*) express him as they flow.[123] Ilā, Bhāratī and Sarasvatī, the

117. 3.10.9.
118. 1.73.2.
119. 3.26.8.
120. 6.9.4 and 6; 6.5.5; 7.4.4.
121. 6.9.6.
122. 4.56.5.
123. 1.141.1.

deities representing divine speech in its various aspects or forms present food to Agni, or nourish him. "He knoweth thy (Agni) favour who gave an impulse to this high devotion."[124] "Who (Agni) comprehends by his wisdom the mysterious sacred hymn — reveal to me the hidden knowledge."[125] Knowing the truth Agni reveals it to man. He showers the rays of truth within man. He sheds divine light, or floods as it were the human heart with the light of divine knowledge.

Agni is intimately connected or deeply involved in the process of destruction of Vṛtra, and the resultant discovery or attainment of *go* (divine speech or hymns). This aspect of Agni is fully discussed in the last chapter. As we discuss the nature and sources of divine inspiration in an independent chapter we do not discuss here the symbolic significance of the recovery of *go*. As a central and running theme of the *Ṛgveda*, the destruction of Vṛtra and the resultant recovery of *go* signify the spiritual process involved in attaining divine light or inspiration, and winning of divine speech or wisdom, and Agni is closely connected with that process.

The divine knowledge of which the Veda is an expression in language is indicated by the term Bhāratī, the corpus of sacred literature. She along with the other two deities of divine speech, Ilā and Sarasvatī are related to Agni. They are food to him, as they nourish him and help in expressing him. They are the means of expressing Agni experienced as divine light. Agni is often described as being kindled in the place of Ilā. The Veda is an expression in language of the divinely inspired wisdom, and Agni represents the divinely illumined consciousness of man.

The spiritual nature of Agni is also known from his capacity to fulfil the higher aspirations of man, for which he is prayed in all worship. At the phenomenal level, Agni as the principle of heat sustains all, and helps the growth of all living beings. It is

124. 4.4.6.

125. 4.5.3.

to be kindled every moment so that human life and growth are possible. It is explained in a Brāhmaṇa text that Agni as life principle is kindled without any effort by all the living beings all through their lives;[126] that is *yajña* at one level in which all the living beings participate. Similarly, at the cosmic level the importance of Agni as the principle of heat and light is recognised. It is kindled every moment to sustain the world. And finally at the spiritual level Agni as the principle of immortality, or divine light within, or knowledge of the divine is to be kindled by the wise, or by those who want to liberate themselves from spiritual darkness and evil. The seekers of truth seek Agni, the divine light, within themselves, and kindle it there.[127]

---

126. 8.43.19.

127. 8.44.19; 8.103.3; 10.91.14.

4

Indra

INDRA represents a phenomenon which is abstract and all-pervasive. Agni is also pervasive as he is present in almost all the phenomena of nature in which the element of fire or heat is present inherently. But the phenomenon represented by Indra is so universal and pervasive that without it nature cannot sustain itself. Nature is an integrated whole in which various phenomena are interrelated and intermixed. It is an interplay of different phenomena, and no phenomenon of nature stands by itself. Nevertheless, a phenomenon of nature can be distinguished from the rest in terms of certain dominant characteristics which characterise it. As every natural phenomenon is universal, the deities that represent them are also universal and pervasive. But Indra is unlike other deities in that he does not represent any one specific aspect or phenomenon of nature. He is inherent in all. Hence Indra is described in the *Ṛgveda* as associated with or related to all the deities. In all the manifestations and functions of all the deities the presence of Indra is seen and praised. He is principally responsible for the destruction of Vṛtra, while all other deities participate in it, and help Indra in accomplishing it. He is the chief agent of the act of destroying Vṛtra and the consequent release of "waters" and "cows". Thus Indra is a deity who is central to Vedic thought and worship. Apart from these considerations Indra is great and mighty as in and through him the divine manifests itself more comprehensively. While each deity is a self-expression or manifestation of the divine, Indra is supreme among them as he stands to reveal the divine in its intrinsic nature which is not limited to any one particular manifestation of it. He is revealed commonly in all the manifestations of the divine, or he stands for that divine principle which is inherently present in all. And yet he is conceived as distinct from all other deities. At the same time he is not the divine in itself. As each deity is an individual expression of the divine, so also is Indra. He is also a manifestation of the divine though all-comprehensive in nature. Although every deity reveals the divine by manifesting the divine qualities, Indra excels them all in revealing the divine. More than any other deity, Indra reveals the nature of the divine more fully, and hence to him are attributed all the divine qualities superlatively. In the *Ṛgveda* deification of Indra is more complete when compared to other deities. He is addressed and praised as if he is the divine, and all the attributes proper to the divine are attributed to him.

Indra stands to represent the divine power which manifests itself in diverse ways and forms within the phenomenal world. It is not the divine reality, but what is intrinsic to it. Indra is divine but the divine is not Indra. The divine manifests itself variously in terms of its power of self-expression or self-manifestation, and Indra represents that power of the divine. It is abstract in nature, and is known through the diverse forms of its manifestation at various levels of creation. Therefore, Indra in himself is not known or revealed directly to man. He is known through his acts of self-manifestation. He is at the same time not identical with any of the manifestations of power, but his presence is felt equally in all the manifestations of power of which he is the common name and source. He is the power itself, and manifests himself in and through all the phenomena of nature in diverse ways and forms. Although the self-creative or expressive power of the divine is distinct from its other attributes, it is not devoid of divine qualities. Therefore, Indra possesses all the divine qualities, though he represents primarily the divine power of self-manifestation.

In the *Ṛgveda*, the divine power is indicated by the words *sahaḥ*, *sahasaḥ*, *savasaḥ*, *kṣātram*, *vīryam* and *ojas* and Indra stands for that which is commonly denoted by all these terms. They express the varied forms of manifestation of Indra power (*indriyam*). Although all these terms mean generally the power or might (*bala*), each term stands to mean a different aspect of power. The power that manifests itself through nature is distinct in the mode of its manifestation, or in the manner of its operation from the power which is revealed within the animate sphere, and especially within man. But it is the same power which manifests itself within the whole of nature, including man, though known differently because of its distinct forms of manifestation at different levels, and also in relation to various functions with which it is associated.

The power constitutes the nature of Indra, or it is his being (*indriya*). The term Indra is the substantive form of the word *indriya*, and the *indriya* or the power that constitutes the being of Indra is characteristic of all the phenomena of nature which manifest power in various ways and degress. In several contexts of its usage the term *indra* is used to mean a powerful being, or one who possesses power supremely. The deity Uṣā is addressed as *indratama*, or possessing Indra to the utmost degree.[1] So also are the Aśvins. The different deities like the Maruts, Viṣṇu and Agni are described as possessing Indra (*indravantaḥ*).[2] All such expressions show that the various deities possess and manifest divine power (Indra) in different degrees, and it constitutes their greatness and strength. Likewise, the seers also pray for it, and seek to possess it. They want to be full of Indra (power) (*vayam śyāma indravantaḥ*).[3] All the deities partake of the power that is Indra, and he in this respect is their chief or prototype (*jyeṣṭha*).[4] The various deities manifest in their own individual ways the power that is Indra. They are the sources of manifestation of the power that is Indra which they possess derivately; whereas power is the very nature of Indra, or he is power itself. As

1. 7.79.3.
2. 10.128.2; 4.36.5; 10.35.1; 5.57.1.
3. 1.105.19; 1.103.1.
4. 10.120.1; 8.16.3; 8.51.2.

representing power Indra is conceived in abstract terms, and is therefore not an object of anyone's experience. What is experienced are his varied manifestations which are known in relation to various functions or acts of the deities. Because of the abstract character of the power which Indra represents, doubts are entertained in the *Ṛgveda* regarding the existence of Indra, which is not however the case with regard to the existence of other deities. While the different phenomena of nature represented by the various deities are individualised and visible, the power which the deities manifest is not an individual phenomenon which can be identified and distinguished from other phenomena. Agni as the principle of heat, Vāyu as the principle of motion and Āpaḥ as the principle of moisture are phenomena of nature, and man has no doubts about their existence. Whereas the power that is inherent within these phenomena, and because of which they are able to manifest themselves in various ways and forms is not an individual phenomenon given to direct observation of man. It is an abstract reality, and is known through its manifestation; in itself it is not open to man's observation.

Yet Indra is also a deity and represents a phenomenon of nature in the sense that Indra power manifests itself within the phenomenal realm, though known indirectly through its manifestations. It is known to all as the capacity to manifest which is inherent within all the phenomena of nature. It manifests itself within all the deities as their capacity to manifest themselves variously. While the term "Indra" stands to mean power in its abstract and unmanifested condition, the other terms that are used to mean power or strength indicate the diverse forms of its manifestation. The various terms denoting power like *ojas* and *vīryam* have their specific connotations, and refer to different aspects of power, or power as revealed in relation to its various operations. They do not have the same significance though what is indicated by them all is the same reality. For instance, the creative power or the power of intellect is distinct in its nature and functions from the power that operates within nature. Thus the various terms like *sahaḥ, balam, ojas,* etc., are used to indicate the nature of power that is represented by Indra. The nature of power that is indicated by these terms is to be determined mostly in terms of the functions with which power is associated. In terms of its manifestation, the power may mean either the power of the intellect or the creative energy in man, or the vital energy (*prāṇa-śakti*) which manifests itself within the animate sphere or the power that manifests itself within nature. In addition to these several forms of manifestation at different levels, power is also seen in its divine aspect which manifests itself in and through certain supernatural acts which Indra as a deity performs. While the words *vīryam* and *kṣātram* are generally used to mean vigour and valour respectively, the word *ojaḥ* is used to mean either vital energy or creative power, besides power in general. The term *balam* is also used to mean power in general, unless it is qualified and made to mean some form of power. Thus power reveals itself in and through all the phenomena of nature, and also in man, and Indra stands to represent it. When a doubt is expressed with regard to the existence of Indra (There is no Indra. Who has seen him?), Indra himself is said to have responded by saying: "Here I am, worshippers, behold me, I overpower all beings by my might."[5] He is the ultimate measure or archetype (*pratimānam*) of power (*ojas*).[6] His might or power (*savasaḥ*) is measureless and infinite (*na antaḥ*).[7] He is the measure of strength (*savasaḥ mānam*), and his power is limitless (*apāra ojaḥ*). He is the lord of power, and derives his lordship over all because of his power (*ojas*). He is the giver of power and might to all, as all power and might belong to him, and flow from him. There is no one second to him in power and strength. He is the lord of the universe because of his power (*ojas*) which is unequalled and unrivalled. He is glorified and worshipped through all the acts, as well as through all the agents. "People worship me as acts

---

5. 8.89.3 and 4; 1.102.8.
6. 1.102.8; 1.52.12 and 13;1.100.14.
7. 1.54.1; 1.54.8.

and the agent" (*mām āryanti kṛteṅa kartvena ca*),[8] as his presence is revealed in and through them all. To realise that Indra manifests himself through all acts and agents is to glorify him and worship him. His greatness flows from his nature, and he is well known by nature (*sa na śrutaḥ*).[9] He is born with power and wisdom, and is matchless in his valour (*kṣātram*). The whole universe does not exceed him in power, and all the power that is revealed in it is but a part or fraction of his power. He is revealed to man by his own power and strength, and the whole universe acknowledges him as the source of all power. His being is power as the being of the sun is light,[10] and the others derive their power from him. As the ultimate measure of all power he sustains the whole world, and "without his might this world is naught."[11]

The power that is Indra is beyond the comprehension of man (*etat te indriyam aceti*).[12] In himself Indra is not known to man. Power is not known to man directly; it is known through its manifestations. The presence of Indra as the embodiment of all power is felt in all the instances of its manifestation at all levels of creation. He is known by his mighty acts (*karmobhiḥ mahadbhiḥ suśrutā bhūt*).[13] His manifestations are varied. All the manifestations of power reveal his glory. He is known to the whole world by his might and power. He is the lord of each and everything that manifests power and strength, or he is the prototype of everything that is endowed with power. Thus the whole universe, or the three regions display his manifested form. They reveal his greatness by manifesting his power. "Heaven, earth and mid-region display his phenomenal form (*darśatam vapuḥ*), and the sun and the moon perform their revolutions so that we may see

8. 10.48.3. It can also mean : "People worship me for what I have done and for what I shall do."

9. 10.23.3. See Sāyaṇa's commentary thereon.

10. 8.6.10; see also 1.84.1.

11. 2.16.2.

12. 6.27.4.

13. 3.36.1

and have faith in him."[14] Because of him the heaven and earth are upheld in their respective places. "Behold this the vast and extensive might of Indra (*vīryam*), have faith in his *vīryam*."[15] "Making himself by his power the sovereign over all the worlds, he sustains them therewith."[16] He is the power that manifests itself in all the deities (*deveṣu dhārayadhā asūryam*). All the power that is there in all the deities is his (*indrasya nu sukṛtam daivyam sahaḥ*).[17] By partaking of the power of Indra, Viṣṇu is able to traverse the three worlds. Indra pervades and comprehends all that is born by his power (*abhi bhū asi viśvā jātāni ojasa*).[18] He has become all this by his power (*viśvājātāni savasā abhibhūḥ*).[19] He supports the strength of the world as a father the strength of his sons.[20] He has become the form of each and everything for the sake of manifesting himself, or to reveal his form to all (*rūpam rūpam prati rūpam babhūva tat asya rūpam prati cakṣaṇāya*).[21] He fills full both the worlds with his might, and as the earth is encompassed by space, he encompasses and upholds the three worlds. They are not separated from him, from the strength of whom the world derives its lustre. Because of the all-pervasive nature of power, the whole world is an abode of Indra. His presence is felt everywhere. So he is like a hawk without a nest.[22] He lords over the whole world by being the principle of its sustenance. Thus everything in the world acknowledges his greatness, and participates in his power.

The infinite power that is Indra is more than and beyond the power that is manifested in the world in various forms. His being is not exhausted by the power that is manifested in the

14. 1.102.2.
15. 1.103.5.
16. 2.17.4.
17. 10.100.6.
18. 10.153.4; 8.86.9.
19. 8.86.9.
20. 10.23.5; see also 8.45.20.
21. 6.47.18.
22. 10.55.6.

world. The whole world is not fit or sufficient to contain his power (*ojas*). On the other hand, all the worlds are contained in his power. The greatness of his power exceeds that of heaven and earth. He is Śakra (almighty) and, therefore, there is nothing which is not within his power to do.

The different manifestations of power whereby Indra is known to man are either benevolent and auspicious or terrible. He is both *ghoram* (terrible) and *bhadram* (auspicious).[23] While in his terrible aspect he is the source of destruction of all evil, in his benevolent aspect he is the source of protection and happiness to the righteous. He is described as fearlessness and good (*abhayam svasti*).[24] He is prayed to keep away from his worshippers the divine wrath (*daivyam bhayam*).[25] As the sole source of power he is described as Bhīma, as the whole creation feels the terror of his power. "Through fear of him mountains remain firm, heaven and earth tremble."[26] As the born enemy of all powers or forces that obstruct light and wisdom, and are the sources of evil, he is the destroyer of all such powers. The *vajra* which symbolises his irresistible wrath (*manyu*) is always with him, and it is the source of fear as well as of protection.[27] It causes destruction of evil powers, and provides protection for the good, or to those who follow the path of *ṛta*. "He is the strength of the feeble and the fall of the mighty (*acyutam cyutam*)."[28] He protects the wise and righteous with his divine protection (*daivyana avasā*). The major divine deed of Indra for which he is extolled and worshipped, and in which all other deities participate is the destruction of Vṛtra. Killing of Vṛtra and the consequent liberation of *āpaḥ* and *go* are the chief achievements of Indra. He along with other deities is prayed and invoked to

23. 2.12.5; see also 8.81.5.
24. 3.38.9; see also 6.47.8.
25. 8.50.16.
26. 1.61.14; 6.31.2.
27. 10.83.1. Often Soma is described as the *vajra* of Indra.
28. 2.12.9; 8.84.4; 6.47.15.

destroy Vṛtra, which is the central and running theme of the *Ṛgveda*. All other acts for which Indra is extolled and worshipped are not so significant in comparison to the act of killing Vṛtra. The significance of this event is discussed fully elsewhere.[29]

Indra is able to accomplish all his mighty deeds, including the destruction of Vṛtra, by virtue of his Māyā. However, according to the *Ṛgveda*, the power of Māyā is not peculiar to Indra alone. It is possessed by all other deities, and all their acts reveal it. They are able to accomplish deeds similar to those of Indra because of it. Besides the deities, the dark and evil forces represented by Vṛtra and his allies mentioned in the *Ṛgveda* also possess it, though in relation to them its nature and functions are conceived differently. But the basic character and meaning of Māyā remain the same whether it is employed by the deities or by the demonic forces. It is that creative power by means of which the deities manifest themselves variously, or become many. It means a mysterious creative power by means of which a deity manifests itself variously. It is the creative power inherent within the nature of the divine by which it manifests what is inherent within itself. In other words, Māyā is that creative power whereby the divine becomes many, or manifests itself variously in the form of deities. The problem as to how the multiplicity of the phenomenal world has come into existence out of the oneness of the divine was felt by the Vedic seers, and they sought to explain it in terms of Māyā. It is indicated in the *Ṛgveda* that the divine has become many, by way of self-manifestation, because of the power of Māyā which is inherent within itself.[30] And as all the deities manifest themselves variously in nature they also possess it. Likewise, the powers that are inimical to the deities, and work against their manifestation, or obstruct the revelation

29. See chapter VI.

30. The term *māyā* is used in the *Ṛgveda* to signify the creative power inherent within divine or the deities whereby they manifest themselves variously. It is also used to mean wisdom (*prajñā*), and is so interpreted often by Sāyaṇa. In relation to man it is used to mean ignorance or spiritual blindness.

of the divine also manifest themselves in nature in various forms and ways. This process of one becoming many is due to the power of Māyā. It is the ultimate explanation of the process of diversification, or the reason for self-manifestation of the divine. It is also the explanation of self-manifestation either of the deities or of the demonic powers. Without the manifestation of the deities as nature, and in and through them the divine, there would have been no existence of the phenomenal reality. Even the etymological definition of the term Māyā indicates the same. It is that wisdom or power of the divine because of which it measures or determines itself into the phenomenal reality. It is that creative power because of which measureless reality becomes measured or determined. It is the self-measuring principle inherent within the nature of the divine, as the divine gets itself measured or determined in the process of its becoming many. Now, the power of Māyā manifests itself fully in Indra, the primary manifestation of the divine. Thus it is one thing to know Indra as power, and another to understand how that power manifests itself in different forms. Similarly the deities as universal principles of nature manifest themselves in varied forms, and to explain the process of becoming many, some creative power is to be admitted as being inherent within them.

Indra manifests himself in the world in various forms. He is present throughout the nature. Now, Indra becomes many, or assumes any form he wills, because of his Māyā. His victory over all the evil and dark powers is due to his *āsurī* Māyā (inauspicious or undivine wisdom). Thus Māyā is the creative power or wisdom that is inherent within Indra, and because of which he is able to assume various forms at will. Because of it he becomes all that he wills, or assumes whatever form he wants to assume. He manifests himself variously in terms of his Māyā which is great (*puru*) and co-extensive with himself. And his manifestations are for the purpose of revealing himself. The infinite forms he assumes (*viśvarūpa*) are for revealing himself (*asya rūpam prati cakṣaṇāya*), and these he is able to assume because of his Māyā (*indra māyābhiḥ puru rūpaḥ īyate*).[31] In the expression that Indra is the prototype of every form (*rūpam rūpam pratirūpam babhūva*), the term *pratirūpam* may mean the ideal form or prototype of everything, which are inherent within the wisdom of Indra. And the world of actual forms is a manifestation of the wisdom of Indra. The actualisation of the ideal forms is due to Māyā. At will he becomes all, and Māyā is the reason for becoming so. That is to say, all the forms of the world in their ideal condition are eternally present within the wisdom of Indra, and their actualisation in the phenomenal realm is due to Māyā (*rūpam rūpam maghavā bhobhavīti māyayā kṛṇvantaḥ tanvam parisvām*).[32] The assertions that Indra assumes all the forms at will, and he is the prototype or ideal form of all the forms may mean that all the forms of the world are ideally contained in Indra or in his wisdom before they are actualised (*aprāmisatya maghavān tadhā it asat indra kratvā yadhā vaśaḥ*).[33] To measure the world is to intellectually comprehend and determine its nature in terms of ideas or concepts, and this process is due to Māyā. Each form is a determinant of the reality, and if what is there is not determined in terms of forms, reality remains formless, and then there will be no knowledge of it. Anything that is formless is inconceivable, and hence unmeasured. To measure is to determine, and that is possible only when the reality has assumed some form. And as all the forms of the world are the phenomenal manifestations of the divine, they help to measure it, or determine its nature. Thus to be formed is to be measured, and the process of becoming many is spontaneous on the part of the divine. And in assuming various forms the divine reality gets itself self-measured or self-determined. This process of self-differentiation and self-determination is due to Māyā which is inherent within the nature of the divine. Thus throughout the Indian tradition, Māyā is essentially connected with the process of becoming,

31. 6.47.18.

32. 3.53.8.

33. 8.50.4; see also 3.48.4.

despite differences in the conception of its nature. At the same time the process of becoming is a mystery to human understanding, and this sense is also conveyed by the concept of Māyā. The concept of Māyā conveys both the senses; the reason for becoming, and the sense of mystery associated with the process of becoming. This mysterious and creative power is not peculiar to any particular deity in the *Ṛgveda*, as all the deities are involved in the process of becoming, and also perpetuate it. The dark and evil powers represented by Vṛtra and his allies also possess the power of Māyā, as they also manifest themselves in nature in various forms and ways. Their forms of manifestation are not always the same.

Although Indra assumes various forms at will because of his Māyā, in himself he transcends it (*pareṇa māyābhiḥ ruta āsa nāma te*).[34] Because of his Māyā power he manifests himself variously, but in himself he transcends all his manifestations. His being cannot be determined completely in terms of his manifested forms. He is the lord of his Māyā. All that is known about him through his manifestations is only an expression of his greatness or glory (*mahimā*); and he is more than his glory. All that is known about him is only a part of his being. All that is there is contained within his being. All the things are determined in him, or are measured out of him, while he is not measured by any of them (*yasmin viśvā adhiśritā; indreḥ viśvā bhuvanāni yemire*).[35] He is the measure of all things, but he is not measured by any. He is beyond all measure (*paro mātram*).[36] Thus what is revealed of Indra in and through his mighty deeds of power is only his phenomenal form of existence. In all the acts ascribed to him, both natural and supernatural or divine, only his glory or greatness (*vibhūti* or *mahimā*) is revealed. All the forms in which power manifests itself, either at intellectual, or vital, or physical levels reveal Indra, and point to his existence. He is known through them indirectly. The whole world manifests

34. 5.44.2.

35. 8.81.20; 8.3.6.

36. 8.57.6. He is *amātram* 1.102.7.

his power and wisdom, and thus helps to reveal his nature (*devasya paśya kāvyam mahītva*).[37] "The heaven and earth have not grown equal to half of me (*pakṣam na prati aham asmi*).[38] "I am greater than all greatness, or greater than any greatness (*mahāmaha*)."[39] The expression *mahāmaha* which occurs several times in the *Ṛgveda*, and is used to describe the greatness of Indra indicates the transcendence of Indra over his greatness that is revealed in and through the world. The same idea is poetically expressed when it is said that hundred heavens and hundred earths are no comparison to Indra's greatness. Even thousand suns shining together cannot reveal his splendour and glory fully.[40] In other words, no created being can determine his greatness, and contain his glory fully. The whole world is due to his Māyā, and he is beyond it. In his true nature he is incomprehensible (*agohya*).[41] "We wish to know thee, but here we know thee not."[42] "How can I comprehend thee wise, immature in understanding."[43] "Who are seers (*ṛṣi*) who comprehended before our time the limits of thy greatness, or thy greatness completely or comprehensively (*mahimnā samasya*)."[44]

It is only with regard to the existence of Indra doubts are expressed in the *Ṛgveda*. Power is such an abstract phenomenon and all-pervasive, that it is not possible to identify it in terms of any one phenomenon of nature, and determine its nature adequately. It manifests itself through such diverse forms as the divine acts of grace, the working of nature, and as vital energy within the world of living beings and as creative power in man. It is not the case with regard to other deities who can be identified

37. 10.55.5.
38. 10.119.7; see also 6.30.1.
39. 10.119.12; 10.134.1; 10.111.4; 8.33.15.
40. 8.59.5.
41. 8.98.4.
42. 8.80.3.
43. 10.28.5.
44. 10.54.3.

in terms of various natural phenomena which they represent; whereas Indra as the self-creative or self-expressive power of the divine is so comprehensive that it is revealed in and through all the deities. He is everywhere, and there is no phenomenon of nature which is without him. He is like a bird without a nest, or he has no fixed abode. The scepticism expressed with regard to the existence of Indra, and the way it is met are significant in this connection. "True praise to Indra if he truly exists, Nama says, verily there is no Indra, who has ever seen him, whom shall we praise?" To this Indra himself responds: "Here I am, worshippers, behold me, Here I overpower all beings by my might. The offices of *ṛta* increase me. Rending with strength I rend the worlds asunder" (*ayamasmi jaritāriti paśya mā iha viśvājātāni abhi asmi maha, ṛtasya mā pradiśaḥ vardhayanti. . .*).[45] "Have faith in me, O worshippers, for by my greatness I encompass the whole world" (*śrat asme dhatta saḥ janāsaḥ indra*).[46] This may be adequate to prove the existence of Indra by way of pointing to him as one whose power manifests itself within the world in various ways, but the Indra who declares himself as "it is I", or as one who is above and beyond the manifestations of his power is not given to man's knowledge. Accordingly, Indra may be seen as expressing himself in many forms, and hence having many names. But in himself he is more than and beyond those names and forms. In himself or in his true nature, he is known to himself only. We know only his three names that reveal his glory in the three regions of the world, but not his fourth and hidden name. Indra is known to us in his threefold manifestation, or by his three names, whereas he knows all his names; and yet they are his functional names only (*catvāri te asūryāni nāma adabdhāni mahinasya santi, tvam aṅga tāni viśvāni vitse yābhiḥ karmaṇa cakartha*).[47]

Now to Indra are attributed all the attributes that properly belong to the highest reality or the divine. But he is not the highest

45. 8.100.3. and 4.

46. 2.12.5.

47. 10.54.5.

reality. Ontologically his status in the *Ṛgveda* is the same as that of any other deity. He is one among them. The only difference between Indra and other Ṛgvedic deities is that while the latter can be identified in terms of different natural phenomena, Indra as divine power does not represent any phenomenon of nature. He is inherent within all the deities. He is all-pervasive as there is no phenomenon in nature which does not reveal his presence. As the primary manifestation of the divine, Indra enjoys the status of first-born among the deities. Here again the status of being first-born is true of many other deities besides Indra. However, the birth of Indra is logically prior to the birth of other deities. His birth from the divine is spontaneous and instantaneous (*sadya*), and is similar to the manifestation of light from the sun (*aham sūrya iva ajāni*). As the self-creative power of the divine, Indra is inherent within the divine. He is co-eternal and co-extensive with the divine, and manifests himself along with the manifestations of the divine. The various deities other than Indra come into existence out of this creative process, and hence the birth of the deities follow logically the birth of Indra. As the creative power of the divine, the divine matrix (*mātṛkā*) of all that is there, Indra's existence is not only logically prior to that of all other deities, but also forms the basis of their existence. In this sense Indra is also born, but not a self-subsisting reality. He is born of the highest in the manner of self-expression; and manifests himself along with or through all the manifestations of the divine. There are numerous passages in the *Ṛgveda* indicating the birth of Indra from the highest. He is born of the Divine, or in the highest realm (*parame vyoman*). And as soon as he is born he entered into all. "Born in the highest (*parame vyoman*) you have entered (*āviveśa*) earth and heaven."[48] His coming into existence has no temporal dimension. His birth from the highest is instantaneous (*sadyaḥ api jātaḥ parame vyoman; bhuvaneśu jyeṣṭham sadyaḥ jajña*).[49] The existence of the divine is only logically prior to its manifestations.

48. 3.32.10.

49. 3.32.10; 10.120.1.

Indra is also described as born of the deities. "Whom the heaven and earth and the deities brought into existence."[50] In manifesting Indra power the deities may be regarded figuratively as the sources of his birth. He is addressed as *triṣu jātaḥ* or born in the three regions as they are the sources of his manifestation. Besides being born in the three regions, he manifests himself within the living beings including man. All the power that is inherent within the deities is of Indra (*indrasyāhu sukṛtam daivyam sahaḥ*).[51] He has become all the deities (*devāḥ bhavadha viśve indra*).[52] "All the deities become powerful and wise by thine power and wisdom."[53] He is born to lord over all that is there, the world of animate beings and the world of inanimate objects. He is the creator of all, as he is the creative power of the divine. He supports all himself being unsupported by anything created.

Indra is born of *ṛta*. He is the protector of *ṛta*, and also manifests it within himself. He is the increaser of *ṛta*, or extends it to all the realms, and *ṛta* in all its manifestations reveals him. He is full of *ṛta*, and is, therefore, prayed to fill the devotees with it. And to be born of *ṛta* is the same as to be born of truth. As the dynamic side of the divine, *ṛta* is the source of all that is there, including the deities, and in revealing *ṛta* the whole creation reveals the divine. Indra is also addressed as born of truth (*satya*). He is the child of truth (*satyasya sūnum*), and truth is his birthplace (*satya yoni*).[54] At the same time he is identified with truth (*indra satyam; tvamhi satyaḥ*). "All truth is inherent in you both Indra and Bṛhaspati."[55] "We address you or praise you as truth (*satyamiti vayam indra stavāma*).[56] "You are truth (*tvam hi satyam*)."[57] All such

---

50. 3.49.1.
51. 10.100.6.
52. 3.54.17.
53. 8.51.7; see also 6.36.1.
54. 8.58.4; 4.19.2.
55. 2.24.12.
56. 8.51.12.
57. 8.79.4; 10; 111.1

expressions in which Indra is addressed as truth are to be taken in their secondary sense, as not only Indra but all the deities are identified with truth. At the same time all the deities are described as born of truth. All the deities are born of truth, and reveal it in themselves. Similarly *ṛta* is present within all the deities, but none of them by himself is *ṛta*. "You are the abiding place of *ṛta*, so reveal it to us."[58] So also, all the deities are divine, but the divine is not identical with any of them. Thus *satya* or *ṛta* or the divine inhere in all the deities and contain them, but none of the deities can contain *ṛta* or *satya* or the divine. These are more than what is revealed in and through all the deities. Each deity in its own individual way reveals the divine, *ṛta* and *satya*. Each deity manifests the divine, and gets itself manifested in and through a phenomenon of nature. Thus every deity, including Indra, is born twice. They are first born of the highest or the divine and then in nature, nature is the source of their manifestation at the phenomenal level. Thus, though all the deities, including Indra, are addressed and praised in terms which are appropriate to the divine, they are not identical with the divine. And at the same time they are not other than the divine, as the divine is not known apart from them. As self-manifestations of the divine, the deities cannot exist without the divine.

Indra who in himself is changeless (*aprāmi satya*) assumes various forms at will, and shines through them. He is known as one who shines and reveals in and through every phenomenon of nature exhibiting power and strength (*śriyaḥ vasānaḥ carati svarochihi*).[59] He is *svarāj* or self-shining, and hence self-revealing. He is also addressed as *svarāt* or self-ruler. As the source of all power he moves everywhere in his greatness, and there is none who can rule over him (*mahān caṛati ojasā nākti niyāmat*).[60] What is revealed of him to man is only his manifested state, or the various

58. 1.132.3.

59. 3.38.4.

60. 8.33.8.

forms he assumes because of his Māyā. In this connection the following passage is significant. The wise or the seers have given a form to Indra who in reality abides in all the forms by his Māyā (*anyat anyat asūryam vasānan hi māyinaḥ memire rūpam asmin*).[61] All the forms in which Indra manifests himself are his, but in himself he is formless. Before assuming various forms at will, Indra has no form, and the term Indra refers primarily to such formless state of power. As the source of all power, Indra manifests himself in various forms, and the reason for his self-manifestation, as well as the manner of his manifestation are a mystery to human understanding. He is, therefore, described as full of Māyā (*māyinam*). Thus Māyā as representing the self-creative and self-determining power of a deity is a mystery, and the real nature of a deity as the lord of Māyā is not really known to man whose capacity to know is limited to the phenomenal world.

The divine power or Indra is revealed to man directly within himself. In man also Indra power manifests itself in different forms at different levels. In whatever form and at whatever level it manifests itself within man, the energy is the same. However, it is known differently according to the modes of its manifestation, or in relation to various functions with which it is associated. It manifests itself at the physical or bodily, vital, mental or intellectual and spiritual levels, and at each level the mode of its manifestation is distinct. It is the same power which impells or inspires the various faculties and senses of man to perform their respective functions. It inspires the different sense organs (*indriya*) and the mind or the intellect. In one of the many etymological definitions given of the term "Indra", it is analysed to mean that which inspires the different sense organs and other faculties of man to their respective functions (*indriyāni śatakrato iti śatakrato yāte janeṣu pañceṣu indra tāni te āvruṇi*).[62] By being within man inherently Indra is the real agent of all functions and actions done by man

61. 3.38.7.

62. 3.37.9.

(*śakriḥ āpaḥ narya yat kariṣyan*).[63] He upholds or sustains all actions (*viśvasya karmaṇā dhartā*).[64] He is present or revealed in all actions (*karmaṇi karmaṇi sthiraḥ*).[65] He moves along with, and is revealed by every act of wisdom (*kāvyena samācakre*). He witnesses all men in terms of their actions (*sam yat janān kratubhiḥ sūraḥ īkṣayate*).[66] He is not only the real agent of all actions, but is also their fulfiller (*kratuprā*), as he has become all this, or the lord of all by his power (*tvamindra abhibhū asi viśvā jātāni ojasā*).[67] He judges all men by their actions, and rewards each according to his own deeds (*vibhakta bhāgam*).[68] Besides being the lord of the whole world, he is also the lord of all living beings, including man. He is the universal impeller or inspirer (*viśvaminvaḥ*).[69] He is the ruler of men, as their sustenance. He witnesses the truthfulness and faith within the hearts of men. "The various doings of men are ordered by thee in thy wisdom."[70] He dwells within the consciousness of all (*sahasracetaḥ*) and inspires the five classes of beings with vigour. He is the inner source of their sustenance. Not only the deities but men also possess his power and wisdom. He is present within all beings, both mortal and immortal. He is the source of development and perfection of all the powers that are within man. The full development and perfect expression of man's creative power is due to his inspiration. Without his help and inspiration the creative power within man may remain unexpressed fully and perfectly.

The divine aspect of Indra power is revealed to man within his spiritual life. Although its presence is experienced in all the

63. 1.169.2. Indra is described as *nṛtamaḥ* and *naryaḥ*, best among men and dweller among men (10.29.1). He is addressed as *vaiśvānarāya* (10.51.1).
64. 1.11.4.
65. 1.101.4.
66. 1.132.5.
67. 10.153.5.
68. 3.49.4.
69. 7.28.1. He is addressed as *sāvitre* (2.30.1) or inspirer of all.
70. 1.169.2.

operations of nature and the doings of man, in its divine aspect it is not known through them. It is within the spiritual life of man, or in the act of inspiring man's will and intellect divinely, the divine nature of Indra power is revealed to man directly. Or man comes to know the divine nature of Indra power when he is divinely inspired. Divine inspiration is also a form of manifestation of divine power. While all the human beings experience power in one form or other, a *kavi* or a *ṛṣi* knows it in its divine nature. In its subtle or spiritual form divine power illumines human intellect, inspires his will to act in accordance with *ṛta*, and evokes devotion in him. All creative power within man either of the will or of the intellect is a manifestation of Indra. It is the creative or spiritual power of man which helps him in knowing the divine. We may thus identify Indra, at the spiritual level, as the power of man's intellect and will. When the heart and intellect of man are inspired and illumined, he becomes aware of the divine as that which inspires and illumines his heart and intellect. Hymns are spontaneously born out of divine inspiration, or are created by a divinely inspired or illumined intellect. Therefore a hymn is also known as *dhī* or *mati*. Now, Indra is described as the lord of intellect (*dhiyaspati*).[71] He is also described as one who sees everything through the eyes of man (*sahasrākṣa*), and knows everything through the consciousness of man (*sahasracetasa*). The power of Indra (*ojaḥ*) inspires man to worship and prayer, and to create hymns. By possessing it one becomes a *kavi*, and all the ancient seers possessed it (*tat te indriyam paramam parācai ādhārayantaḥ kavayaḥ*).[72] The seer-poets of the *Ṛgveda* pray for it. "May we be possessed of Indra power (*indravantam syāma*)."[73] Because of it Soma is shed and offered to Indra (*ojasā arcan arcanti ojasā*). Indra is described as the creative power of the holy synod.[74] His power prevails in the

71. 1.23.9.
72. 1.103.1.
73. 1.105.19.
74. 1.56.2.

hearts of the worshippers, and inspires them to the holy act of worship. The spiritual power of Indra that dwells within all is the source of inspiration for the poets to experience devotion and to create hymns. It surges forth spontaneously in the form of devotion, and is expressed is the form of a *mantra* (hymn). It springs up in man bringing with it divine light and joy. All the deities, and especially Indra, are prayed for divine light. "Let power swell high like rivers for the singer."[75] Thus the Indra power manifests itself in its subtlest or spiritual form within the spiritual or creative life of man, and is experienced by those who are wise (*indram nicikyuḥ kavayaḥ manīṣā*).[76] One has to be a seer to know the divine aspect of Indra. To know a deity in its spiritual or divine aspect one has to be spiritually awakened or divinely inspired, and that is a divine gift. And whatever one does to receive it is only a preparation, but not the cause of it. Perfect mastery over one's mind or intellect (*manīṣā*) prepares man to become a *kavi*. But it is not sufficient to become a *kavi*. To become a *kavi* one is to be divinely inspired, and the deities are the sources of divine inspiration. The seers see their glory as a gift of Indra (*tvādattam it yaśaḥ*).[77] Indra is worshipped and prayed with the wisdom which is his gift. "We worship you with the wisdom granted by you (*tava kratvā saneyam*)."[78] "The gift of ours which Indra likes and welcomes, even that he makes for us."[79] The auspicious, purifying or sanctifying spiritual power is a gift from Indra. He inspires devotion in man, and makes him divine (*devavantam*). "May we abide in thee and be yours (*tve indra abhūma viprāḥ* or *syāma te indra*)."[80]

Although Indra is known primarily for his power and strength he is not devoid of other divine qualities like *kāvya* and

75. 4.21.7.
76. 10.124.9.
77. 3.40.6; see also 4.22.1; 4.32.15.
78. 8.19.20.
79. 4.22.1.
80. 2.11.12 and 13.

kratu. All the divine attributes are fully integrated in the nature of the divine, and are, therefore, revealed in all the deities in an integrated way. Nevertheless, in each deity a particular divine quality manifests itself more prominently than in others. Each deity is known or seen as a more perfect expression of a particular divine attribute which does not preclude it from expressing at the same time all other divine attributes. As each deity is a manifestation of the divine, it possesses all the qualities of the divine though it is known primarily for revealing a particular divine quality more fully. Therefore, Indra though represents primarily the power of the divine he is not devoid of divine wisdom. He is full of intelligence and wisdom. He is born with power and wisdom (*sākam jātaḥ kratunā sākam ojasā*).[81] He is addressed as great mind (*mahā mate*). He is described as *vidvān* (wise), *medhira* (intelligent), *kavi, vipra, pracetasa, ṛṣi, ṛtavān* and *trātā*. He is matchless in wisdom and supremely intelligent (*cetiṣṭha*).

At the spiritual level, power manifests itself together with wisdom and righteousness. As all the divine qualities are integrated in the nature of the divine, so also in a *kavi* or a *ṛṣi* all the divine qualities find their expression together. A *kavi* is also a *manīṣā*, a *ṛṣi* and a *vipra* and is full of righteousness (*ṛtavān*). Thus though Indra is known primarily as the source of strength and power, he is equally a source of divine wisdom to man. He inspires devotion and worship among his worshippers. "You reward with understanding those who praise you."[82] "He is the inspirer of understanding with which a *kavi* composes his songs or hymns."[83]

Worship of Indra is due to two reasons. He is the lord of all that is there by virtue of his power, and everything depends on him for sustenance. None can resist his power, and all are naught without him. In this sense of dependence on him all are devoted to him naturally. The whole creation pays homage to him, or acknowledges its dependence on him. Wherever power is

81. 2.22.3

82. 1.173.8.

83. 1.109.1; 1.173.8.

exerted Indra is worshipped naturally. "The entire universe is engaged in thy worship."[84] "Both heaven and earth worship him."[85] The whole creation bows down to him as it were in reverence, and acknowledges its dependence on him. He is the lord of all that is there, or the lord of animate and inanimate worlds (*jagataḥ prāṇataḥ pati*). Even those who are not divinely inspired or spiritually awakened worship him in submitting themselves to his power. Whether one addresses and worships Indra by name or not, by submitting oneself to power in any form of its manifestation, Indra is acknowledged and worshipped. Everyone in the world feels dependent upon something great and mighty, and that feeling of dependence generates naturally the sense of worship. The whole world manifests his power and feels dependent on him, the source of all power. The whole creation perpetually pays homage to Indra in the sense of acknowledging its dependence on him. Thus Indra is an object of worship universally. All worship him and feel dependent upon him, the phenomenon of strength and power. The weak and the strong, the victor and the vanquished, the robber and the gentle worship him and seek him. The highest and the lowest and the middle, those going and those stopping, those staying at home or going to battle worship Indra.[86]

Although all men recognise power and submit to it in various ways, that act of submission or bowing down is not real conscious worship which comes spontaneously when one is divinely inspired. The real worship is not due solely to a sense of helplessness and dependence. It is born out of love, and is spontaneous and irresistible. It is like the feeling of love which a son has for his father. It is as spontaneous as water seeking declivity. It is based on kinship and friendship. There is joy in such devotion and worship. "In Indra they rejoice who love

84. 1.57.3.

85. 2.12.13.

86. 4.25.8; 8.55.8; 1.101.6.

devotion."[87] "The ties by which worshippers are bound to him (Indra) are not bonds but ties of love."[88] Such spontaneous and loving devotion to Indra is a gift of Indra to his devotees. He is inspirer of devotion, as well as the object of it. He stirs the worshippers to devotion and worship like wind the forest.[89] He is generator of all worship and prayer, and also abides in them (*yā viśveṣām janitā matīnām; viśveṣu gīrṣu āyatam*).[90]

Devotion sustains the worshipper spiritually; and what is sought through it is the loving benevolence (*pramati* or *sumati*) of Indra (*te mahīm sumatim vevidāma*).[91] "Thy devotees cling to thy feet for glory."[92] And the prayers are also meant to glorify him. "For your pleasure are made these praises."[93] "Thou art our *pramati* (benevolence) even as a father."[94] "We repeatedly glorify with praises him who is greatest among great (*mahāntam mahinā*)."[95] In him all the praises and hymns are concentrated like the rivers in the sea. "As water goes to lower places my songs go to you."[96] "To Indra our praises are due as debt."[97] One cannot resist from worshipping Indra when one is inspired by him. "Directed unto thee my spirit never strays."[98] The worshippers feel so attached to Indra, when they are awakened to his presence, that they feel bound to him as a child clings to the hem of its father's cloth. "I will send forth my songs in flow unceasing, like waters

87. 3.34.8.
88. 6.24.4.
89. 10.23.4.
90. 6.69.2; 8.81.7.
91. 7.24.6.
92. 6.29.3.
93. 7.3.5; 1.25.3; 7.29.3; 1.102.1.
94. 7.29.4.
95. 10.134.1.
96. 8.6.34; 8.32.22.
97. 8.50.12.
98. 10.43.2.

from the depths of ocean, to Indra."[99] The devotion to Indra, as to other deities, is deeply touched with emotion. "You are more to me than my father or niggard brother. You and my mother appear alike to me."[100] "Through devotion I fashioned a hymn to you."[101] "I bend down with devotion to you."[102] "You are our dearest, and no one is dearer to us than you."[103]

Devotion to Indra is his gift, and he is prayed to inspire and increase devotion in his worshippers. He is described as the form of Gāyatrī (*gāyatra vepasam*), the deity of creativity or inspiration.[104] He is regarded as the power of inspiration of the deity of inspiration (Savitā).[105] Gāyatrī as the source of divine inspiration is identical with Sāvitrī or Savitā, and Indra is seen as the form of Gāyatrī. His divinity consists in his capacity to inspire man divinely. He is inspirer of devotion and prayer universally (*viśvaminvaḥ*).[106] He illumines human intellect with divine light, and inspires devotion in man. He is prayed to sharpen the intellect of his worshippers (*śiśīḥ mā śiśimān tvā śṛṇomi*).[107] "From Indra have I measured a song faithful to *ṛta*."[108] He is the abode of all songs of praise and prayer. The birth of divine inspiration, or its upsurge in the heart of man removes from within it the darkness, and leads man to divine light; and Indra is seen as the remover of darkness from within the hearts of man (*hṛdā varadaḥ tamāṁsi*).[109] "You impel a poet to win light."[110] In you is my wisdom,

99. 10.89.4; see also 10.43.2.

100. 8.1.6; see also 7.32.23.

101. 8.6.23.

102. 7.32.20.

103. 7.32.19.

104. 8.1.10; 1.142.12.

105. 2.30.1.

106. 7.28.1.

107. 10.42.3; see also 8.4.16. *codaya dhiyam ayasā na dhārām* (6.47.10). Sharpen my thought as it were a blade of iron (Griffith).

108. 8.65.12.

109. 5.31.9.

110. 6.26.3.

or you are my wisdom (*tve api kratu mama*)."[111] He consecrates or sanctifies man and makes him divine. "Inspire our intellect and make us divine (*devavantam*).[112] He is described as the lord of intellect, as well as its inspirer (*patindhiyam* or *dhiyaspati* and *codaya dhiyam*). He is light amidst darkness. He is a *kavi* among the *vipras*. He is a *ṛṣi* and a *dhīra*, and matchless in his wisdom. He is prayed to lead man to divine light which is good (*svasti*) and confers fearlessness (*abhayam*), or it is itself fearlessness.[113]

He is identified with devotion (*brahma*) and is also awakened by it. He is full of *kratu* (wisdom) and ordains all. He inspires in people the sense of sacrifice (*yajña*), devotion (*brahma*) and hymns (*gira*). He presides over every act of worship. When man is fully awakened to the divine, whatever he does will be an act of worship. Then Indra is glorified by all the acts of man (*yoge yoge tava staram vāje vāje havāmahe*).[114] Even such mundane acts like harvesting will then have the significance of worship. In one of the hymns of the *Ṛgveda* it is said that the glory of Indra cannot be praised adequately by man.[115] His greatness is ineffable. He cannot be attained by works and sacrifice. The only appropriate and befitting way of expressing one's devotion to Indra is to bow down to him in reverence, and take refuge in him, like a bird flying to its nest. All the offerings made to Indra, and the various ritualistic acts performed in his honour are of secondary importance only. "Soma shed without prayer is not acceptable to Indra."[116] "Whether the simple or the sage has offered praise to thee by his love has gladdened thee."[117] Prayer which is mainly of the form of praising the glory of Indra is a fit means of expressing one's devotion to Indra. It touches his heart, and

111. 7.31.5.

112. 6.47.10.

113. 6.47.3 and also 12; 2.27.11 and 14.

114. 1.30.7.

115. 6.47.15. He is described as *ajūrya* or beyond all praise. 6.21.9.

116. 7.26.1.

117. 9.50.9.

awakens him to his worshippers. Devotion is increased by devotion, and Indra increases devotion in those who are devoted to him (*namaḥ namasi īryati*).[118] Indra himself has chosen devotion (*brahma*) as the supreme form of his worship, as well as the means of his increase (*aham brahma kṛṇvam, mahyam vardhanam*).[119] He is attained by devotion (*brahmavāḥ*) which is his gift to man (*imā brahma brahmavāḥ kriyante*).[120] "He is to be worshipped with bowed down head as respect is paid by prostration to a holy sage."[121] Simple and spontaneous act of bowing down in reverence, which the act of prostration indicates, is the supreme form of expressing one's devotion, and is done by man spontaneously when devotion springs up in him. "All these libations you make effective, and of which you are the supporter."[122] And the devotion increases his glory and makes him great (*bhuva tvam indra brahmanā mahān bhava*).[123]

Devotion is an end in itself. By it nothing other than its increase and consummation are sought. In all the hymns of the *Ṛgveda*, devotion is extolled and glorified in divine terms, and is sought for its own sake. It is divine, and its perfect realisation is the highest end of man. It is the revelation of the divine within man. To be in Indra, or to possess his divine power is the quest of the worshippers. To be divinely inspired, or to experience devotion is the supreme quest of the Vedic seers. Prayer is a means of attaining devotion, as well as a means of expressing it. We will discuss this fully in the next chapter. "One man worships Indra to augment his power by sacrifice, another who is insincere worships with mind averted. To the former he is like a lake to a thirsty pilgrim. To the other a long road which retards the end of the journey.[124]

118. 4.21.5.

119. 10.49.1; see also 6.23.6.

120. 3.41.3.

121. 1.132.2.

122. 10.50.6.

123. 10.50.4.

124. 1.173.11; see also 1.175.6.

The presence of a deity in a phenomenon of nature is not something given to man's empirical observation. The divine presence is seen in nature when man is divinely inspired. Hence birth of devotion in man means the birth of divine, and with the growth and maturity of devotion within man his awareness of the divine becomes more and more comprehensive. Thus the increase of a deity in terms of devotion and prayer mean the growth and fulfilment of devotion in man. Devotion increases devotion. It is *brahma* (devotion) that inspires *brahma*, and helps its growth and maturity. Along with the growth in devotion man's awareness of the divine becomes comprehensive and gains clarity. The divine is not something that is there to be observed, but is something that is experienced within man or within his divinely inspired devotion. In this sense devotion helps the growth (*vardhana*) of a deity. The deities grow in terms of man's devotion and reverence (*namaḥ vr̥dhāsaḥ*). "You (Indra) have displayed the first great powers when propitiated by prayer."[125] "Vigour has been perpetually imparted to him by his worshippers."[126] Even in the ordinary sense also man and nature continuously help the growth or increase of the deities, in the sense that they help the deities to manifest more and more fully in newer forms all the time. Growth of a deity then comes to mean the manifestation of a deity more and more fully, and in the process of self-manifestation and self-extension of the divine the whole universe is involved. Increase of a deity means the fuller manifestation of a deity. When the presence of the divine is seen in nature, or when nature is seen as the manifestation of the deities, nature in its varied forms becomes a source of divine revelation. The role of man is to help the extension of this process to all the spheres of his life; and that is the real significance of *yajña*. All the deities are born out of *yajña*. They perpetuate it and extend it and are also extended by it. Man performs *yajña* or extends it when the sense of *yajña* is divinely inspired in him.

125. 2.17.3.

126. 2.20.8.

As indicated earlier, Indra power is holy and righteous or full of *ṛta*. It not only inspires human heart to devotion, but impels human will to move in accordance with *ṛta*. It is full of *ṛta* (*ṛtasā pipyuṣīm*). "You (Indra) are the abiding place of *ṛta*, do thou declare it to us, or make it known to us, so that men may see it within themselves with the rays of its own light (*antariti paśyanti raśmibhiḥ*)."[127] Indra teaches mankind the ways of *ṛta*, and unfolds thereby all his portals. He is born of *ṛta* and is its protector.[128] His power sanctifies man. He is prayed to lead man in righteous ways, and to inspire his will for doing things in accordance with *ṛta*. He is addressed as *trātā* (saviour from sin), and is known as *taraṇi*. He saves men from sin, and inspires them for truthful conduct. He does not turn away from the sinner. He saves men from great sins (*trātā indra enasaḥ mahācit*).[129] He saves men from sin which Varuṇa finds in them. "Let us be liberated from sin by your grace."[130] He not only saves men from sin, but guides them to go by the path of *ṛta* (*ṛtasya padā naya ati viśvāni dūrita*).[131] Indra is like a ship who takes man across sins. He saves man from divine wrath which he may incur by not following the path of *ṛta*. He awakens wisdom in man, and is the lord of his *yoga* and *kṣema* (conduct and welfare).[132] He inspires even a niggard to liberality. "On good and evil paths be thou our leader. All blessings (*saubhāga*) are in you. Your truth (*ṛtam*) be our protector."[133] In following the *ṛta* man and nature magnify or glorify Indra, and manifest his wisdom.

Among the deities of the *Ṛgveda* Indra is praised as if he is the supreme reality. He is addressed as *dhātā* and *vidhātā* the ordainer and sustainer of the whole world. He is truth. He is Brahma. He is wisdom and devotion. He is chief among the

---

127. 1.132.3; see also 2.27.3.

128. 3.31.21.

129. 7.20.1; see also 5.34.4.

130. 8.18.7; 6.74.3; 7.86.7.

131. 10.133.6.

132. 10.89.10; see also 8.37.5.

133. 6.21.12.

hymns (*jyeṣṭha mantraḥ*). In a dialogue between Indra and the seer Viśvāmitra, Indra says that knowledge of himself is the highest for man, and hence man should try to know him only. And such knowledge saves man from all sins. Further he identifies himself with the divine and its creative power (Brahma and Brahmāṇī) or the divine and its dynamic aspect.[134] Out of the several etymological definitions traditionally given of the "Indra", we present two important definitions here. According to one definition, as soon as born, Indra entered into all men as the inspirer and internal ruler of all the senses and faculties of man. Therefore, he is known as Indra.[135] According to this definition, Indra is the spiritual power in man because of which all the senses are able to know their respective objects. He inspires them to perform their respective functions. In another illuminating definition it is said that after the creation Indra entered into all. "Born he looked through all beings to see whether any one wished to proclaim another self. He saw his person as the most widely extended *Brahman*. "I have seen it", so he said, and therefore he is Indra by name (*idam darśa* and *so idamdra* or *indra*)."[136] According to this conception of Indra, he is comparable to the concept of *Īśvara* of the later Hindu tradition. Ontologically *Īśvara* is the same as *Brahman*, but in conception he is distinct from *Brahman*. He represents *Brahman* in its creative aspect, or he is *Brahman* viewed as the creator. Thus Indra is the primary and first manifestation of the divine, and manifests himself in and through all the manifestations of the divine. As the creative power inherent within the reality of the divine, he is the creator and lord of all that is there. Without him there is no creation. He is the lord of both animate and inanimate worlds. By being within all the beings he sustains them. The entire universe is contained in him as spokes within the felly. As the

134. *Śāṅkhāyana Āraṇyaka* 1.6.

135. See Sāyaṇa's commentary on 1.2.4; see also 3.37.9.

136. *Aitareya Āraṇyaka* 11.4.3. translation by Arthur B. Keith.

creator, or as the divine in its creative aspect, he is not fully realised in what is created. Creation cannot contain his glory fully. All the glory that is revealed in creation is his. At the same time, all that is there reflects only a part of his glory and greatness. In himself or in his true nature he is inconceivable, and no praise is adequate to express his glory and greatness. "His greatness the heaven and earth cannot comprehend."[137] He supports all but is unsupported by any. He contains everything and rules everything, but is not contained and ruled by anything. "Far is that secret name by which in terror the worlds invoke thee."[138] "Thy form held in secret by men with averted faces is far from hence."[139] "When alarmed heaven and earth call upon thee for sustenance."[140] Four are his mighty divine names which reveal his glory, and he himself knows them all (*catvāri te asūryāni nāma adābhyāni mahiṣasya santi, tvam aṅga tāni viśvāni vitse*).[141] That aspect of Indra which transcends human knowledge constitutes his fourth name. Three of his names which are given to him according to his manifestations within the three regions are known to man. However, the divine nature of Indra is revealed in and through all his manifestations at all levels. He is revealed in all his deeds both natural and supernatural. Man can only contemplate in wonder the true divine nature of Indra, the source of all power. The divine aspect of Indra is revealed more fully to the wise who are attached to him in love and devotion.

In the above sense, Indra is first-born among the deities, or his birth is logically prior to that of all the other deities. All the deities share his glory and participate in his divine power which they manifest in their own individual ways. As he pervades all creation, he is inherent within all the deities as divine power, and hence all the prayers addressed to various deities are

137. 10.112.4; see also 8.6.15; 1.52.14; 1.61.8.

138. 10.55.1.

139. 10.55.1 and 2.

140. 1.63.1.

141. 10.54.4.

addressed to him also. In worshipping all other deities he is being worshipped. The various rites done in honour of the various deities, and all the virtuous acts of man (*dharma*) are devoted to Indra. As the sustaining power inherent within all the deities, he is Viśvadeva or of the nature of all the deities. He is their inner unity. He is identified with almost all the deities, and worshipped along with all other deities, as all the deities are powerful and wise by his power and wisdom. He is incomparable and one, and the most divine among the deities (*na tvā vān anyaḥ divyaḥ na pārḍhivaḥ na jātaḥ no janiṣyate*). He is *apūrva*, or there is none like him. He is incomparable. He is Viṣṇu, he is Prajāpati, he is Viśvakarmā, he is Varuṇa and Sūrya (*yaḥ devāḥ devatamam; devāḥ bhavadha viśve indra*).[142] In him is concentrated all devotion. All worship and hymns proceed to him as their sole object, as all the rivers join the sea. He is the truth in its dynamic aspect, and all that is there is a manifestation of truth. So whatever is there as the manifestation of Indra is also true. What he looks upon is true. He is the supreme revelation of truth (*ketum parām svaḥ dr̥śām*).[143] "That which he knows is truth, but not false" (*yat ciketa satyam it tat na mogham*).[144] As the primary manifestation of the divine he reveals it by manifesting its glory in all the worlds. He is worshipped as the source of all bliss, or as bliss itself.

His reality is true and objective, but not imagined or mentally constructed (*akalpaḥ*).[145] His existence is independent of human conception and imagination. He is not the creation of poetic imagination, though poetic imagination may try to determine his nature or measure him. He is known to all through his manifestations. However, in his divine aspect he is known to the wise or the seers. He is the source of all wisdom, but not a

142. 6.22.3; 3.54.17.

143. 1.33.1.

144. 10.55.6.

145. 1.102.6.

product of it. In the moments of inspiration man's understanding is divinely illumined, or his vision is divinely transformed, and what is not revealed to ordinary understanding of man is then revealed to him. In all this process of knowing the nature of the divine, nature acts on man's creativity. It is the immediate source of divine inspiration to man.

5

Divine Inspiration

In the previous chapters we have discussed the nature and meaning of the divine as revealed to the seers of the *Ṛgveda* in and through the various deities. As the deities dwell in nature, or as nature is the immediate source of their revelation, nature is viewed by the Vedic seers as the visible form or phenomenal manifestation of the divine. To a divinely inspired person or a seer, who sees or experiences the divine through its presence in nature, nature is something more than what it is known ordinarily or empirically. It is a manifestation of the divine, or the abode of the deities. It reveals the divine as its inner unity. According to the Ṛgvedic mode of expression, to see nature as divine is to see it as the abode of the deities, the primary forms of self-manifestation of the divine. Each deity dwells in a phenomenon of nature, and manifests itself through it. Although each deity has an identity of its own, and is distinct from the rest of the deities, as manifestations of the divine they find their unity in the divine. The divine is what is commonly revealed in and through them all. It is their inner unity. Thus nature as the abode of the deities represents the cosmic form of the divine (*virāṭ*). Nature is divine because of its capacity to reveal the divine to man, or to inspire him divinely. This vision of the seers which is central to *Ṛgveda* is expressed in a language which is poetic, devotional and mostly symbolic.

We now turn our attention to the seers (*ṛṣi*) and seer-poets (*kavi*) of the *Ṛgveda*, who receive divine revelation, to understand the nature and meaning of divine inspiration, the source of Vedic wisdom expressed through hymns. The hymns of the *Ṛgveda* are essentially prayers and praises addressed to various deities, either individually or collectively, and with the exception of a few speculative hymns, they describe, by way of praising the deities in terms of their divine attributes, the nature of the divine as revealed to the seers. And as prayers the hymns also express the deep devotion of the seers experienced in response to their awareness of the divine. Each phenomenon of nature reveals the nature of the divine in its own way, and together all the phenomena of nature reveal the infinite richness of divine glory and splendour. Thus what is revealed directly to the seers are the various facets of the divine as manifested in nature, and the divine in itself, the ultimate source of these manifestations is a matter of intellectual abstraction and generalisation based on what is directly experienced. The problem of the nature of the divine in itself has not exercised the understanding of the seers, and the few hymns in which it is reflected upon do not, however, form the core of the *Ṛgveda*. The general tone of the speculative hymns, which are a few in number considering the total number of the Ṛgvedic hymns, is one of scepticism, though intellectual enquiry reflected in them is deep and sincere. Intellectual understanding of the nature of the divine in itself follows logically the direct apprehension of it in and through its manifestations. When the presence of the divine is experienced in nature man may try to understand the nature of the divine abstractly. Such a theoretical approach to understand the nature of the divine, with which the post-Saṁhitā tradition is concerned, is not the central theme of the Vedic hymns. We are, therefore, concerned in this chapter mainly with the nature of divine inspiration, the source of vedic hymns.

The object of this chapter, is to understand the nature and meaning of divine inspiration, the source of Vedic wisdom, its sources and the forms of its expression as presented in the hymns of the *Ṛgveda*. What does Veda speak about itself and its wisdom? Apart from the later Hindu tradition in which the Veda is regarded as the infallible source of our knowledge of the divine, the Veda itself speaks in clear terms about its revealed character. The *R̥gveda* is a collection of hymns which try to express and communicate the truth as revealed to the seers. Although the seers are the authors of the hymns, as often they speak of creating or fashioning new hymns, the wisdom they embody and express is not born out of their own understanding. The hymns express in human language the divinely inspired "Word" or Speech (*vāk*), and nowhere the seers have claimed to themselves the source of the wisdom contained in the hymns. The truth or wisdom conveyed through the hymns is not due to their own understanding. The hymns not only contain the divinely inspired wisdom or speech, but also express the devotion that is divinely inspired. To be divinely inspired, or to become a *r̥ṣi* or a *kavi* is the supreme quest of the seers, and this is fully reflected in their prayers to the deities. All the knowledge the hymns convey about the nature of the deities is conveyed by way of praising the deities in terms of their divine attributes. The hymns are not simple descriptions of the deities, described for the sake of giving knowledge about them. It is by way of expressing the heart-felt devotion of the seers to the deities, the deities are praised in terms of their divine attributes. Thus the primary purpose of the seer-poets in creating hymns is to give expression to their inwardly experienced devotion to the deities. Each deity is an object of man's devotion and worship, and the deities are prayed and worshipped with the devotion that is inspired by the deities themselves. As primary self-manifestations of the divine all the deities are intrinsically capable of awakening man to the presence of the divine, and to inspire in him devotion and reverence. Anything that can awaken in man the sense of divine, and inspire in him devotion and worship is an object of man's worship. All such objects, however insignificant they may appear to an uninspired understanding of man, are to an inspired person manifestations of the divine, and reveal its glory. The divine manifests itself in various ways and forms in nature, and each of its manifestation is a source of its revelation to man, provided he has attained the purity of vision. A seer who is known for the purity of his heart and subtlety (*aṇu*) of his intellect experiences the divine through its presence in nature, and therefore nature is an object of reverence and worship for him. This explains the general indifference of the Vedic seers towards a metaphysical understanding of the nature of the divine. Their faith in the existence of the deities, and their attachment to them in devotion and reverence cannot also be explained otherwise.

The Vedic seers' knowledge of nature or their vision of it is not based on their speculative or metaphysical understanding of it. When they describe the deities in terms of their phenomenal and divine attributes, the purpose is not to provide a metaphysical explanation of nature in terms of the deities. The hymns of the *Ṛgveda* are not a philosophical study of nature, but express what nature has revealed to the seers in the state of inspiration. A *ṛṣi* or a *kavi* is one who knows nature in its hidden or divine aspect. The divine aspect of nature is revealed to man when nature acts on his finer sensibilities, and inspires in him devotion and reverence. Man experiences the presence of the divine in nature when he is divinely inspired. Divine inspiration influences the whole being of man, and opens to him the depths of his own being. It is often compared to a stream which floods the inner being of man, fulfils his existence supremely and bestows on him bliss. It illumines his understanding and fulfils it. It also influences his will to act according to or follow the path of *ṛta*. The wisdom that is born out of divine inspiration helps man to see nature in a new light, or to see the divine as the inner unity of all that is there. When man is enlightened and his being is flooded with divine inspiration, he is born anew, and becomes a *ṛṣi*, or a *kavi*, or a *vipra*. The immediate source of such inspiration to man is nature. Seeing the divine in nature depends more on the inner purity of man. He sees the divine, or experiences its presence in nature when devotion is born in him. Nature as it is known to an uninspired person is not an object of worship for him, but it is the same nature which inspires a seer, and reveals to him its hidden divine nature. Thus man experiences the divine primarily within the state of devotion, or within the inspired state of his existence, and as nature is the immediate source of such inspiration it is seen as the abode of the deities, or as a manifestation of the divine.

Divine inspiration moves a man deeply, or stirs his inner being, and transforms him totally. The Vedic hymns are a poetic expression of the truth revealed in the state of inspiration. The state of being divinely inspired, or inwardly experienced devotion is indicated by the term *brahma*, the source of Vedic wisdom. The divine wisdom or speech (*vāk*) is revealed to the seers in the state of inspiration. We may render the meaning of divine *vāk* (speech), keeping in view its all-comprehensive character, as divine intelligence or wisdom which finds its creative expression in all the manifestations of the divine. Vāk and Brahma are co-extensive; and from the standpoint of a seer Brahma is what the Vāk expresses."Let the Brahma come from the abode of *r̥ta* (truth), creating by its multiform splendour the hymns (*gāh*) (*pra brahma etu sadanāt r̥tasya viraśmibhiḥ sasruje sūrya gāḥ*).[1] "Through Brahma have we made the hymns"; and Brahma is the supreme abode of all speech.[2] The hymns which express Brahma experienced within are termed variously as *dhītayaḥ*, *manīṣā*, *sūkta*, *stuti*, *stotra* and *mantra*. All these terms are meaningful as expressing the relation between Brahma and the various faculties of man which receive it, and are influenced by it. Brahma inspires all the faculties of man, and in their turn they express it. However, the intellect and heart of man are the seats of its experience, as well as the means of its expression. As the creation of man's inspired intellect the hymns are known as *dhītayaḥ*, and as expressing divinely inspired wisdom they are known as *manīṣā*. Hymns are created by an intellect that is

1. 7.36.1.
2. 8.6.33.
   Brahma in the sense of the divine or the ultimate reality is the ultimate source of all speech or wisdom. The limits of speech are the limits of Brahma, or both are limitless. Speech extends as far as Brahma extends. And Brahma as devotion is the direct manifestation and revelation of the divine in man. Divine wisdom or speech is born in man when he is inspired to devotion.

divinely inspired or illumined. Although the heart of man (*hṛdayam*) is mentioned several times in the *Ṛgveda* as the seat of divine inspiration, human mind or intellect, which is more comprehensive in its functions than the heart, is seen at times as comprehending the heart, or the term mind is used to mean both intellect and heart. Thus the term *manīṣā* (wisdom or hymn) which means the wisdom of a *manīṣin*, literally lord of one's mind, does not only express what is grasped by human mind, but also indicates what an inspired heart intuits. Although the chief purpose of the Vedic hymns is to give expression to inwardly experienced devotion of the seers, as prayers and praises they also communicate the nature of the divine as revealed to the seers.

As Brahma is divine, the hymns that express it are also divine, and hence sacred. The divine is revealed within the state of Brahma, and as the hymns are an expression of Brahma in human language, they convey the knowledge of the divine as revealed. And the Veda as a collection of hymns is a repository of divine wisdom or *vāk* as revealed to the seers. In this sense, the divine Vāk as expressed in the hymns of the Veda is an abode of the deities, or the deities dwell therein. In the speech of the Veda abide all the deities. What the Veda can do, if one does not know that? Or in the imperishable word of the Veda, the highest realm, dwell the deities; and the Veda is not intelligible or meaningful to those who do not know this (*ṛcā akṣare parame vyoman yasmin devāḥ adhi viśve niṣeduḥ, yaḥ tannaveda kim ṛcā kariṣyati*).[3] "He knows well thy favour who gave an impulse to this high devotion (Brahma)."[4] One who is divinely inspired knows the divine, as well as the true meaning of the Veda. Veda is therefore, helpless to reveal the divine to those who are content only with the verbal meaning of the Veda, or those who deal only with its words. On the other hand, to those who can see through the words the wisdom of the seers, or can discern their real and

3. 1.164.39.
4. 4.4.6.

intended meaning, the real meaning of the Veda reveals itself as a loving wife offers herself willingly to her loving husband. "Brahmaṇaspati recites the sacred hymn (*mantra*) in which the various deities dwell, or have made it their place of dwelling (*pra nūnam brahmaṇsapati mantram vadati uktam yasmin indraḥ, varuṇaḥ, mitraḥ, aryamā devāḥ okāṁśi cakrire*)."[5] The deities are described as born of hymns (*mānasya sūnuh*) which clothe divine inspiration. In this connection it is significant to note that all the deities are attainable by devotion (*brahmavāḥ*). They are also increased by it, or devotion is the source of their growth. Man is awakened to the divine presence in nature when devotion is generated in him, and in terms of its growth and maturity he is able to know the nature of the divine more clearly and fully. It is the unfailing source of man's knowledge of the divine. Indra is described as abiding within hymns (*mānasya kṣiyaḥ*).[6] Similarly, Viṣṇu is also addressed as dwelling in hymns (*giri kṣitaḥ*).[7] Agni is addressed as the child of hymns (*mānasya sūnuḥ*).[8] In a significant hymn it is stated that spiritually awakened, the seers (*ṛṣi*) looked around when first they beheld that heaven allotted treasure, and all the deities came to all their respective dwellings.[9] This we may explain to mean that with the dawn of divine wisdom, or with the birth of divine inspiration within themselves, the seers are able to see the presence of the deities in nature, or nature reveals itself as the dwelling place of the deities. In another hymn it is said that the various deities have entered into different Vedic metres, and a person who knows this truth is a *ṛṣi*.[10] The various metres in which the hymns are arranged mean figuratively either the hymns or the Veda. The purpose of expressing the inspired wisdom through hymns is to help future generations to know

5. 1.40.5.
6. 8.63.8; 8.81.7.
7. 1.154.3.
8. 1.189.8.
9. 4.1.18.
10. 10.130.4 to 6.

it. "Let us proclaim with a stirring or inspired voice (*vipanyayā*) the birth of the deities that one may see them when the hymns are recited in a future age."[11]

The terms *divya* (divine), *satya* (truth or reality) and *ṛta* (truth or cosmic order) are often employed in the *Ṛgveda* to mean the same reality. And the terms *param* or *parame vyoman* (the highest or the supreme), *pitā* (Father or supreme Father), *ekam* (one) and even Brahma are used to indicate the ultimate or the divine reality. However, a subtle distinction can be made between their meanings in terms of their actual usage in different contexts of the *Ṛgveda*. The term *divya* which is used both substantively and adjectively can mean either the divine reality in its varied manifestations, or as a quality inherent within things. In the latter sense it is used in relation to all the deities. It is also used to qualify inspiration or inspired intellect, human thoughts and speech. It is not used in its abstract sense, or to mean the divine in itself (*divyatva* or *devatvam*). In almost all the cases of its usage it means the divine in its manifested or embodied form of existence, such as the deities. The term *satya* which in its common usage means the truthfulness or veracity of an utterence or a statement, is used to mean the highest reality or truth. *Ṛta* is also used to mean the truth or the highest truth. However, in the sense of truth it has its distinctive meaning, and indicates the divine in its dynamic or revelatory aspect. It is the divine order and purpose revealed in the universe at all levels. The terms *Father* or *supreme Father*, the creator or matrix of all, the Supreme and One and also Brahma are often used synonymously, and mean the highest reality or the divine.

The Vedic hymns express and communicate divine knowledge or wisdom (*dhītiḥ*) as revealed to the seers. They are songs of prayer addressed to various deities, and praise their divine glory and splendour. The whole universe is an abode of the divine, or a means of its creative self-expression (*dhāman te*

11. 10.72.1.

viśvam bhuvanam adhi śritam).[12] In its splendour and glory, the divine is present throughout the universe as that which illumines and reveals all. It is the illumining consciousness in all living beings, as well as the lord and fulfiller of man's intelligence (*pracetasā viśvasya; īśānaḥ pipyatam dhiyaḥ*).[13] All that exists phenomenally is a self-manifestation of the divine, and, therefore, is a source of divine revelation. It is a sign (*ketu*) of the divine or the supreme or the immortal, and is known in that aspect by the wisdom it inspires in man. All the deities are described as *jyotiradhāḥ*, or the vehicles of expression of the divine light. They approach man on vehicles of divine light. They are revealed to man as inspirers or illuminers of his intellect or understanding, and as the likeness of divine light (*svaḥ druk*).

The source of the Vedic hymns is the wisdom inspired by the divine or the deities. They are born out of divine inspiration, or in them is yoked the ancient or timeless divine wisdom.[14] They are born of *ṛta* (*ṛta jātā ṛta prajātam*), and express it. The hymns which express divine wisdom or speech (*vāk*) are arranged in or bound by the seven principal Vedic metres. With their minds full of truth, the seers living in communion with the deities have discovered or attained the hidden light of the Father; hence their speech or hymns are true (*te devānām sadamādaḥ āsan ṛtamānaḥ kavayaḥ pūrvāsaḥ gulham jyotiḥ pitaraḥ anuvindan satyamantrāḥ ajanayan uṣasam*).[15] The light of truth so discovered or attained is co-eternal and co-extensive with the divine; and the Vedic seers constantly refer to this fact when they speak of ancient or timeless inspiration (*dhīyam prātnam*) and its first recipients, their forefathers. The thought or wisdom which the hymns contain is ancient or

12. 4.58.11.
    The whole world is an abode of the divine, as the deities, the primary and universal self-manifestations of the divine, dwell in nature and manifest themselves within nature.
13. 5.71.7.
14. 10.13.1.
15. 7.76.4.

timeless, while the seers or those to whom it is revealed belong to various times and places. "Where is *ṛtam*, who is its new diffuser, or who holds it anew (*bibharti nūtanaḥ*)."[16] It is only when the thoughts of man are inspired and quickened by the divine or truth, he knows the divine and becomes a *ṛṣi*. The seers are divinely inspired (*devajūtaḥ*),[17] and call themselves the children of the divine (*devaputrāḥ*).[18] They are divine born (*devajā*). They are knowers of truth as well as its upholders. Although the source of inspiration is the same for all the seers, the mode of its revelation, or the manner in which it is apprehended by different seers may not be the same. Each seer holds the truth according to his own capacity and maturity of understanding, and adopts his own mode of expression to convey it. This explains the differences in the form of expression of truth as found in the *Ṛgveda*, and the different symbols and metaphors employed by the seers to convey the revealed truth. The different forms of expression, and the various symbols and metaphors employed by different seers are according to individual differences among seers (*manīṣinaḥ prabharadhvam manīṣām yadhā yadhā matayaḥ santi nrīṇām*).[19] The inspired or the poet-seers express differently in terms of their speech the divine light which is one (*suparnam viprāḥ kavayāḥ vacobhiḥ ekam santam bahudhā kalpayanti*).[20] The Real is one, and the inspired speak of it differently (*ekam sat viprāḥ bahudhā vadanti*).[21] The ancient or timeless thought or wisdom which is full of light (*ghṛtsya pipyuṣīm*) is developed or nourished variously by the seers (*kanvāḥ uktena vavridhuḥ*), by means of their hymns.[22] The hymns release or give expression to the thoughts which are bound as it were in a seer's understanding (*yat mocati bandhāt*

16. 1.105.4.
17. 3.53.9.
18. 10.62.4; see also 3.53.9.
19. 10.111.1.
20. 10.114.5.
21. 1.164.46.
22. 8.6.43.

baddhem iva).[23] The seers who are self-refulgent, and of profound wisdom (*svabhānavaḥ viprāḥ; kavi iti gambhīra cetasa*) try to express the glory of the deities with commendable thoughts each in his own individual way.[24] Comprehending the hidden mysteries here on earth the seers have through their power of understanding made manifest heaven and earth in their true divine significance or nature. They are the people to whom nature has revealed its hidden divine nature. They are men with well-governed minds (*manīṣinaḥ*) and of pure thoughts (*sudhītayaḥ*). They are steadfast in their understanding (*kavīnām manodr̥tāḥ*). They discern the truth which is hidden to ordinary or uninspired understanding of man (*dhīrāḥ ninya ciketa*).[25] The hymns glow with truth. Therefore, the truth or wisdom which the Veda contains is not within the grasp of man's immature (*apakka*) or uninspired understanding. It is only when the understanding of man is divinely illumined or inspired he comes to know the truth. "I know not if I am all this, for I go perplexed and bound in mind, when the first-born perception of the truth reached me. Then immediately shall I obtain a portion of the meaning of the sacred word."[26]

Truth is not apprehended, as the Vedic seers claim, by man's ordinary or unillumined intellect, or simply by his intelligent questioning and enquiry. "Not all learn by questioning what the sage (*dhīra*) has grasped as it were with his own mind."[27] "We have not known the truth by our own efforts and understanding (*na tasya vidma puruṣatavatā vayam*)."[28] The real meaning of the Veda is not, therefore, revealed to those who are not mature in understanding, or to those who are satisfied with a verbal understanding of it. To those who deal only with the words of the Veda, the meaning of it is not revealed. "They call

23. 8.56.7.
24. 1.82.2; 1.82.2; 10.62.5.
25. 7.56.4.
26. 1.164.37.
27. 1.145.2.
28. 5.48.5.

one man firmly established in the friendship of speech, in whose heart the sweetness of truth is firmly seated. He is not excluded from the company of the wise. Others wander with an illusion (*māyā*) that is barren bearing speech which is fruitless and unflowering."[29] The same idea is expressed differently in a hymn addressed to *jñānam* or divine knowledge. One, though seeing or thinking about divine knowledge or wisdom yet do not see it, one, though hearing it yet do not hear it (*uta tva paśyan na dadarśa vācam uta tvaḥ śruṇvan na śruṇoti enām*).[30] But to one who can penetrate the words to grasp the wisdom communicated through them, Veda opens itself up, or shows its meaning like a loving well-dressed woman shows her beauty to her husband. It is by the wisdom that Soma grants to man, he can know the divine, but not by his own understanding.[31]

The seers speak of darkness that is present within man, and hinders him from knowing the truth. It envelops man's intellect or understanding like mist, and is the basic reason why man is not able to apprehend the divine though it is eternally revealed. The seers pray to the deities to lead them to the great divine light which is full of bliss and fearlessness, and to liberate them from the inner darkness.[32] The hymns are attained by him, or they approach him who is spiritually awakened (*yaḥ jagāra tām ū iti sāmāni yanti*).[33] Him Soma approaches in friendship, or divine Soma approaches him who is awakened and loves his friendship. "Men filled with understanding find him there when they have sung prayers formed within their hearts."[34] Being born of truth (*ṛta*) and expressing its glory, the hymns can destroy sins of man, and confer bliss on him.[35] The thoughts of *ṛta* destroy sins of

29. 10.71.5.
30. 10.71.4.
31. 1.139.2.
32. 6.47.8.
33. 5.44.14.
34. 1.7.2.
35. 4.23.8.

man (*ṛtasya dhītiḥ*). As expressing divine joy experienced by the seers, the hymns can bestow joy and bliss on others.

The seat of divine inspiration is man's intellect (*dhī* or *dhiyam*) or mind. The term *puraṁdhi* which is generally used to mean knowledge or wisdom is related to intellect as the etymology of the word shows; (*puram yāsu dhīyate*) that which is thought out in or by man. According to the *Ṛgveda,* human heart is also a source of wisdom expressed through the hymns. However, it is appropriate to make a fine distinction between the intellect and heart, and note their respective places in the formation of the hymns. Though a finer distinction between the mind or the intellect and heart is not clearly made in the *Ṛgveda,* we can yet discern a distinction between them based on their usage in different contexts of the *Ṛgveda*. Both are involved in the creation of a hymn. The hymns flow from one's heart, and are formed within one's mind or intellect. In the *Atharvaveda* it is said very significantly that the Ṛṣi Atharvan sewed the head and heart together.[36] This indicates that the nature and functions of head and heart are conceived differently in the Veda. But in the formation of a hymn, understanding of man and the intuitions of his heart are harmonised and integrated. The wisdom of the hymns reflects the contributions of both, or in their formation both play an important role. Therefore, the wisdom of the Veda is not purely based on intellectual understanding, nor does it simply express the feelings of heart. The harmony of head and heart reflected in the wisdom of the Veda is due mainly to the nature of divine inspiration, which influences both of them equally. Both the intellect and heart are inspired or illumined by the same divine light, and in the state of inspiration the distinction between them may not be there, though in normal life their areas of operation as well as their functions are distinct. The gulf between them as ordinarily experienced is not felt in the state of inspiration. Both of them or rather all the faculties of man fully participate in the divine light, and are equally

36. *Atharvaveda Saṁhitā* 10.2.26.

influenced by it. It floods the whole being of man. This explains the expressions like *antaḥ hṛdā manasā pūyamānaḥ*, purified within the heart and mind.[37] "Men filled with understanding find him there when they have sung prayers formed within their hearts.[38] The hymns are known as *dhītayaḥ*, or *dhīṣāṇa* or *manīṣā*, and the seers of the hymns are known as *dhīrā* and *manīṣā*. They are known for the purity of their intellect or thought (*sudhītayaḥ*), and are illumined in their understanding (*dīdhyānāḥ*). Hymns are formed when one is intellectually inspired (*dhiya iṣitā*). The hymns are created by intellect (*dhiyā cakre*). The seers think out a hymn, or a hymn is born out of contemplation (*āmanmahi*). The hymns express the truth that is apprehended by the intellect. The wise (*dhīrā*) with their minds or understanding formed the hymns discerning the truth from the untruth, just as barley is winnowed to separate it from husk.[39] With a true mind or understanding (*satyena manasā*) the seers have known the truth, and pray that their speech or hymns be true. The hymns are true as they present the truth (*satya mantrāḥ*). The *ṛṣis* are of true speech (*satya vācaḥ ṛṣyaḥ*).[40] "Let my thoughts or hymns be true (*dhiyā satyamastu*)."[41] The hymns are an expression of an inspired mind, or are born of it. The power of Indra prevails in the thoughts or intellect (*dhiyā*) of his worshippers. The seers constantly pray to the deities to inspire or illumine their understanding. The hymn popularly known as "Gāyatrī" is an invocation to the deity Savitā to inspire the intellect of the worshipper. "Let my intellect be inspired (*dhīyo yo naḥ pracodayāt*)."[42] The deities are prayed to sharpen one's intellect, as a stone the knife.[43] The truth is apprehended by those who are mentally illumined or

37. *Ṛgveda Saṁhitā* 4.58.6.
38. 1.67.2.
39. 10.71.2.
40. 3.54.5.
41. 1.185.11.
42. 3.62.10.
43. 2.39.7.

enlightened (*manasā vipaścitāḥ*).[44] The sacred knowledge contained in the Veda is mentally apprehended by the seers (*manasā bibharti*).[45] The deities are perceived mentally by those who can discern (*apaśyam tvā manasā cekitānam*).[46] The deity Sarasvatī is known to accomplish or fulfil one's understanding (*sādhayanti dhiyam naḥ*), or achieves a hymn for the seer.[47] Pūṣan is described as a means of achieving hymns (*matīnām sādhanam*).[48] The term *mati* may mean either the mind or understanding or its creation, the hymns. Thus the hymns as creative expressions of an inspired mind or understanding are known as *dhītayaḥ, manīṣā* and *mati*. Inspired intellect is likened to a milk cow from which wisdom can be drawn, or it milks divine wisdom to man.

The hymns are equally connected with the human heart. They are formed within the heart of man (*hṛdā taṣthaḥ*).[49] They are spoken from within the heart, or are spontaneous outpourings of a heart that is divinely inspired (*hṛdā āvacaya-mānaḥ*). "We utter a hymn that is well formed within our hearts (*hṛdā ā sutaṣṭham mantram vocema*)."[50] The seers perceive the truth within their hearts, or discern it there (*hṛdā paśyanti; hṛdā vicaṣṭhe*).[51] The prayers are touched by heart (*hṛdāspṛśa*) and are intended to awaken the deities to the prayer. "Prayer born of heart goes to the presence of the deity, and is its awakener."[52] In the post-Saṁhitā literature, especially in the Brāhmaṇas and the Upaniṣads, the heart of man is regarded as a source of knowledge, for by means of it man knows love,

44. 10.171.1; see also 10.181.3; 8.95.5.
45. 10.177.2.
46. 1.173.1.
47. 2.3.8.
48. 10.26.4.
49. 1.171.2; see also 1.67.3.
50. 2.35.2.
51. 1.24.12.
52. 3.39.1.

faith, devotion and reverence.[53] It knows certain things the meaning of which the mind of man cannot grasp. The streams of inspiration in the form of hymns flow from within the ocean of heart (*etā arṣanti hṛdyāt samudrāt*).[54] In the *Ṛgveda*, the term *samudra* is often used as a symbol for human heart. The hymns flow like streams being purified within the heart and mind of man (*samyak sravanti saritā na dhenāḥ antaḥ hṛdā manasā pūyamānaḥ*).[55] When the mind comprehends what is felt or formed within the heart, and when the latter is guided by the former, the truth is known; and the wisdom expressed through the hymns reflects the contributions of both. "Prayer connected with pure heart's desire of the worshipper is not disappointed, and where the mind is known to be attached to the pure (heart)."[56] The prayers are stirred within the heart of a seer, and are expressed with the help of the mind (*hṛdi spṛśa manasā vacyamānaḥ*).[57] Devotion which springs up in the heart is connected with the mind also (*haviṣmatā manasā*), and the hymns are equally connected with the heart (*hṛtsu dhītayaḥ*). Thus the hymns are formed with the help of both heart and mind (*hṛdā manasā taṣṭhaḥ*). The seers desiring to attain the highest see the truth within their hearts (*samudre antariti kavayaḥ vicakṣate maricīnām padam icchanti vedasaḥ*).[58] The darkness that envelops the inner being of man and obstructs his vision of the divine resides in the hearts of man, for it is prayed that the darkness within their hearts be dispelled. It is even said that the deities unfold or reveal themselves within the heart of man (*virunoti hṛdā*) and give birth to devotion thereby.[59]

Now a distinction is made in the *Ṛgveda* between understanding that is divinely illumined or inspired, and

53. *Aitareya Āraṇyaka* 2.6; *Bṛhadāraṇyaka Upaniṣad* 3.9.21 and 23; *Taittirīya Brāhmaṇa* 2.8.87; *ṚV* 10.151.4.

54. 4.58.5.

55. 4.58.6.

56. 5.44.9.

57. 10.47.7.

58. 10.177.1.

59. 5.48.5.

ordinary or uninspired understanding. While human understanding when it is divinely inspired can apprehend truth, ordinary or uninspired understanding of man cannot apprehend it. To indicate the distinction between ordinary or spiritually immature understanding of man, and the understanding that is divinely inspired, the latter is qualified by the term *divya* or *devya* (divine). The intellect that is the source of divine knowledge or wisdom is known as divine intellect, or intellect that is made divine (*devyā dhiyā* or *devīm dhiyam*), and the wisdom or speech that is born out of such an intellect is known as *devī vāk* or *devī dhīṣāṇa*. Divinely inspired intellect is described as pure (*śukra*), bright (*śociṣa*) and illumined (*dīdhyānaḥ*). The divine is revealed to one whose intellect is pure, subtle (*aṇu*) and divinely inspired or illumined. "We do not know him by ourselves or by our own efforts." He is known by the supreme wealth that is bestowed on us by Savitā (*na tasya vidma puruṣtvatā vayam yataḥ bhāgaḥ savitā dāti vāryam*).[60] "In the seats wherein ye dwell have we beheld the golden one or of golden form not with our own minds but with the eyes or sight that Soma gives."[61] Thus the Ṛgvedic seers have not claimed to themselves the wisdom that is expressed through the hymns. It is always attributed to the inspiration which they receive from the deities, and it is their constant prayer that they be blessed with it.

When the inspired wisdom is expressed in language which is arranged in or regulated by metres the hymns are born. As each Vedic hymn is arranged in a metre, figuratively metres also stand to mean the hymns. In most of the contexts of its usage, the Vedic figure seven (*sapta*) stands for the seven principal Vedic metres. Therefore, the ability to know the application of metres mean the ability to compose hymns. In this sense the knowledge of metres makes a man a *ṛṣi*. Hymns are metred verses. Thus the knowledge of the metres, and their application is the same as the sacred knowledge of the Veda (*yatra brahma*

60. 5.48.5.

61. 1.139.2.

pavamāna chandasyām vācam vadan).[62] "What sage has learned the metres' application? Who has gained *vāk*, the spirit's aim and object (*kaḥ chandasām yogam ā veda dhīraḥ*).[63] The various deities have entered into different metres and those who know this truth are the seers.[64] As the hymns express in language the divine wisdom they also reveal the deities, or the deities dwell among them.

Divine speech or wisdom (*vāk*) is revealed to man when he is divinely inspired. When the intellect and heart of man are divinely influenced or informed they become fit to receive divine knowledge, or know the divine in and through its varied manifestations. Then man's understanding of himself, and of nature will undergo a radical transformation. He comes to know the precious treasure hidden within himself, and sees nature in its hidden divine aspect, or as the abode of the deities. The divine reveals itself to man in various ways and forms. *Ṛta* (truth), the dynamic side of the divine, or its revelation in nature, manifests itself in diverse forms. All the deities manifest it, and reveal it in their own individual ways. *Yajña* which reveals the divine purpose involved in creation also manifests *ṛta*, and reveals its meaning, especially at the human level. The term *ṛta* also means *yajña*. In extending *yajña* to all the spheres of his life man realises the divine purpose in his own life, or follows the path of *ṛta*. *Ṛta* will then permeate the whole of man's life, and will help him in realising the divine fully. All that exists phenomenally, including the deities, is due to the process of divine *yajña*, and in extending it to all the spheres of his life, man in his own way participates in it, and perpetuates it. In extending it man becomes a conscious agent of the divine process within the phenomenal realm, and realises thereby the divine purpose in all that he does. Thus *yajña*, which is divine, reveals the divine purpose involved in creation, and in this sense it is not different from *ṛta*.

62. 9.113.6.
63. 10.114.9.
64. 10.130.5 to 7.

As out of the process of *yajña* the divine has become all this, to know the divine is to realise the significance of *yajña* and to participate in it and extend it. In realising the meaning of *yajña* the meaning of *ṛta* is also comprehended.

Ṛta is not revealed independently of its manifestations. The splendid forms of its manifestation are varied and many (*ṛtasya dhṛlhā dharunāni santi purūḥ candrā vapuṣe vapūmṣi*).[65] The deities, and man, or the whole of creation reveal it. As the dynamic or self-revelatory aspect of the divine, *ṛta* is the source of divine wisdom to man. The hymns are due to its inspiration. They shed the sweetness of *ṛta*, like a cow yielding milk. The knowledge of *ṛta* liberates man from his ordinary type of existence, and illumines all his faculties. It destroys the sins of man (*ṛtasya dhītīḥ vṛjināni hanti*).[66] The splendour or knowledge (*śloka*) of *ṛta* awakens a person spiritually, and opens his ears or faculties (*ṛtasya ślokaḥ badhirā tatardha karṇā budhānaḥ sucamānaḥ āyoḥ*).[67] The term *śloka* is a synonym of knowledge or wisdom, according to *Nighaṇṭu*. The deities as the primary and universal manifestations of *ṛta* share this function of *ṛta*.

In its creative function or aspect, the divine is known as Savitā or Sāvitrī, the deity of creativity and inspiration, and all the deities manifest the creative power of Savitā. The root meaning of the term *deva* includes the capacity to illumine and inspire (*dyotana* and *dīpana*), and what they illumine and inspire are the various faculties of man, including the heart. According to the *Ṛgveda*, the power to inspire man divinely is inherent in all the deities. They are the immediate sources of divine revelation to man, and by inspiring in man divine wisdom or speech (*vāk*) they make him a *ṛṣi* or a *kavi*. In the *Ṛgveda*, Savitā is both identified with and distinguished from the Sun. In most of the hymns addressed to Savitā he is identified with the Sun, but even in his identification with the Sun, Savitā is described

65. 4.23.9.

66. 4.23.8.

67. 4.23.8.

in spiritual terms as the source of divine inspiration and illumination. In his functions he comprehends the functions of the Sun. He impels the Sun to his functions (*sūraḥ cit asme anu dat apasyām*).[68] He goes to all the regions of the world with his light, and moves along with the rays of the Sun (*sūryasya raśmibhiḥ ṣamucyasi*).[69] In the symbolic narration of Sūryā's marriage with Soma, the spiritual or divine significance of Savitā as the source of divine knowledge is made clear. According to *Nighaṇṭu*, the term Sūrya is a synonym of knowledge.

Savitā is the lord of all creativity or inspiration (*īśiṣe prasavasya*).[70] Creative power of Savitā manifests itself in man as divine illumination, or it indicates the birth of divine light or consciousness in man. He is the creativity in man (*prasavai janānām*), or the source of illumination of human consciousness (*bhūtasya pracetasaḥ*).[71] His gifts to man are highly precious. He is the lord of all precious things, both earthly and divine. He is the source of inspiration and animation to all living beings. In the form of his manifestation as the Sun he impels all living beings to their respective functions, and as Varuṇa he guides people to righteous life, and thus knows all the actions of man. He is the countenance (*anīkam*) or collective expression of the deities.[72] And as the eye of them all he knows them all. As the inner source of inspiration he dwells within all. He sees all and knows all. He is the self of all the deities, or in him all the deities are one (*viśvadevam*). He is the source of happiness to all (*viśva śambhuvam*). He is the inspirer of truth in man, or due to his inspiration truth is revealed to man (*satya savam*).[73] In this sense he is the generator of divine speech in man (*janitrīm dhīṣānam*).[74]

68. 7.45.2.
69. 5.81.4; see also 10.139.1.
70. 5.81.5.
71. 10.85.17.
72. 1.115.1.
73. 5.82.7.
74. 10.35.7.

He is the face or expression of *ṛta* (*ṛtasya anīkam*). By his creative power he inspires all beings to divine knowledge, and thus glorifies them, or he inspires all beings to know and glorify truth (*yaḥ imā viśvā jātāni āśravayati ślokena pra ca suvāti savitā*).[75] "He who by his creative power inspires or produces the object of the song of praise" (Ludwig).[76] He proclaims his glory to all by inspiring them to knowledge. He is prayed to remove all evil, and to inspire man to what is good or auspicious (*viśvāni deva savitaḥ duritāni parāsuva yat bhadram tan naḥ āsuva*).[77] The wise apply their minds and intellect to him, and are in turn inspired by him to compose hymns, and to perform holy acts. He knows the functions of the various priests, and guides them to perform their respective functions. No deity can violate his wisdom or will (*kratu*), and in a significant passage it is said that all the deities proceed from him sharing his greatness and power.[78] The seers pray for the invaluable gift of Savitā, the divine bliss or enjoyment (*devasya bhojanam*). In the famous Gāyatrī hymn addressed to Savitā, he is prayed to inspire the intellect or understanding of the worshippers.[79] He is prayed to bless man with his power of inspiration (*devasya savituḥ savimāni*).[80] The seers pray to Savitā to inspire them to attain the supreme and adorable wealth, which among other things consists of divine speech or wisdom (*śreṣṭham naḥ adya savitaḥ vareṇyam bhāgam āsuva, saḥ hi ratnadhā asi rāyaḥ janitrīm dhīṣānam*),[81] and want to be great by sharing the creative power of Savitā (*śreṣthe syāma savituḥ savamāni, tat devaṇam avaḥ adya vṛṇīmahe*).[82] He is addressed as *gnāspati*, which according to Sāyaṇa,

75. 5.82.9.

76. See Griffith's note on 5.82.9.

77. 5.82.5.

78. 10.36.13.

79. 3.62.10.

80. 6.71.2.

81. 10.35.7.

82. 10.36.12.

can mean the lord of metres, or figuratively hymns.[83] Even in his identification with the Sun, he means the divine light which one receives in the state of divine inspiration. Otherwise the description of Sūryā (daughter of Savitā) as the bride of Soma, inspired state of existence of man, will be unintelligible. Mind is her carriage or vehicle of expression (*manoratha*), thought (*chitti*) is her resting place, and the *Ṛk* and *Sāman* hymns are the oxen yoked to her carriage to carry her.[84]

The inspired sages (*vipra*) touch the lovely (*vena*) and caress him as an infant with their hymns, where the "waters" (*āpaḥ*) and the Sun mingle (*apām samgame sūryasya śiśum na viprāḥ matibhiḥ rihanti*).[85] The symbolic meaning of the term *āpaḥ* is discussed elsewhere. "What is truth and what is not truth we do not know; may he inspire our thoughts (*dhiyaḥ hinvānaḥ*) and help or protect our thoughts or praises (*dhiyaḥ it naḥ avyaḥ*).[86] All the deities praise him being inspired by him. Aditi praises him rejoicing in his inspiration, and likewise all other deities praise his glory (*abhi yam devī aditiḥ gṛṇāti savam devasya savituḥ juṣānā, abhi samrājaḥ varuṇaḥ gṛnanti abhi mitrāsaḥ aryamā sajoṣā*).[87] The prayers of the seers addressed to the deities, and especially to Savitā, for precious riches or treasure, which in most cases mean divine wealth, describe Savitā as the giver of most desirable and adorable divine wealth. Savitā, who is described as the collective form of all the deities, and in whose nature all the deities participate, is the source of divine wisdom to man. He inspires or generates divine knowledge in man whereby he is supported or glorified (*ślokam devaḥ kṛnute svāya dharmane*).[88] It is when nature acts on man, and inspires his faculties divinely he sees in nature the presence of the divine, the real source of inspiration, and the deity Savitā

83. 2.38.10.
84. 10.85.10 to 12.
85. 10.123.1.
86. 10.139.5.
87. 7.38.4.
88. 4.53.3.

represents the creative aspect of that divine power. He is the deification of the power of inspiration, as Brahmaṇaspati is the deification of devotion. And the deities are the immediate sources of divine inspiration to man as they partake of the nature of Savitā. "All the deities partake of the nature and functions of Savitā".[89] It is because of Savitā's inspiration, or by means of the wealth he grants man, man is able to know truth, but not by his own effort (*na tasya vidma puruṣatvatā vayam yataḥ bhāgaḥ savitā dāti vāryam*).[90]

While Savitā is the deity of divine inspiration, Brahmaṇaspati is the deity of devotion which finds its expression through hymns. Man experiences the presence of the divine in nature when devotion is born in him. The birth of devotion in man and his awareness of the divine go together. They refer to the same experience. Devotion is born in man when he is divinely inspired, or it is his response to his awareness of the divine. As varied self-manifestations of the divine, the deities are the immediate sources of divine inspiration to man. They reveal the divine to man by inspiring in him devotion and reverence. Brahmaṇaspati recites the sacred prayer (*mantram*) in which all the deities reside or make it their abode. His glory or knowledge (*śloka*) pervades the heaven and earth like the light of the Sun, and that illumines man's intellect and generates devotion in him. Man becomes aware of the divine when devotion is born in him, and Brahmaṇaspati as the deification of devotion is regarded as most divine among the deities (*devānām devatamam*). He is regarded as the father or matrix of all the deities (*devānām pitaram, pitā viśve devāya*).[91] The famous hymn addressed to Brahmaṇaspati, and which is recited at the beginning of all Vedic rites describes him as the lord of all the deities (*gaṇāṇām tvā gaṇapatim*), seer of all seers (*kavim kavīnām*) and lord and chief of all devotion or prayer (*jyeṣṭha rājam brahmaṇām brahmaṇaḥ pate*).[92] As, according to *Nighaṇṭu*,

89. 10.36.1.

90. 5.48.5.

91. 2.26.3; 4.50.6.

92. 2.23.1.

the word *gaṇa* is a synonym of knowledge, we can interpret Brahmaṇaspati as the deification of sacred knowledge and devotion. He is the generator of all devotion (*viśveṣām janitā brahmaṇāḥ asi*).[93] From him flow forth streams of devotion unobstructed, and one who receives them is the first to attain divine speech or hymns (*goṣu*).[94] All truth (*viśvam satyam*) is inherent in him and proceed from him. He awakens (*prajñāpayati*) in man Uṣas, Sūrya, *gam* and *arkam*. He inspires in man divine speech or wisdom which is luminous (*dyumantam*) and faultless or pure (*anāmivam*) and dynamic (*iṣiram*).[95] Generating holy thoughts in man Brahmaṇaspati awakens him to wisdom (*jigṛtam puraṁdhī*). He is of the nature of light (*mahājyoti*), and is born of truth.[96] He is prayed to grant wonderful wealth (*draviṇam citram*) wherewith pious people can worship him exceedingly. The lustrous wealth which he grants to man shines amidst men or within them. It is the means of performing holy rites, and invigorates its possessor with divine strength. The wonderful wealth that Brahmaṇaspati grants men, shines within them as the light of knowledge or wisdom. It is the wealth of divine knowledge (*dyumat vibhāti kratumat janeṣu yat dīdyat savasā tat asmāsu dehi draviṇam citram*).[97] He is described as awakener of hymns in man (*uktasya bodhi*).[98] He is the source of devotion and prayer, and is increased by them as well. The nature of devotion is such that as soon as it is born in men they spontaneously bow down to Brahmaṇaspati (*svayameva namante*). The Vedic wisdom, and its expression in the form of hymns arranged in metres are his gifts, or he makes man attain them (*imaṃ dhiyam sapta śīrṇām pitā naḥ ṛtā prajātam brihatīm avindat*).[99] Among the deities, with the

93. 2.23.2.
94. 2.25.3.
95. 10.93.3.
96. 4.50.4.
97. 2.23.15.
98. 2.23.19.
99. 10.67.1.

exception of Indra, Brahmaṇaspati is actively connected with the destruction of Vṛtra, and the resultant attainment or recovery of divine speech or *go*. This, as we shall soon interpret, also shows the importance of Brahmaṇaspati in discovering divine speech or wisdom expressed through hymns.

While the sun in his divine nature stands for divine light, the state preceding the emergence of divine light in man, or heralding it to man is signified by the symbol of Uṣā. Although Uṣas (dawn) indicates light yet it has its own spiritual or psychological significance to man. Uṣā, as dawn of divine wisdom in man before it gains fullest clarity and illumines his being totally, means for him the end of his inner darkness, and the beginning of the life of light. By unfolding the inner riches of man, it heralds the rise of the sun of divine knowledge. All this it accomplishes by dispelling the inner darkness of man that conceals the divine from his vision. It means the moment of great joy for man as it means the end of his dark and sinful state of existence, and the beginning of a life of truth and divine illumination. It signifies the threshold of divine light, and is consummated in the life of light and wisdom. It is the first glimpse of divine light, and emanates from the same source of all light.

All the Ṛgvedic hymns addressed to Uṣā reflect the joyful mood of the seers, and express their creativity at its best. Though the description of Uṣā in most of the hymns addressed to her refers to the phenomenon of dawn, as it is the case with Savitā or the Sun, its symbolic meaning as the birth of divine consciousness in man is also well presented in them. We have to admit the symbolic character of Uṣā as otherwise most of the hymns addressed to her would be utterly unintelligible. Their meaning cannot be explained in terms of dawn, a natural phenomenon. Just as light is used as a symbol for divine knowledge or divine illumination of consciousness, so also Uṣā is used symbolically to mean the destruction of inner darkness of man. The divine dawn, the bride of the immortal (*amṛtasya patni*), and the sign of immortality (*amṛtasya ketu*) is the first manifestation of truth in man. Shining bright with truth Uṣā reveals it to man (*ṛtam āvasan uṣasaḥ vibhāti*).[100] She is born of truth. Spreading the rays of truth, or appearing along with the brilliance of truth (*ṛtasya raśmin anuyaśchamānā*) Uṣā bestows on us sacred and auspicious wisdom (*bhadram kratu*).[101] As the female counterpart of a deity, a *devī* represents the dynamic side of the deity, and helps to reveal it. Similarly Uṣā is seen as the bride of the immortal. She represents the self-revelatory aspect of the divine. She is described as the face or expression of the undivided divine principle, the mother of the deities (*aditeḥ anīkam*).[102] She is a sign of the divine. Preceding the full emergence of divine light within man, Uṣā heralds the birth of divine in man by dispelling his inner darkness. In this sense Uṣā is not only a first manifestation of Savitā, but she is his gift to man. "Uṣā is the divine gift of Savitā".[103] With the appearance of Uṣā man's faculties (doors) open themselves to receive divine light, and he is enabled to see things in their divine significance; he is also roused from his ordinary or unillumined state of existence. Man's inner darkness is destroyed with the appearance of Uṣā, and his inner spiritual treasure concealed by darkness is made manifest to him. "Dissipate the concealing darkness of the cave (heart) and show us the light we long for."[104] She is described as the brilliant guide of the truthful (*sūnṛtānām*). When she appears, the sins of man are destroyed along with the inner darkness. Inner darkness of man is destroyed by Uṣā who shines bright manifesting her splendour; and is followed by the emergence of the great (*bṛhat*) Sun who watches good and evil in mortals.[105] She bestows on man the most desirable and wonderful treasure

100. 4.2.19.
101. 1.123.13.
102. 1.113.19.
103. 1.159.5.
104. 7.90.4.
105. 4.1.17.

of divine wisdom which is to be glorified by man. "These dawns diffuse the knowledge (*vāyunānai*) that is apprehended by the pious men, and overspread the whole world with light."[106] Uṣā sheds her light on the worship of man, produces in him the sense of holy and inspires him to religious or spiritual life, or to follow the ordinances of the divine (*daivyāni vratāni*). She also helps their fulfilment. She bestows on man the supreme bliss or great fortune (*mahā saubhāgya*), and awakens wisdom in him (*ajīgarti marteṣu mānuṣi; jigr̥tam puraṁdhi*).[107] The auspicious (*sumaṅgalī*) Uṣā who is born of *r̥ta* and sustains it, awakens in man shining wisdom (*revatī puraṁdhi*).[108] Therefore, it is said that the wisdom expressed through hymns shines like the divine dawn (*uṣasam na devīm*). She awakens the worshipper spiritually (*citayanta*) and confers on him riches of inspiration (*aṅgirastama sukr̥tā vasūni*).[109] The symbolic character of Uṣā and her divine significance are further evident from the following expressions. "The poet-seers who are full of truth have discovered the hidden divine light by their communion with the deities, and generated the dawns (*ajanyan uṣsam*)."[110] It is with the appearance of Uṣā the divine is seen by man, or she indicates the birth of divine in man. "All the deities follow or are revealed after the shining of divine dawns (*anuprayānam uṣasaḥ virājati*)."[111] It is with the help of Uṣā R̥bhus had attained divinity, and could accomplish their deeds of wisdom.

Uṣā is described as the mother of the deities (*mātā devānām*). Awakened in the place of *r̥ta* (truth) the divine dawns flow like hymns, or awakened in the place of *r̥ta* the divine dawns praise (truth) as the flow of hymns (*r̥tasya devīḥ sadasaḥ budhānāḥ gavām na sargāḥ uṣasa jarante*).[112] It is while praising the divine nature of the

106. 5.48.2.
107. 7.75.2.
108. 1.158.2.
109. 7.79.3.
110. 7.76.4.
111. 5.81.2.
112. 4.51.8.

divine dawns the assertion is made that the great divine nature or glory of all the deities is one. When the earliest dawns break forth in the place of hymns, the great imperishable or truth is born, and then the worshippers are illumined or influenced to observe the divine ordinances. The great divine nature or glory of the deities is one (*uṣasaḥ pūrvaḥ adha yat viūṣuḥ mahat vi jajñe akṣaram pade goḥ, vratā devānām upa nu prabhūṣan, mahat devānām asuratvam ekam*).[113]

The emergence of the divine Uṣā is related to the recovery or attainment of *go*, the divine speech or wisdom expressed in the form of hymns. The breaking forth of Uṣā is connected with the birth of divine consciousness in man, or his being awakened to the presence of the divine. When the divine Word or speech is revealed to the ancient seers (*aṅgīrasas*) they came to know the divine, and praised Uṣā as the source of revelation of divine speech. "All the deities manifest themselves with the shining of Uṣā."[114] "When for us the divine dawns, the brides of the immortal overspread the world with (divine light)."[115] With the emergence of Uṣā Aṅgīrasa seers behold the divine treasure, and then all the deities are revealed in their respective abodes. In other words, man's awareness of the divine in nature, or seeing nature as the abode of the deities is due to the dawn of divine light in man. "Awakened they looked around when first they beheld that heaven allotted treasure. Then all the deities came to their respective dwellings. May my vision be true."[116] Hymns are born when man is awakened to the presence of the divine either within himself or in nature, and Uṣā generates such awareness. The divine Soma, the flow of divine inspiration in man, is described as the face or expression of Uṣā. The divine Uṣā is connected with the creation of hymns. "The hymns (divine speech) bear the auspicious, expanding illustrious Uṣā."[117] Through

113. 3.55.1.

114. 5.82.2.

115. 4.5.13.

116. 4.1.18.

117. 6.54.3.

the favour of Uṣā Aṅgīrasa seers received the hymns from the summit of the mountain by prayer and worship (*arkena* and *brahmaṇa*).[118] Accordingly, Uṣā is seen as the matrix of the divine speech or hymns (*gavām mātā*). She is also their leader (*gavām netā*). She is the expression or face of Aditi, the mother of all deities. She is the eye of all the deities. She awakens divine knowledge in man, and is the sign of *yajña*. She is full of inspiration (*aṅgirattama*), divine vigour and speech (*aśvavatī* and *gomatī*), and is capable of destroying the sins of man (*uṣā ucchanti apabhādatam agham*).[119] Thus in its root meaning the term *uṣā* means that which dispels or destroys the inner darkness of man. She symbolises the dawn of divine light in man, or divine light in its function of dispelling the inner darkness. It is thus the deities Savitā, Brahmaṇaspati and Uṣā are associated with the birth of divine consciousness in man, and represent its various aspects. While Savitā and Brahmaṇaspati have no representation in nature, except in their manifestation within the spiritual life of man. Uṣā stands to represent symbolically the dawn of divine light or consciousness in man, and the resultant destruction of his inner darkness. The hymns addressed to these deities are our sources to know the nature of divine inspiration, or the birth of divine in man, and its sources.

We now discuss the birth of divine in human consciousness which is due to divine inspiration. The various deities representing the diverse manifestations of the divine in nature are the immediate sources of divine inspiration to man. When man is divinely inspired, nature reveals itself in its divine aspect which is hidden to ordinary or uninspired understanding of man. A divinely inspired person or a seer sees the presence of the divine in nature or sees nature as the dwelling place of the deities who manifest themselves in and through the workings of nature. To see nature as the abode of the deities is the same as

118. 6.55.5.

119. 10.35.5.

to see the presence of the divine in nature. Therefore, each phenomenon of nature, as a self-manifestation of the divine, is represented by a deity, or is seen as the abode of a deity. When the sense of divine dawns in man due to divine inspiration, his vision of himself and of nature is divine transformed, and he sees the presence of the divine everywhere. And, as nature is the source of divine inspiration to the Vedic seers, it is to them more than what it is known ordinarily. To be able to inspire man divinely nature must be divine. Thus to see the deities as the various self-manifestations of the divine in nature is the same as to see nature as a creative self-manifestation of the divine. To see the divine in nature is to see the deities as representing nature in its diverse phenomena. Or to see the deities as dwelling within the various phenomena of nature is possible only when the presence of the divine is seen in nature. And the idea of the divine in itself is arrived at as a result of intellectual abstraction based on direct experience of the divine in nature. Thus we can understand the Vedic scepticism about the nature and existence of the divine in itself expressed whenever it is talked about in the *Ṛgveda*. According to the *Ṛgveda*, each phenomenon of nature, or the deity that dwells in it is a source of divine revelation to man. There is no deity in the *Ṛgveda* which is not a source of divine inspiration to man. Each deity in its own way inspires in man the sense of divine, and awakens him to the presence of the divine in nature. Therefore, every deity is an object of devotion and worship which the deities themselves inspire in man. As self-manifestations of the divine all the deities possess inherently all the divine qualities, especially the capacity to inspire man divinely. The capacity to illumine the faculties of man and to inspire him divinely is the primary characteristic of what is divine. All the deities participate in the nature of Savitā, the deity of inspiration. Similarly, Brahmaṇaspati as the deification of devotion and Vedic speech or wisdom, in which all the deities dwell, is the source of all the deities. He is described as the father of the deities, or he gives birth to all the deities (*devānām yaḥ pitaram; devānām janmāni samadādat karmarā iva*).[120] Therefore, the deities share the nature of Brahmaṇaspati also. Thus the deities are the immediate sources of divine inspiration to man, and inspire in him devotion and divine *vāk* or wisdom.

The birth of divine in human consciousness is the same as the birth of devotion in him. Devotion is man's spontaneous response to his awareness of the divine. The nature and meaning of divine are revealed to man in the state of devotion. While devotion is more on the affective side of man, and stirs his heart and fulfils it, divine *vāk* or wisdom, the source of divine knowledge, is more on the intellectual side of man, and is born of enlightened human understanding. However, they are the two aspects of the same wisdom, and point to the same source. Both of them are important sources of divine knowledge, and influence each other in knowing the nature of the divine. What is immediately felt within the heart is comprehended by the intellect and, therefore, both of them play an important role in the creation of a hymn. The hymns are created with the help of both heart and mind (*hṛdā manasā taṣṭhaḥ*), and reflect the heartfelt devotion, and what is comprehended by an illumined mind or intellect.[121] The wisdom of the Veda, therefore, reflects the harmony of what is directly felt within the heart of man, and what is comprehended by his intellect. While the heart that is flooded with divine inspiration is the fountain of creativity that is expressed through the hymns, the illumined intellect helps man to know the nature of the divine as revealed in and through its varied manifestations. Divine inspiration floods the being of man completely, and influences all his faculties. However, the heart and intellect of man are his sources of knowledge of the divine, and are sought to be inspired by the deities. While divinely illumined intellect is the seat of *vāk* (divine speech or wisdom), divinely inspired heart is the seat of faith, reverence and devotion. Divine *vāk* is described as comprehending within itself all that is there, including the deities, and in its essence it is the wisdom of the divine. The divine is the source of *vāk*, as well as its object.

---

120. 2.26.3; 10.72.2.

121. 1.171.2.

The hymns flow from the ocean of heart (*etā arśanti hṛdyāt samudrāt*).[122] They are inspired and purified within heart, and flow from there (*samyak śravanti saritā na dhenāḥ antaḥ hṛdā manasā pūyamānaḥ*).[123] The truth is revealed within the ocean of heart (*antariti samudre hṛdi*).[124] Prayers born within the heart of man go to the presence of the deities and awaken them. "Prayer is connected with pure heart's desire of the worshipper where the mind is known to be attached to the pure (*pūtabandhinī*)."[125] *Śraddhā* (faith) which means holding on to truth when it is revealed (*śrat dha*) also arises in the heart of man (*śraddhām hṛdayya ākṛtya śraddhayā vindate vasu*).[126] The divine is seen or experienced within their hearts by those whose understanding is divinely inspired (*hṛdā paśyanti manasā vipaścitāḥ*).[127] The seers see the divine within their hearts. Divine inspiration touches the heart, and stirs it (*spṛśa* and *ejati*), and is expressed with the help of the mind (*hṛdāspṛśā manasā vacyamānaḥ*).[128] "We speak the hymns which are well formed within ourselves or within our hearts (*su asme āsutaṣṭham mantram*)."[129] The prayers addressed to Indra are spoken from the heart (*indram matiḥ hṛdā āvcyamānaḥ*).[130] The seers hold within themselves the hymns which are formed within their hearts (*ṛcā hṛdā taṣṭham bharāmasi*).[131]

With the same emphasis the understanding or intellect of man is also regarded by the seers as a seat of divine inspiration and knowledge. The hymns are connected with or created by

122. 4.58.5.
123. 4.58.6.
124. 4.58.11.
125. 5.44.9.
126. 10.151.4.
127. 10.177.1.
128. 10.47.7.
129. 2.35.2.
130. 3.39.1.
131. 6.16.47.

an intellect that is divinely illumined (*dhītayaḥ*). The seers are known as *dhīrā* and *manīṣinaḥ*, or those who have achieved complete mastery over their minds, or lords of their minds. A seer is one whose intellect is made divine or divinely illumined (*devīm dhiyam; daivyā dhiyā; daivyena manasā*). He can discern what is hidden to ordinary understanding (*dhīrā ninya ciketa*); or one who discerns is a seer (*yaha ciketa sa sukratuṛ*).[132] Seer-poets are those whose thoughts are pure (*kavayaḥ sudhītayaḥ*) and who are firm in their understanding (*manodhṛtāḥ*).[133] They are self-luminous by their knowledge (*svabhānavaḥ*), and their minds are full of devotion (*haviṣmatā manasā*).[134] They are men of mature understanding (*pākena manasā*). The hymns express the well-discerned thoughts of the seers, and full of truth (*cikitvāt manasām dhiyam; prātnam ṛtasya pipyuṣīm*).[135] The intellect is divinely illumined, or is made divine by worshipping Agni. The thought that is expressed through hymns or arranged in metres is born of truth, and is discovered by the ancient seers. The seers are those who are intellectually illumined, and the inspired intellect is like a milk cow that yields truth (*duhanā dhenu*) or (*manīṣā dhenu*).[136] The deities are apprehended by a discerning intellect (*apaśyam tvā manasā cekitānam*); they are born out of austerity, or made manifest by it (*tapasā jātam tapasā vibhūtam*).[137] Man's wisdom is according to his mental capacity. Men hold wisdom within themselves according to their mental capacities (*prabharadhvam manīṣām yadhā yadhā matayaḥ santi nṛnām*).[138] The hymns are made according to the wisdom of each seer. The hymns are also known as *matiḥ* (born of or expressing mind), and the mind of a man can create a hymn when it is divinely inspired. Sarasvatī, the

132. 5.65.1.
133. 1.159.4; 3.38.2.
134. 6.67.1; 7.12.1.
135. 8.95.5.
136. 3.57.1.
137. 10.183.1.
138. 10.111.1.

deity of speech, achieves a hymn for the seer (*sarasvatī sādhayanti dhiyam naḥ*).[139] The deities are prayed to inspire and fulfil one's intellect or thoughts (*codaya dhiyā* and *pinvatam dhiyā*).[140] The Indra power is experienced within one's intellect. And the benevolence of the deities is also experienced by it. The mind of man becomes pure, auspicious and holy when it is divinely inspired. That which is blessed by the deities is holy and auspicious. One has to praise or speak about the deities or meditate on them according to one's wisdom, and they are to be apprehended by a mind which is ever growing and comprehensive, or that which is supreme and ever growing is to be apprehended mentally (*svena kratunā sam vadet śreyāṁśam dakṣam manasā jagṛbhyāt*).[141] However, the ordinary or uninspired intellect of man cannot apprehend the deities. They are intuited by an intellect which is inspired or illumined by divine Soma. The seers are divine-born (*devajā*), and are moved or inspired by the divine (*devajūta*). They call themselves the children of Savitā. Thought or wisdom of man is sharpened and purified by divine inspiration, or divinely illumined or inspired intellect and heart of man purify his thoughts (*mārjayanti*).[142] Divine inspiration that springs up in heart is clarified by the intellect. The seers often claim that they have made or created new hymns, and pray for divine inspiration to create new hymns. The wise or intelligent (*dhīra*) make the speech or create the hymns through their understanding (*manasā vācam akrata*) discerning truth, and separating it from falsehood like barley is winnowed to separate it from chaff.[143]

Ordinary or unillumined or uninspired intellect and heart of man are not capable of apprehending the divine. An uninspired man can know only the phenomenal aspect of nature but not the divine that is hidden within it. The presence of the

139. 2.3.8.

140. 6.47.10; 10.3.92; 5.71.2.

141. 10.31.2.

142. 9.63.20; 9.89.4.

143. 10.71.2.

divine in nature is experienced by man when his inner darkness is dispelled. Because of its presence in man he does not see the divine though it is eternally revealed. It is not by means or one's rational understanding one comes to know what the seers have known as it were with their own minds. It is with the sight or vision granted by divine Soma, or with the eyes of the indwelling divine principle (*vaiśvānarasya cakṣasā*) the seers apprehend the divine.[144] When the divine that is present in nature acts on the divine within man he is inspired to see the divine. Although the seers differ in their experiences of the divine, they are of profound piety, and are deeply stirred by the divine, (*virūpāsaḥ et ṛṣayaḥ te iti gaṁbhīra vepasā*).[145] "Let us praise each deity with divine intellect."[146] They sing the devotion which is a divine gift to them (*devattam brahma gāyata*).[147] "Through devotion (*brahma*) we have made these hymns."[148] Brahma or devotion is regarded as the inner or spiritual protection of man (*brahma varma mama antaram*).[149] It saves man spiritually, and makes him bow down in reverence to the deities spontaneously (*devāḥ naraḥ savitāram viprāḥ yajñe su uktibhiḥ namasyanti dhiyā īṣita*).[150] The power to inspire in man devotion is inherent in all the deities. They are the sources of its inspiration, as well as its object. It is a favour done to man by the deities. However, the ultimate source of devotion or divine inspiration is the divine itself, though it is mediated to man through the deities. "I have acquired or attained the favour of intelligence of the father of truth (*pituḥ ṛtasya*)."[151] Even a seer claims that he is taught the mysteries of the divine directly by the deity Varuṇa of whom he considers himself a student

---

144. 6.7.6.
145. 10.62.5.
146. 8.27.13.
147. 8.3.27.
148. 8.6.33.
149. 6.75.19.
150. 3.62.12.
151. 10.67.1.

(*antevāsī*).[152] It is due to the inspiration of Agni man is made a *kavi* or a *ṛṣi* or a *vipra*. And it is by the wisdom granted by Agni man attains immortality (*tava kratubhiḥ amṛtatvamāyan*). From him flow wisdom and knowledge, and hymns are inspired by him. The Ṛk and *Sāman* hymns seek him who is inspired or awakened by Agni. From Agni are born knowledge, wisdom and hymns (*agne tvāt kāvyā tvāt manīṣā tvāt uktaḥ jāyante*).[153] The Ṛk and *Sāman* hymns seek him who is spiritually awakened (*yaḥ jagāra tam ṛcāḥ kāmayante yam jagāra tam ū iti sāmāni yanti*).[154]

The seers constantly pray to the deities to dispel the darkness from within themselves, to fulfil their vision, and to free them from the bonds that bind them. Man is divinely born, or divine is born within man when the deities inspire and quicken his understanding. The hymns are a revelation from the divine, and provide light that guides man. "He knows well thy favour (as one) who gave an impulse to this high devotion; one who is inspired to sing the prayers knows the divine gift of the deities (*saḥ te jānāti sumatim yaviṣṭha yaḥ īvate brahmaṇe gātum erat*)."[155] The hymns are created when the seer is moved by devotion, or when he is gripped by the spirit of the divine. "I have brought forth a song when longing seized me."[156] "When shall thy glory as a deity, Agni, be shown forth to us suddenly (*devasya cetanam*)."[157] Indra is prayed to inspire the seer for winning devotion and hymns (*tvam kavim codaya arka sātau*).[158] He is prayed to sharpen the intellect like the stone a knife, and make him divine (*deva vantam*). He is regarded as increaser of hymns (*stoma vardhana*). Varuṇa has made Vasiṣṭha a *ṛṣi*, or a maker of hymns. Pūṣan is described as the means of achieving hymns, and the inspirer of the wise

152. 7.87.4.
153. 4.11.3.
154. 5.44.14.
155. 4.4.6.
156. 3.32.14.
157. 4.7.2.
158. 6.26.3.

(*matīnām sādhanam viprānām ādharam*).[159] It is by the greatness and glory of Indra the wise grow in their wisdom (*viprāḥ vardhanti*). Agni is described as the source or awakener of wisdom in man (*manīṣām prārpaṇaḥ*).[160] Varuṇa awakens man to devotion, or causes it in man (*brahma kṛnoti varuṇaḥ*).[161] He unfolds within the hearts of men a prayer (*vivṛnoti hṛdā matim*), or he unfolds within the hearts of men the knowledge of hymns. The graceful disposition of the deities, which they bestow on man, is the source of the hymns. "I have only that *pramati* which is given by you (with which I make a hymn)."[162] Agni is described as the awakener in man the bright speech (*śukrasya vacasaḥ manota*).[163] He is maker of human intelligence (*medhākāram*), and a means of attaining devotion and worship (*vidadhasya prasādhanam*). He rules over every thought of man, and stirs his mind. The deities in general awaken man to the divine, and inspire prayer in the awakened. Being within man the deities witness the inner world of man, and judge him in terms of right and wrong (*ādityāsaḥ antariti paśyanti vṛjinā uta sādhu*).[164] They approach man with divine light (*cardhi*). The seers hold within themselves divine inspiration, and come under the protection of the deities because of it.

The divine speech or wisdom (*vāk*) is co-extensive with the divine or the deities. The deities are the sources of its revelation to man. They are the centres of its manifestation. They move with divine wisdom, or are created out of it (*samācakre kāvyena*). The term *cakre* can mean both motion and creation. The hymns or prayers are meant to glorify the divine greatness of the deities, and a seer-poet is one to whom the glory of the deities is revealed (*asya mahaḥ viprāḥ vardhanti*).[165] The deities themselves have chosen

159. 10.26.4.

160. 10.45.5.

161. 1.105.15.

162. 1.109.1.

163. 2.9.4.

164. 2.27.3.

165. 10.43.7.

the prayers or hymns as the source of their increase (*aham kṛnvam brahma mahyam vardhanam*).[166] "I am the inspirer of the devotees (*yajamānasya codita*)."[167] "I have measured a hymn from Indra."[168] From Indra hymns flow unceasingly (*indrāya giraḥ aniśiṭa sargāḥ*).[169] It is often stated in the *Ṛgveda* that the deities inspire or generate and increase devotion in man, and along with its birth and maturity, the deities are also born, and are increased. The birth of devotion in man and his awareness of the divine or the deities are simultaneous. They go together and increase each other, and in this sense devotion is phenomenologically the meaning of divine. In the state of devotion man comes to know the meaning of divine and experiences it. It is also the source of man's knowledge of the divine. It is the means of divine revelation to man, and being co-extensive with the divine it holds within itself all the deities, or comprehends them within itself. Therefore anything that can inspire man divinely and generate in him devotion is divine. And as nature is the immediate source of divine inspiration to man, it is divine. It is the primary source of divine revelation to man because of its capacity to inspire man divinely, and generate in him devotion and reverence. But there are deities in the *Ṛgveda* who have no representation in nature. However, they represent the various aspects of divine inspiration or devotion experienced by man. There are other deities in the *Ṛgveda* who are divine by virtue of their association with worship or *yajña* which is divine.

Thus the deities are the immediate sources of divine inspiration to man. They reveal to man divine wisdom and make him divine. This they do by inspiring or illumining his intellect and heart divinely. The hymns are born when the seers try to give expression to divinely inspired devotion. They are primarily an expression of man's devotion to the divine or the deities.

166. 10.49.1.

167. 10.49.1.

168. 8.72.12.

169. 10.89.4.

The devotion makes man bow down in reverence to the deities, and in its birth he sees the supreme fulfilment of his life. It is the source of wisdom communicated through hymns. With its birth the faculties of man fully unfold themselves, and receive divine light. It enables man to know the hidden divine presence in nature. What is so experienced is so wonderful and profound, man's speech may fail to express it adequately. Devotion is really ineffable (*acittam brahma*).[170] "Mine ears unclose to hear, mine eyes to see him; the light that harbours in my spirit broadens. Far roams my mind whose thoughts are in the distance. What shall I speak, what shall I now imagine?" Or "mine ears are turned to hear him, mine eyes to behold him, this light that is placed in the heart. My mind, the receptacle of distant objects hastens towards him. What shall I declare him? How shall I comprehend him?" (*vi me karnā patayataḥ vi cakṣuḥ vi idam jyotiḥ hr̥daya āhitam yat; vi me manaḥ carati dūre adhīḥ. kim svit vakṣyāmi, kim ū iti nu maniṣye*).[171]

170. 1.152.5.

171. 6.9.6.

6

Soma

In this and the next chapters we continue the discussion on the nature and meaning of divine inspiration, and the birth of divine in human consciousness. The present chapter on the nature and meaning of the deity Soma and the next one on the various symbols associated with divine inspiration and its expression are intended to substantiate and elucidate further the meaning and mode of divine revelation according to the *Ṛgveda*. As shown in the previous chapters, nature is the immediate source of divine revelation to the Vedic seers, or they experience the divine through its presence in nature. Therefore, nature is viewed by them as the abode of the deities, who as primary self-manifestations of the divine, reveal themselves in and through nature. The reason for seeing the presence of the divine in nature, or for regarding it as the abode of the deities is its capacity to inspire man divinely. Nature in all its phenomena has the power to inspire man divinely; and when a person is inspired divinely the sense of divine is born in him. And devotion is man's spontaneous response to his awareness of the divine, and the Vedic hymns are an expression of it. They are spontaneous outpourings of a heart that is divinely inspired, and are addressed to the divine revealed in and through the various deities. Thus the difference between a *ṛṣi* or a *kavi* and an ordinary person is the fact of inspiration.

The object of this chapter is to present and discuss the nature of divine inspiration, and the mode of its expression in the form of Vedic hymns. The state of being divinely inspired, or the divinely inspired state of man's existence is what is symbolically represented by the deity Soma. At the outset it may appear far-fetched to interpret Soma as representing the essence of divine inspiration, but a closer study of the symbolism involved in the use of the terms *go* and *dhenu*, which will be discussed in the next chapter, and the hymns devoted to divine Soma will reveal the symbolic character of Soma, and its real meaning as intended by the Vedic seers. The whole of the ninth *maṇḍala* of the *Ṛgveda* is devoted to the deity Soma.

Apparently Soma stands to mean a herbal juice shed by the Ṛgvedic priests, and offered at the time of sacrifice to the various deities for their vigour and enjoyment. Guided primarily by such an understanding attempts have been made to identify the herb from which the *soma* juice is extracted. But if we confine ourselves to the text of the *Ṛgveda*, the information or evidence which we get about the physical nature of *soma* as a herb is very scant. *Soma* as the juice of a herb is not the prime concern of the Ṛgvedic seers and, therefore we obtain little or no evidence regarding its nature as a herb, except that it is born and grown on mountains. Here also as we shall soon discuss the term *gira* (mountain) does not always mean a mountain, especially when used in relation to Soma. Only occasionally the word *parvata* (mountain) is used in relation to Soma, and only on one occasion the name of the mountain on which the *soma* is supposed to grow is identified as *muñjavan*. Even in other Vedic literature the identity of Soma as simply a herb is not unambiguously stated. Soma is often described as being born of *go* (*gojā*), mountain (*adṛjā*) and truth (*ṛtajā*), and in these contexts the word *adri* does not always mean a mountain. The word *adri* is defined etymologically even within the *Ṛgveda* as having something to do with *adhvara* (sacrifice). It is a symbol for *yajña* or *adharva*. It is defined as the form of sacrifice (*adhvarasya peśa*).[1] The other evidence available within the *Ṛgveda* to show that Soma is a herbal juice is that it is shed and made to flow through a sieve or filter into a vessel meant for its collection. In its description as being grown on the mountain *mauja* or *muñja*

1. 7.42.1

(*somasya iva maujavatasya bakṣya*), the term *mauja* besides referring to the name of a mountain can also mean, according to Yāska, that which liberates (*vimuñca*).[2] Further evidence to identify *soma* as a herb is the fact that its juice is taken in by the priests. It is described as the queen of all plants or herbs, or they have *soma* as their queen and source. But Brahmaṇaspati is also described in the *Ṛgveda* as the source of all herbs. Even when it is stated that *soma* juice when taken in produces joy in the hearts of priests, as well as in the deities, it need not be taken literally as one may be intoxicated with the joy (*mada*) of divine inspiration or poetic inspiration. As we shall soon see most of the terms and expressions used to indicate the fact of divine inspiration, and the mode of its expression in the form of hymns, are symbolic in character. Instead of trying to understand certain of these keywords and expressions either in their etymological or literal senses, if we try to grasp their meaning on the basis of actual usage in different contexts of the *Ṛgveda*, their symbolic character and value becomes clear. If we adopt this method and follow the meaning of a word emerging out of its usage in differnt contexts of the *Ṛgveda*, we can clearly comprehend the intended meaning of the word which its etymological definition cannot convey. This is the method that is mostly adopted here. One advantage of this approach is that it not only shows the limitations of the etymological method, but also helps to reveal more and more clearly the deeper meaning of the words, and their symbolic value. They are used symbolically to convey a sense which they cannot otherwise convey. Therefore, in trying to understand and explain these words symbolically we are not trying to force a particular interpretation on the *Ṛgveda*. The purpose is to grasp the intention of the seers in using them which cannot be known otherwise. The symbolic significance of the various words and expressions used in relation to Soma and their real or spiritual import will become clear when we can identify first of all the real meaning of Soma, and its place

2. Sāyaṇa's commentary on 10.34.1

and importance in the spiritual or divine life of the Vedic seer-poets. It will also shed light on the meaning of various concepts associated with Soma, and they in their turn will help us in comprehending the real meaning of Soma.

In almost all the earlier interpretations of Soma, with one or two exceptions, the spiritual or divine significance of Soma, and hence its symbolic value are overlooked in an attempt to identify the herb of which *soma* is considered to be the juice. The general tone and intention of the ninth *maṇḍala* of the *Ṛgveda* which is entirely devoted to the praise of Soma, besides references to it in all other books of *Ṛgveda* are not to describe Soma as merely a plant juice effective in producing in its drinkers joy and enthusiasm, but to express symbolically or even analogically the nature of divine inspiration, and its creative influence on man. The nature of divine inspiration and its expression through Vedic hymns are well presented in the hymns addressed to Soma. The divinely intoxicating *rasa* of inspiration which swells within the heart of man, floods or soaks his being (*siñca*), transforms his vision of himself and of nature, and finally how it flows through the hymns, which embody it, are symbolically represented by Soma and its shedding. This symbolic meaning of Soma is overlooked by most of the interpreters mainly because all the aspects of Soma, as presented in the *Ṛgveda*, which tend to show its symbolic value have not been taken into serious consideration. Thus if all the aspects of Soma as presented in *Ṛgveda* are taken note of, and if we are to interpret them comprehensively so that no aspect of Soma is overlooked or ignored, then we have to view the significance of Soma in divine terms. Then we will find in the hymns addressed to Soma the attempts of the Ṛgvedic seers to express a somewhat nebulous spiritual force or power called inspiration which springs up within their hearts, and enables them to see in its light the divine presence in nature. It is this inspiration which sustains a seer-poet spiritually, transforms his vision divinely and presents to him the world in a new light, or reveals something more in nature than what is ordinarily known.

The peculiarity of the deity Soma in relation to all other deities of the *Ṛgveda*, with the exception of some other deities like Savitā and Brahmaṇaspati, is that he has no representation in nature. Other deities manifest themselves in nature, and thus have phenomenal representation in nature. Although Soma is described in the *Ṛgveda* as descending from heaven (*divi*) to earth, it is not strictly speaking represented by any natural phenomenon. Even the *soma* plant or its juice does not stand in relation to divine Soma, as the phenomenal fire stands in relation to the deity Agni. The earthly representation of divine Soma in the form of a plant juice is more a matter of symbolism, or even we can say of analogy, for in several hymns of the *Ṛgveda* Soma is said to be present in all the plants or herbs as their queen and source. Moreover, its presence on earth is not limited to plants only; it is described as being born in waters, rivers and even in ocean.

The reason why the juice of a particular plant or herb is extolled as Soma in its earthly form, supposing that Soma means the juice of a herb, must be due to the fact that the properties of the plant juice can help to describe symbolically or analogically the true character of divine Soma. It is mostly for the purpose of communication, and also to serve the ritual purpose of performing *yajña*, Soma is symbolically represented by a herbal juice which is known for its property of quickening the ordinary spirit of man. *Yajña* as ritually performed by the Vedic people is a symbolic representation of the divine or cosmic *yajña*, which is to be extended but not performed by man, and Soma is regarded as the soul of *yajña*. The use of *soma* juice is restricted to ceremonious or ritual occasions only. It is shed as an offering to the deities during the performance of *yajña*; whereas the real divine *Soma* is known for its functions of illumining the intellect of man, opening his doors of knowledge and inspiring in him divine speech or wisdom. It reveals the deities to man, and is at the same time the food or sustaining principle of the deities.

When we compare the deity Soma with other deities, we

observe that the divine attributes of Soma preponderate over his phenomenal attributes. While other deities are described in terms of their phenomenal and divine natures, and both are given equal importance, the description of Soma in terms of its phenomenal or earthly qualities is almost insignificant and scant. His divine nature and significance are prominently described in the *Ṛgveda*. While the other deities reveal themselves to man in and through their phenomenal manifestations, Soma has no phenomenal manifestation in the above sense. Its description as a herb is so scant that it is very difficult to identify it in definite terms with anything that is found in nature. The juice of a herb known as *soma,* which is clearly distinguished from *surā* (liquor or wine), is not in the strict sense of the term a phenomenal manifestation of the divine Soma. It is used as a symbol for divine Soma mainly because of its exhilarating properties, and is employed during the performance of *yajña* in which almost all the accessories or elements employed have only symbolic value. While the divine nature of a deity is revealed to man in and through its manifestations in nature, the divine nature of Soma is not so mediated. It is directly revealed to man, or is directly experienced by him. It is, therefore, meaningful to identify Soma with divine inspiration, which is directly experienced by man inwardly, instead of viewing it as the deification of a herbal juice which can produce in man joy and exhilaration, and inspire him to compose hymns. It refers to the inner state of being divinely inspired, or divinely inspired state of man's existence. Moreover, every deity is a source of divine inspiration to the poets, and nature itself reveals its divine aspect. Every phenomenon of nature, as an individualised self-manifestation of the divine, has intrinsically the capacity to inspire within man the sense of divine. This shows that *soma* as a plant juice is not the exclusive source of inspiration for the poets. We cannot, therefore, say that *soma* juice when taken in produces a sort of inspiration in the light of which nature is seen as divine. Thus if Soma is not the cause or source of inspiration, and yet it is associated with the phenomenon of inspiration in a sense in which no other deity is associated with it, we have to identify it not as the source of inspiration, but as inspiration itself. In all its description *Soma* stands to represent the fact of divine inspiration, or the divinely inspired state of man's existence. The need to symbolise the fact of divine inspiration arises for two main reasons. Firstly to adapt it for the purpose of performing *yajña* ritually in which many cosmic principles are symbolised, and secondly to communicate adequately the meaning of divine inspiration. The *soma* juice, and all the nutrient herbs, for *soma* is the source of all herbs, produce in man a feeling kindred to that experienced when the real divine Soma is tasted. Therefore, instead of the deity *soma* being a deification of a herbal juice, the latter is analogically used to convey the nature of divine Soma. Soma is invariably shed during *yajña*, but not drunk for the sake of exhilaration or joy it produces. It is offered first to the deities, and then taken by man. As we shall soon see the shedding of Soma, its purification and offering of it to the deities are considered as mere ritualistic acts in the *Ṛgveda*. If we do not, on the other hand, accept the symbolic character and value of Soma most of the hymns addressed to Soma, and the images used in relation to it remain utterly unintelligible. For instance, Soma is born not only on the mountains, but also in waters (*āpaḥ*), in rivers or floods and in ocean, and also in all herbs. However, its original birthplace is the highest or the divine, and from there it is brought down to earth by a well-winged bird or metres, especially by the divine metre Gāyatrī. In the Brāhmaṇa literature also it is stated that the divine *Soma* is brought down to earth by *vāk* or divine speech.[3] It is the speech that helps to express divine inspiration experienced within.

The exhilaration and joy caused by Soma are distinguished from those produced by wine (*surā*). The exhilaration or intoxication caused by Soma is divine (*amartyam madam*),[4] whereas the intoxication caused by wine, which is bad or evil in nature

3. 1.80.2; 8.89.8; 9.71.6 *Śatapatha Brāhmaṇa.*

4. 1.84.4; see also 2.37.4.

(*durmada*) is not known to produce any of the divine or sublime feelings which are associated with Soma. While Soma illumines the intellect of man, awakens in him the sense of divine and is the source of Vedic wisdom or hymns, the intoxication caused by *surā* is opposed to all these. While the deity Soma confers immortality on man, guides him on righteous paths and enables him to know the divine, wine or *surā* is not known to accomplish any of these. It is opposed to the divine or spiritual life of man. A *surā* drunk person cannot create hymns and devote himself to the deities. The deities are not to be attained by the rich and the drunk.[5] Wine cannot inspire man to know the divine or the deities, or for any creative activity. It cannot make a person a *kavi* or a *ṛṣi*; whereas Soma, being of the nature of a *ṛṣi* or being *ṛṣi*-minded, and being the ruler of the *ṛṣi*s makes a man a *ṛṣi* and a *kavi*. Thus Soma is not any kind of wine, and the exhilaration and joy it gives rise to in man are in no way similar to the intoxication produced by wine. This distinction between Soma and *surā* maintained in the *Ṛgveda* will help us to know clearly that Soma, which is often described as great *rasa* (*mahān rasa*), and is said to flow universally, is not wine. It is the same as the *rasa* of the Upaniṣads (*rasovai saḥ*), and the *rasa* of classical Sanskrit literature in which it stands to mean creative inspiration, the fountain of poetry and literature. While the *rasa* that is experienced and enjoyed by poets and other creative people in its various forms is a manifestation of Soma, Soma in its divine nature is the primary *rasa* of the divine, or the essence and source of all creativity. As pointed out earlier the description of Soma as a plant juice is very scant in the *Ṛgveda*, while its description as divine *rasa* is profound and elaborate. And the Vedic seers are mainly concerned with the description of divine Soma in all the hymns addressed to Soma. The distinction between Soma as the great or divine *rasa*, the essence of all creativity, and Soma as the sap of a herb which is symbolically used in *yajña*, which itself is a symbolic act, is maintained clearly in the *Ṛgveda*. Their

5. 8.21.14.

identities are not confused, for the seers explicitly state that the divine Soma is not the same as the *soma* that is shed during *yajña*. The Soma that is divine is experienced and enjoyed by the wise or the seers (*dhīrā cit samanakṣanta*).[6] "The wise by their striving have attained it."[7] It is to be attained by truthful speech (*ṛtavākena*), faith and austerity.[8] Only men of high moral perfection (*sukṛttamāḥ*) attain it, and enjoy it.[9] The divine Soma which gives birth to divine *vāk* or wisdom in man, and makes him a *kavi* is the guide and controller of the sacred knowledge of the Veda (*śloka yantrāsaḥ*).[10] It is not attained by those who are spiritually blind or sightless (*anakṣāsaḥ badhirā*) and bound, have no faith in divine wisdom, and are sinful.[11] They reject it. It is difficult to tread the path of *ṛta*, and without living a life of *ṛta* one cannot taste divine Soma. It is experienced by those whose understanding or intellect is both comprehensive and subtle (*viśvā* and *aṇu*). It is shed by the wisdom of the wise (*kṛtvā ayam asmāt āsuta*).[12] It cannot inspire or illumine a person who is untruthful and sinful. Only those who are spiritually mature can attain it, but not those whose bodies are not purified by austerity (*tapa*), and are immature spiritually (*ama*).[13] It does not stir or inspire all, though it is present everywhere, and is capable of inspiring all (*āviśvaminvam*).[14] While the Soma employed in *yajña* passes through a hairy filter for its purification, the purifier of the divine Soma is present everywhere (*pavitram te vitatam brahmaṇaspate*).[15] Here divine Soma is significantly identified with

6. 9.73.9.
7. 9.73.9; see also 9.83.4.
8. 9.113.2.
9. 9.83.4; see also 9.48.1.
10. 9.73.6.
11. 9.73.6; see also 9.104.13.
12. 10.144.6.
13. 9.83.1.
14. 2.40.3.
15. 9.83.1.

Brahmaṇaspati. It is purified or refined by human devotion and faith (*punāti te pariśrutam somam sūryasya duhitā vāreṇa śāśvata tanā*).[16] The hymns that are born out of it also help to refine it. The distinction between the divine Soma and *soma* juice is made further clear when the Vedic seers proclaim that the real divine Soma which is experienced by them is not known to those who take it to be the juice of a plant and drink it (*somam yam brāhmaṇā vidhuhna tasya āśnoti kahcana*).[17] Only the wise or divinely inspired persons taste it, and know its real divine nature (*na te āśnoti pārdhivā*). Here the term *pārdhivā* need not necessarily mean earthly or human beings, as in the light of the above assertion it may mean ordinary or spiritually immature mortals, for its real nature is known to the wise. Thus it is sufficient for the present to assert that the Soma of which the seers speak, and for whose description the whole of ninth *maṇḍala* of the *Ṛgveda* is devoted, is not simply the juice of a herb, but a divine principle which the wise experience within their hearts. Also it is essential to keep in mind the distinction made in the *Ṛgveda* between divine Soma, and Soma as a plant juice to comprehend the meaning of most of the Soma hymns, and the various epithets employed to describe Soma. This distiction also helps us in understanding and appreciating the symbolic value of the various epithets employed to describe Soma. Almost all the attributes of Soma refer to divine Soma which is neither the deification of a plant juice that is symbolically shed during *yajña*, nor an abstraction of something that is experienced in nature. It refers to an inward experience.

Our interpretation of Soma primarily refers to the divine Soma, and the object of the following discussion is to present and discuss the nature and meaning of Soma as a deity. The real abode of divine Soma is the highest or the divine, and it is brought down to earth from there (*parāt*).[18] While Soma in its divine existence is present everywhere, when it is brought down

16. 9.1.6; see also 9.113.3.
17. 10.85.3.
18. 9.68.6.

to earth it has made plants, waters or floods and the hearts of inspired poets and their creation, the Vedic hymns, as its abode.[19] Divine Soma which produces divine or immortal joy in the wise (*amartyam madam*) is addressed as a divine child (*divaḥ śiśu*).[20] It is born in the highest (*ucchā te jātam andhasā divisat bhūmiḥ ādadhe*), and from there it is brought down to earth (*padam yat asya parame vyomani adhā viśvā abhi samyati samyataḥ*).[21] It is brought down by men from the top of heaven (*eṣa nrībhiḥ vinīyate divaḥ mūrdhe*). The divine is the dwelling place of Soma (*bṛhat gabhīram tava soma dhāma*).[22] It is the essence of the divine or divine nectar (*divaḥ pīyūṣam*) that sustains the whole universe.[23] It upholds and sustains all the regions; it is also their measure. Soma is described as milking the divine udder, or shedding for man the divine essence (*duhānaḥ ūdhan divyam*).[24] It is the essence of heaven and earth which they contain as a mother the embryo. It milks from old the divine essence or nectar and fills the whole world with it, or it sheds what is divine (*vṛṣṭhim na arṣa divyam*).[25] "Thy perpetual streams descend or flow like rain from the divine."[26] "Thy streams that never fail flow forth like showers of rain."[27] Soma sheds for man the divine essence that is inherent within all the regions, and it is itself that essence. Being the divine essence of all that is there, Soma pervades the whole creation, and hence assumes various forms in manifesting itself. Its creativity and joy flow in infinite ways and reveal it. Soma goes round both worlds instantly or at once (*sadya*) being present within them as their essence.[28] *Soma* is the support and sustenance

19. 9.68.7.
20. 9.33.5; 9.38.5; 9.102.1.
21. 9.61.10.
22. 9.88.8; 9.91.3.
23. 9.85.9; 9.110.8; 9.51.2.
24. 9.107.5
25. 9.97.17.
26. 9.57.1.
27. 9.57.1.
28. 3.46.5; 9.18.5.

of heaven and earth. Being the divine essence, without which the world cannot sustain itself, Soma unites or integrates the divine with the phenomenal reality, or the visible realms with their source.[29] When brought down from the highest and experienced by the wise within their hearts, Soma reveals the divine in nature, and is thus the matrix of the deities or their progenitor. It is the source of all creative knowledge (*dhāra vedhasaḥ*), or the wisdom or knowledge of the wise, if we take the meaning of the term *dhāra* as knowledge or wisdom. Although the divine is inherently present in all nature, it is Soma that reveals its presence to man. Soma is the divine illumination or inspiration which enables man to see the presence of the divine in nature. He is the inner light of inspiration which guides man in infinite ways (*sahasra nīdhaḥ*). He is the supreme path-finder (*gātuvittamaḥ*). Being present everywhere he unites all. "I offer that juice flowing through the regions of heaven and earth commonly, or which has risen to earthly and heavenly regions, or this visible world and what existed before it."[30] Soma is addressed, accordingly, as the lord and ruler of all that is (*viśvasya bhuvanasya rājā; īśānaḥ viśvataḥ; rājānam asya bhuvanasya; viśvasya īśānaḥ ojasā*).[31] All the worlds therefore offer themselves in worship to him. They abide in his glory which pervades and encompasses them all (*tubhya imā bhuvanā kave mahimnā soma tastire*).[32] He fills both the worlds with his splendour. He measures all the regions of the universe, and from which no single creature is excluded. All the worlds are under his influence and control. It is by participating in his wisdom that all the deities create all that is there (*māyāvinaḥ mamire asya māyayā*).[33]

The essential nature of the divine Soma is light. He is self-luminous, and the whole universe shines with his light. In his

---

29. 10.17.11; see also 9.74.1.
30. 10.17.11.
31. 9.97.56; 9.61.6; 9.85.3; 9.101.5.
32. 9.62.27.
33. 9.83.3

brightness he is like the sun (*ayam sūrya iva upadhṛk*).[34] He illumines the heaven, and comprehends all the forms on earth with his light, and yet transcends all the three regions (*ati tri rocanā rohan bhrājasā divam*).[35] Soma is therefore prayed to place the devotees where there is light eternally, or where light is eternal, or in the immortal and undecaying world of light.[36] He shines with divine splendour, and illumines all (*virocayan sarvam*). In his splendour he is like the Sun, and fills the rays of the Sun with his light (*sūryasya raśmibhiḥ parivyata*).[37] The streams of all-knowing Soma flow like the rays of the Sun (*pavamānasya viśvait prā te sargāḥ asrukṣata sūryasya iva na raśmayaḥ*).[38] He is the brightness of all that is bright. He makes brightness as his form. He is born as light that is adorable, and hence is the increaser of light everywhere (*jyotiḥ jajñānam ukthyam; dyumna vardhanam*).[39] He is the illumination of all that is bright and shining. Through his mighty power his face or form shines with divine splendour, and he finds for man the auspicious or sublime light (*vidat svaḥ mānave jyoti āryam*).[40] He is the divine ray of light (*divyā suparṇā*), and is ever wakeful with his rays of light.[41] The seers shed him or milk him for the bright light eternally. The seers milk him, the *ṛṣi*, his bright essence after his ancient splendour for spiritual sustenance of man (*asya prātnam anudyutam śukram dūduhe*).[42] He milks for man the divine udder, and sheds forth divine (*duhanā ūdhaḥ divyam*).[43] The seers milk him for the great light (*mahe dyumnāya*). He milks the divine essence from the profound depths of the divine that is

34. 9.54.2.
35. 9.17.5; see also 6.44.23.
36. 9.113.7.
37. 9.86.32.
38. 9.64.7.
39. 9.29.5; 9.31.2.
40. 10.43.4.
41. 9.48.3; 9.71.9
42. 9.54.1.
43. 9.107.5.

worshippable and praiseworthy (*divaḥ pīyūṣam pūrvyam yat ukthyam mahe gahāt divaḥ anidrikṣat*).[44]

The light that is the nature or essence of divine *Soma* is the light of truth and righteousness. Light is a symbol for knowledge as it illumines and reveals all. As divine inspiration Soma is the source of divine knowledge for man. As divine light Soma reveals the divine to man through its presence either in nature or within himself. He shines with the splendour of *ṛta*, and is the abode of immortality (*ṛtasyā śukraḥ vibhāsi amṛtasya dhāma*).[45] The noble and bright Soma flows with the streams or knowledge (*dhāra*) of *ṛta* (*ārya śukraḥ ṛtasya dhārayā akṣaran*).[46] His splendour is that of *ṛta* (*ṛta dyumna*). He is the central source of its manifestation. He is the source of immortality and righteousness to man, and proclaims immortality to man (*amṛtatvāya ghoṣya*). And those who have tasted or experienced Soma attain divine light, become immortal and know the deities (*apāma somam amṛtā abhūma aganma jyotiḥ avidāma devān*).[47] He dispells the inner darkness of man, or men fight against dark forces with the help of his light. He is the destroyer of sins in man, or because of him man can overcome all evil. He is the protector of man against sin. His light or the light that is his nature purifies or sanctifies man. He inspires devotion in man (*brahma sava*), and that purifies man spiritually. This shows that Soma as divine light or inspiration is the source of divine wisdom or knowledge to man which alone can put him across all evil, and make him immortal and righteous. He is the supreme path-finder, and being the guide of man to righteousness, he is addressed as the lord of righteousness (*dharmanaḥ pate*).[48] Dharma is *ṛta* as revealed at the human level. *Ṛta* is the dynamic side of the divine, and Soma is related to or even identified with *ṛta* and *satya*. In the *Ṛgveda* Soma is often identified with *ṛtam bṛhat*, the

44. 9.110.8.
45. 9.97.32.
46. 9.63.14.
47. 8.48.3; see also 6.47.3.
48. 9.35.6.

divine or the highest truth (*pavamāna ṛtam bṛhat śukram jyotiḥ ajījanat*).[49] He is *ṛtam bṛhat* or the truth that manifests itself in all; *ṛtam* is the universal manifestation of truth. Soma is the first manifestation of *ṛta*, and shines with its splendour. He sheds the splendour of *ṛta*, or is the chief vehicle of its expression (*ṛtasya sudughe or ṛtasya nāvam*).[50] He is described as the flow of *ṛta* (*ṛtam ṛtāya pavate sumedhā*).[51] He increases or extends *ṛta*, and is increased by it. He is the protector of *ṛta*, as well as its expression. Soma, the lord of seers (*ṛṣi*), participates in the splendour of *ṛta* and inspires it in man (*hinvan ṛtasya dīdhitim*).[52] He is inherent within *ṛta*, or *ṛta* is his source of origin (*ṛtasya garbhe nihitam*).[53] He spreads everywhere the threads of *ṛta*, and gets purified by them. He is full of *ṛta*, and is even identified with it. Being full of *ṛta* Soma inspires truth and righteousness in people. Similarly he is described as the vehicle of expression of the divine (*divyasya vahne*).[54] Thus Soma shares all the attributes of *ṛta* and the divine. As Soma stands for inner divine light or inspiration, the moment of its birth in man, or man's experience of divine Soma marks the beginning of man's divine or spiritual transformation. It indicates the divine transformation of man's vision, or the birth of divine wisdom in him. Man then becomes aware of the eternal divine order present throughout the universe sustaining it. By transforming man's vision divinely, and by revealing the divine to him Soma makes a man a *kavi* and a *ṛṣi*. He awakens man to the light of *ṛta*, the source of rightousness, and to spiritual life of devotion and prayer. Milking for man the essence of *ṛta* or the divine he generates in him all illuminating divine knowledge. These are the most significant creative functions of divine Soma, the divine *rasa* of creativity.

---

49. 9.66.24; see also 9.107.15; 9.61.16.
50. 9.77.1; 9.89.2.
51. 9.97.23.
52. 9.102.1; 9.102.8.
53. 9.68.5.
54. 9.39.1.

Soma leads men on the path of righteousness in diverse creative ways. "Your ordinances are like those of royal Varuṇa."[55] Only the wise can follow the path of *ṛta* or righteousness, and Soma is the wisdom of the wise. He purifies the inner being of man by inspiring devotion in him which is the supreme purifier of man (*punāna brahmaṇā*). "Purify us by those sacred flames of yours O Agni which are spread within us as devotion (*yat te pavitram arciṣi agne vitatam antaḥ ā brahma tena punīḥ naḥ*).[56] Here Soma is identified with Agni.

The primary creative function of Soma is to generate within man the sense of divine or to awaken him to the divine. He is prayed to flow for the birth of divine in man (*divyāya janmane*).[57] Born of truth and increased by it, Soma flows in countless streams for the birth of the deities (*devasya janmane*).[58] He is the best of offering (*uttamam havi*) to the deities, or he is most acceptable to them. He is their feast. We can grasp the meaning of the expressions like *divyāya janmane* and *devasya janmane* in the context of several other passages in which Soma is described as the source of revelation of the nature of the deities. Soma reveals or unfolds to man the real or hidden names or natures of the deities (*devaḥ devānām guhya namāni āviṣkṛṇoti*).[59] He discloses the deities to man (*āvṛṇīta devān*).[60] It is with the sight or vision granted by Soma, a *ṛṣi* claims that he is able to know the divine, and his relation of identity with it.[61] The flood of Soma or Soma streams are born of the divine (*devajātaḥ*), and come to the feast of the deities with divine wisdom or knowledge (*divyasya kāvyai*).[62] He is described as the generator or father of the deities (*pitā* or *janitā*

55. 9.88.8.
56. 9.67.23 and 24.
57. 9.85.6.
58. 9.108.8; 9.85.6.
59. 9.95.2.
60. 9.97.41; see also 9.95.2.
61. 1.139.1.
62. 9.91.2.

devānām).[63] And in him are hidden all the deities (*ninye viśve devāḥ*), or he shines along with all the deities (*sam devaiḥ śobhate kavi*).[64] He is born to reveal the divine glory to the devotees who by participating in it or living in it attain immortality. He fills men with the glory of the deities (*deveṣu yaśaḥ martyāya bhūṣayan*).[65] He fills the world with divine wisdom and fulfils the wisdom of man. By that wisdom which Soma inspires in man, man is able to know the divine, and become a *kavi* or a *ṛṣi*. He is the immortal (light) within mortals. The worlds expand for him who from the beginning found light to spread the law of eternal life.[66] He is the *rasa* shed by the deities, and in that form he enters all the worlds (*devebhyaḥ sutaḥ viśvā dhāmāni āviśan*).[67] As the essence of divine inspiration he is present inherently within all the deities whereby each deity is able to inspire man divinely. All the deities share his glory and greatness, and are rich with them. He is the sweetness that sustains the universe, and is in this sense a best or supreme offering to the deities. He is the king of the deities as well as of mortals. He is the best form of divine light, or the best form of all the deities (*devapsara tama*). He is the delight of the deities (*deva avi*). He is the divine strength of the deities, or he fills them with his divine strength (*ojasā devān anuprabhūṣta: somena ādityāḥ balinaḥ, somena pridhvī mahi*).[68] He is the *dakṣa* (vigour) of the deities. The wisdom of the deities is his. In this sense he is identified with all the deities. All the deities are his kinsmen (*soma jāmayaḥ*). He is described as *guru* or the self or essence of all the deities. As shown earlier, all the deities or the entire nature are capable of inspiring in man the sense of divine, and reveal to him the divine as their inner unity. Because of its capacity to reveal the divine, nature is seen as a manifestation of the divine,

63. 9.109.4.
64. 9.25.3.
65. 9.94.3.
66. 9.94.2.
67. 9.28.2.
68. 10.85.2.

or the abode of the deities. Each deity in its own unique manner is a source of divine inspiration, or a source of divine revelation to man. And one who receives divine revelation, or one who is divinely inspired is a *kavi* or *ṛṣi* or a *vipra*. Now Soma represents divine inspiration, or the inspired state of man's existence. The deities are able to inspire man divinely because they share the nature of Soma, or Soma is inherent within them all.

Soma is divine or he is a deity, but like Agni and other deities he is not an individual deity having his phenomenal representation in nature. He represents the fact of divine inspiration inwardly experienced by the seers and poets. He is inspiration as such, and means in relation to man the inner state of being divinely inspired, or the divinely inspired state of man's existence. Inspiration generates in man devotion and flows itself or is expressed in the form of Vedic hymns. And Soma as divine inspiration does not refer to the experience of any particular seer or poet, but refers to what is commonly experienced by all the seers and poets. It is a universal principle, and reveals itself through the experiences of the seers and poets. In this sense Soma represents the creative aspect of the divine which manifests itself not only in nature but within man also as the source of his creative life and wisdom. Thus Soma is not an individualised manifestation of the divine as other deities are. As the creative power of the divine, Soma is inherently present within all the deities. It is their creative power whereby they inspire man divinely, and reveal to him the nature of the divine. While the other deities represent the various manifestations of the divine in nature, Soma represents the divine power of inspiration by means of which man is able to know the divine. Without being divinely inspired man cannot experience the divine either in nature or within himself.

All the attributes of the divine are attributed to *Soma*, the essence of the divine. However, one epithet that is mostly used in relation to Soma, and which characterises him most is *kavi* or *kāvya*. Soma, the wise, the thinker and the seer moves with wisdom (*kāvyena saha cana*), and finds delight in all wisdom (*viśveṣu kāvyeṣu rantā*).[69] He is all-seeing, and comprehends in his wisdom all the regions eternally (*viśvā dhāmāni viśvacakṣuḥ mahān prabho te sataḥ pariyanti ketavaḥ*), or his great rays encompass all the places.[70] He flows with wisdom comprehending all within his wisdom. Divine Soma, the seer, upholds the universe or all the regions by the wisdom (*pariyat kaviḥ kāvyā bharate bhuvanāni viśvā*).[71] He flows with streams of wisdom and discernment. He illumines or reveals all with his light. "The worlds expand to him who from the beginning found light to spread the law of eternal life."[72] He fills both the worlds with his light and dispells darkness, and reveals the true nature of both the worlds for those who seek immortality. By his wisdom (*kratu*) he contemplates mankind. The whole world abides in his glory who is a *kavi*. He generates divine knowledge in man (*ketum kṛnvan*).[73] Soma who is pure and a *kavi* flows or moves within both the worlds with his wisdom and intelligence (*tava kratvā rodasī iti antarā kave śuciḥ dhiyā pavate somaḥ*).[74] He flows with wisdom to make the whole world auspicious and noble (*kṛnvanto viśvam āryam*).[75] He flows everywhere purifying all.

The hymns of the ninth *maṇḍala* of the *Ṛgveda*, which are exclusively devoted to Soma, are known as *pavamāni* hymns. The term *pavamāna* can mean what is spiritually purifying or sanctifying, for it is used in several contexts of the *Ṛgveda* in that sense, and by awakening divine within man Soma is the supreme purifier of man. The divine inspiration transforms man radically, sanctifies his existence and makes him holy. Agni is also described as a purifier (*pavamāna*).[76] Soma's purifying or holy

69. 9.92.3.
70. 9.86.5.
71. 9.94.3.
72. 9.94.2.
73. 9.64.8.
74. 9.86.13.
75. 9.63.5.
76. 8.101.14; see also 9.96.17.

influence is spread everywhere (*pavitram te vitatam brahmaṇaspate prabhu gātrāṇi pari eṣi viśvataḥ*).[77] Here it is significant to note that Soma is addressed as *prabhu* which means one who influences (*prabhāvita*).[78] He is also addressed elsewhere as *mahān prabhu*. His holy influence is everywhere, or the bright rays of Soma that purify are present everywhere (*tapoḥ pavitram vitatam divaḥ pade śocanta asya tantavaḥ vi astiran*).[79] Rays of Soma purify the powers of man, and also of the deities. Soma gives birth to devotion in man which is expressed through hymns or prayers, and in their turn devotion and prayer purify Soma (*punānaḥ brahmaṇa*).[80] Soma is purified by devotion and reverence (*brahmaṇā pūyamānaḥ; namasā punānaḥ*).[81] All creativity is divine, but all the creative people may not be devoted to the divine. All those people who are inspired to creativity, or who have received inspiration of some kind may not see in their creativity the spark of the divine, and hence may not be devoted to the divine. To see in one's creativity the presence or manifestation of the divine, and hence to channel it as one's means of worship of the divine is due to birth of devotion (*brahma*). Devotion is born when one sees in one's creativity the presence or manifestation of the divine. And this also is accomplished by Soma to whom people and the whole universe bow down spontaneously in reverence. He causes worship (*yajña*), and is born in worship. He is the centre or the soul of worship (*ātmā yajñasya*)[82] for without experiencing the divine, which is due to *Soma*, true worship is not possible. He is the sign (*ketu*) or knowledge of worship, as well as the object of it. He is also the means of worship (*yajña sādhana*), and because of him the wise men of ancient times could perform their religious

77. 9.83.1.
78. The term *prabhu* is defined etymologically by Sāyaṇa as one who influences (*prabhāvita*), and *Soma* is addressed as Mahāprabhu.
79. 9.83.2.
80. 9.113.5; see also 9.16.4
81. 9.88.5.
82. 9.2.10; 9.6.8; *yajñasya ketu* 9.86.7; *jyotiḥ yajñasya* 9.86.10.

duties. He is the source of man's spiritual life, and also sustains him in it. He is the lord of righteousness (*dharmaṇaḥ pate*), and guides people on the paths of righteousness and truth.

The best form of his worship consists in *kāvya* (wisdom). He not only reveals the divine to man, but also liberates him from the knots of worldly existence (*grandhim nivisya*).[83] He is the source as well as the abode of bliss (*śamgayum*). He is also the means of attaining it, or its bridge to man. He accomplishes all these for man by illumining and fulfilling his intelligence. Divine Soma who is addressed as *mahāmate* or *bṛhat mate* (great mind), and who has intelligence as his riches, is the embodiment of wisdom itself.[84] His light is the light of wisdom. He is a *ṛṣi*, and the sovereign ruler of all seers (*ṛṣiṣāt*).[85] He is described as *ṛṣi*-minded. He is a *kavi* by his wisdom (*kāvyena*), and his wisdom is like that of Uśna (a *ṛṣi*) who is supreme among the seers, and whose wisdom is incomparable.[86] He is the greatest among the *kavis*, for he is their inspiration. He is a great *kavi* who reveals or pronounces the hymns to man, or he reveals the meaning of divine speech to man (*mahān kaviḥ nivacanāni śamsan*).[87] His wisdom is beyond the reach of man, and is incomparable (*asamastha kāvya*).[88] He abides in the intelligence or thoughts of all (*dhiyā samvasāna*).[89] He dwells within the intellect of man (*dhiyā hitaḥ*), or among the hymns, the creation of an illumined intellect.[90] He bestows on man conscious wealth of inspiration or illumination (*cetanam rayim kurvanti*).[91] As lord of intelligence he flows through the intellect of man or through the hymns. He is purified and

83. 9.97.18.
84. 9.39.1.
85. 9.76.4.
86. 9.87.3.
87. 9.97.2.
88. 9.76.4.
89. 9.26.4.
90. 9.25.2; 9.44.2.
91. 9.31.1.

adorned by all the hymns (*viśvebhiḥ matibhiḥ pariṣkr̥tam*), and he rejoices in them (*dhiyā jūtaḥ*).[92] He flows with the speed of intellect or thought (*dhījavaḥ*).[93]

Soma is also identified with wisdom (*manīṣā*). He is addressed as *manīṣī* (wise). He is purified by wisdom, and flows along with it, or he is purified by hymns and flows through them. As the hymns are an expression of the divinely inspired wisdom, the meaning of both the above expressions is the same. He is *vipra,* lovely (*vareṇyam*) and wise (*manīṣī*). His streams are full of delight (*matsarāsaḥ*) and wisdom. He knows the minds of men, and is also their lord (*manaḥ cit manasaspati*).[94] He is the inner strength or vigour of the mind or intellect, as well as the means of attaining it (*dakṣai sudakṣa; dakṣa sādhanam*).[95] He is the source of mental vigour or strength to those who seek *r̥ta*. He is the all-knower (*viśvavit*) and great discerner (*vipaścita*). He is the flow of creativity, or flows along with or through it (*dhāra vedhasa*), or the knowledge or wisdom of the wise, as according to *Nighaṇṭu* the term *dhāra* is a synonym of wisdom (*prajñā*). He is supreme creativity (*mahān rasa*) and manifests himself in and through all the forms of creativity.[96] All the acts of creativity manifest him. He is the wisdom of the seer-poets (*kavikratu*).[97] Or he is the creative wisdom of the seer-poets. His wisdom is auspicious, or he is auspicious wisdom (*bhadra kratuḥ*). The all-seeing Soma flows everywhere with his wisdom (*abhi priyāni kāvyā viśvacarṣane arṣati*) or (*kāvyā kavi arṣati*).[98] He flows along with or through the enlightened thoughts of the wise, or he flows as the wisdom of inspired people (*viprasya dhārayā kaviḥ*).[99] He is also the lord of sacred speech (*vācaspati*) as

92. 9.64.16.
93. 9.86.1.
94. 9.11.8.
95. 9.27.2; 9.98.8; 9.101.5.
96. 9.77.5.
97. 9.62.13.
98. 9.57.2.
99. 9.12.8; 9.62.13.

well as its inspirer in man. He is, therefore, identified with Brahmaṇaspati, the poet of all poets, and lord of sacred speech. He is the path of the poet-seers, and their ultimate station or end as well (*padavī kavīnām*).[100]

The identification of Soma with divine inspiration, the source of divine speech or wisdom is further justified by the fact that Soma is attained or experienced by the wise. In his true divine nature Soma is known to the wise, or wise experience him as the source of their wisdom. Apart from the assertion that the divine Soma, who is known to the wise is not the same as what people drink, a plant juice, it is stated that the real divine Soma is tasted by those who are morally pure or truthful, and spiritually mature. It is the wise who attain it or taste it. He is known to or experienced by the wise. The wise know the delightful nature of Soma (*mandrasya rūpam vividuḥ manīṣinaḥ*).[101] Soma the *kavi* is milked by means of their religious or virtuous acts by the poet-seers who are morally perfect and wise (*kavim kavayaḥ apasā manīṣinam aṁśum duhanti*).[102] He is shed by wisdom (*kratvā ayam asmāt āsutaḥ*).[103] The inspired thinkers attain him by means of the wisdom granted to them by Varuṇa, which consists of moral perfection, as Varuṇa represents moral order or righteousness (*varuṇasya māyayā dhīrā cit samanaṣanti*).[104] He is to be approached with devotion and reverence. And people who are desirous of knowing the divine, or moved by the desire to become divine impel him mentally to flow (*ahinvire manasā devayantaḥ*).[105] He is impelled to flow by the wise (*tvā hinvire vedhasaḥ*). Purified by the zeal of devotion of the people he flows to the deities. He is made pure, and is adorned by the prayers or hymns. Men with all-comprehensive understanding shed Soma for the sake

100. 9.96.6.
101. 9.68.6; 9.96.6 and 8.
102. 9.72.6.
103. 10.144.6.
104. 9.73.9.
105. 9.74.8.

of worship. He is apprehended by a most subtle intellect (*aṇvā dhiyā*), or he is expressed by most subtle thoughts of man.[106] Being within the intelligence of man, the divine Soma, the delight of the seers (*ṛṣisāna*) and creative (*vedhasa*), milks for man the essence of the divine. He is adorned by those who are inspired, and are knowers of speech by their wisdom (*tvam tvā viprāḥ vacovidāḥ pariṣkṛnvanti vedhasā*).[107] The flow of Soma is connected with the generation of wisdom, and mental vigour or strength in man (*kratvā dakṣaya pavasva soma dhārayā*), for he is prayed to flow generating them in man.[108] He is prayed to bestow on man the gifts of wisdom and mental strength (*bhadram naḥ api vātaya manaḥ dakṣam uta kratum*).[109] By giving birth to divine light of truth in man he dispels the inner darkness of man (*apāvṛṇu vrajam hinvam ṛtasya dīdhitim*).[110] Thus divine Soma is the wisdom of the wise, the creativity of all creative people, and the divine principle that illumines the intellect of man. He is the supreme offering to the deities, and is their delight. He is the source of immortality and bliss to man, and is attained by the wise (*kratu vidam*). All these he achieves for man by illumining his intelligence.

Although Soma is divine, and dwells in the highest realm, he is brought down to earth by divine speech or by metres symbolised as fine winged (*suparṇa*), and he has made the heart and intelligence of man as his dwelling places on earth. In the *Ṛgveda* as well as in the post-Saṁhitā literature it is stated that divine Soma is brought down to earth by divine speech (*vāk*). He is the immortal who has entered into mortals, just as all other deities have entered into and made man their abode. Soma enters into man from all sides or from everywhere (*viśvataḥ*). He ascends into the hearts of men (*āruhat*), or he is held by men within their

106. 9.26.1.

107. 9.64.23.

108. 9.100.5; see also 9.95.5.

109. 10.25.1.

110. 9.102.8; see also 9.86.23.

hearts (*hṛdi bibharti*).[111] The delightful Soma flows from within the hearts of men illumining the Uṣas, the dawn of divine wisdom in all her forms. His power influences or touches the hearts of men, and in this connection he is prayed not to hurt the heart of man with the brightness of his splendour.[112] In other words, it is prayed that the light of Soma should not dazzle the vision of man with its excessive splendour. Soma with his ever alert or wakeful wisdom descends into the hearts of men and stays there generating bliss in them. He is prayed to find delight in the hearts of men (*soma rarandhi naḥ hṛde*). Being the lord of intelligence and speech he dwells within the thoughts of men, and milks for him the divine essence (*dhīnām antariti sabaḥ dugha*).[113] When urged from heaven, the lord of speech, sheds or rains for man the streams of wisdom. He dwells within the minds of the seers, and is clothed by the hymns. He enters all the minds like a swan its group (*haṁsa yadhā gaṇam*), and if we take the meaning of the word *gaṇa* as knowledge, and as *haṁsa* stands for discernment, we may be right in interpreting the above as Soma enters all the minds as the light of discernment.[114] He is among or within the five races of people and is, therefore, known as *pāñcajanya*. He is within man and is guided by them (*nrībhiḥ yemānaḥ*). He is associated with all wisdom, and flows with all wisdom (*manīṣibhi pavate*) from old or always.

However, Soma is not identified either with the mind, or intellect or with the hymns. At the same time, he is not any of the powers of the mind or intellect so that he is present naturally within man. While intelligence is inherent within all men, Soma is not a natural quality or property of human intelligence. All intelligent beings do not taste *Soma* though they are capable of it. As divine light illumines human intellect, or as divine inspiration which enables man to apprehend the divine, Soma is tasted or experienced by those who are morally pure and

111. 10.32.9; see also 9.73.8.

112. 8.68.8.

113. 9.12.7.

114. 9.32.3.

spiritually mature, and whose intellect is made pure and subtle. Only those whose bodies are purified by austerity (*tapa*) attain Soma. Soma is a divine gift, and is born with the competence of the mind (*dakṣeṇa manasā jāyate kavi*).[115] The intellect of man can apprehend or intuit the divine when it is divinely inspired, and Soma is that inspiration. He stirs the heart of man, and illumines his intellect, and releases the flow of creativity.

The birth of Soma within the heart of man is often compared in the *R̥gveda* with the birth of waves in a river or ocean. The creative upsurge of Soma in man is likened to springing up of water from a fountain. Soma flows in waves, and influences the whole being of man. Soma is also described often as entering the ocean, and residing in "waters" (*apsu*), and is even identified with the ocean (*samudra*). As shown in the previous chaper *samudra* is used in the *R̥gveda* as a symbol for human heart or psyche. And within the classical Sanskrit literature poetic inspiration is compared to a stream or spring which swells within the heart of man or floods his whole being. It flows forth or is expressed in the form of creative speech. Soma is described as a fountain (*utsa*),[116] for the creativity springs up spontaneously within man, and flows out in various forms. As the waves rise in a river or in an ocean spontaneously, the upsurge of creativity and its flow are compared with the birth of waves. Both spring up spontaneously. Waves of emotion and passion always spring from within the human heart, the seat of man's psychic life. In the case of an inspired person his inspired heart gives rise to waves of creativity which flow out seeking expression. Divine inspiration transforms a person completely, and fulfils all his faculties. Soma flows with his streams, which are not streams of plant juice, but of poetic inspiration and wisdom. His waves reach the deities and delight them. He is like a well or fountain from which all can drink, and yet it never dries up.[117] The supreme

115. 9.68.5.

116. 9.110.5; 9.107.4.

117. 9.110.5.

quest of the Vedic seer-poets, which is well expressed in all their prayers, is for the gift of divine inspiration which finds its expression through the hymns. They pray to the deities for the birth of devotion in which they see the ultimate fulfilment of their existence. Each deity is a source of divine inspiration, and the hymns are the means of its expression. They clothe it or embody it. Each deity is capable of evoking devotion in man, and with that devotion he worships the deities. Each deity is a source of divine inspiration to man, and man knows the deities in the light of it.

When tasted or experienced Soma gives rise to divine speech or wisdom in man. He is often addressed as the source of inspiration of the hymns, or the inspirer of hymns (*manīṣām uśatīm; ajīgarati* or *udīrayati vācam; sataḥ prasāviṣu matim*).[118] He is generator of hymns (*janitā matīnām*) and flows through them (*pavase mati*).[119] He inspires divine speech in the seers which seeks its expression through hymns (*hinvānaḥ vācam matibhiḥ kavīnām*).[120] He inspires or stirs the mind of a seer, and prepares it for the creation of hymns (*vepate mati sādhate gira*).[121] He moves the mind and inspires speech like a river the waves, and flows through hymns. He inspires the minds of the wise for the birth of divine speech (*viprāṇām matayaḥ vācaḥ īrate*), or he inspires the thoughts and speech of the wise.[122] Creating or showing the paths of *ṛta* he inspires or impels speech, like oars the boat, and reveals the secret names or real natures of the deities (*sṛjānaḥ padhām ṛtasya iyarti vācam aritā iva nāvam; devaḥ devānām guhya namāni āviṣkṛṇoti*).[123] Dwelling within the cave of heart he holds or sustains the hymns (*guhā cit dadhiṣe girā*).[124] Inspiring speech he releases or frees the wisdom of the wise (*iṣanyan vācam visyā*

118. 6.47.3.
119. 9.96.5.
120. 9.97.32.
121. 9.71.3.
122. 9.85.7.
123. 9.95.2.
124. 6.2.9.

manīṣām).[125] He stirs or inspires speech or hymns or wisdom in man (*vācaḥ, giraḥ* and *manīṣā*) as waves by a river. He is eternally the inspirer of the minds of men or of hymns (*sataḥ prasāvisu matim*).[126] In this respect he is identified with Savitā, the deity of inspiration. He flows to stir or shake all (*pavasva viśvam ejaya*), and moves as the leader or chief (*agriya*) of speech.[127] He moves man completely or stirs him like attrition of sticks in causing fire. He is prayed to kindle man's being for divine light, like fire is kindled by attrition of sticks (*agnim na madhitam sam didīpa*).[128] The seers and the wise milk Soma the seer (*kavi*) for light (*aṁśum*).

The birth of divine Soma, the delightful of all *rasas* or the supreme *rasa* (*mahān rasa*) is compared with the rise of waves in a river or in an ocean. As soon as born Soma bestows on man wonderful gifts and wisdom. The wave of creativity that swells or surges forth in man is often compared in the *R̥gveda* with the rise of waves in a river or in an ocean. Soma is like a well or a perennial spring from which people drink, and yet it remains unexhausted. He is ever growing (*sadā vr̥dhaḥ*), and renews himself everytime he is tasted or drunk. The most wise Soma and most dear to people enters the *samudra* or human heart. He is even addressed as *samudra* (ocean). He, the all-knower and a seer, is (like) an ocean (*tvam samudraḥ asi viśvavit kaveḥ*). Being purified he flows in thousand or countless streams to find out for man the paths of devotion (Brahma), and inspires speech in him (*vidat gātum brahmane pūyamānaḥ sahasra dhārā pavate samudraḥ vācam edha svayam*).[129] Or being purified by devotion he inspires speech within *samudra* (heart). He increases or expands the *samudra*. He is the first to uphold or sustain (*vidhāraya*) the *samudra* for the deities. His birth in man means the birth of divine in man. His flow is compared to the flow of a river (*sindho ūrmā viakṣaran*), for

125. 9.95.5.
126. 9.21.7.
127. 9.62.25.
128. 8.48.6.
129. 9.35.2.

he is the flow of inspiration or creativity in man, and dwells within the wise (*manīṣinām āsīna antaḥ*).[130] "Hastening like waves of water our hymns or wisdom (*manīṣā*) are pressing forward to Soma with reverence."[131] The *Soma* which is of *samudra* or belongs to *samudra*, and being its delight, or having water (waves) as his form, and being seated in the wisdom of the wise flows when impelled by the wise, the witness of the mansion (*samudrīyaḥ apsarasaḥ manīṣinām āsīnaḥ antaḥ abhi somam akṣaran ta īm hinvanti harmyasya sākṣiṇam*).[132] He soaks or floods the being of man completely with his flow of inspiration.

The Soma waves are the delight of the deities (*ūrmā deva aviḥ*). The lovely Soma is stirred by the wise in the waves of a river (heart). He reveals the deities who abide in the womb of the flood (of inspiration) (*apām yat garbhaḥ āvṛṇīta devān*), (*madacyut kṣeti sadane sindho ūrmā vipaścitaḥ*).[133] Soma inspires or stirs the human waters, or the waters that are within man (*hinvānaḥ mānuṣī āpaḥ*).[134] He is the chief of the "waters", or flows as the head of them, inspiring speech and moving or shaking all (*tvam samudrīyaḥ āpaḥ agriyā vācaḥ īrayan pavate viśvam ajaya*).[135] He is described as the inspirer of "waters" (*aptūram*), and here Sāyaṇa says that the word *āpaḥ* can mean either waters or light. Therefore, we can interpret the term *āpaḥ* to mean the flood of divine inspiration or creativity. Soma is described as *vibhāvasu* or having light as his wealth. He is amidst the waves of *sindhu* and is soaked by "waters" (*āpaḥ*). The term *sindhu* literally means that which flows. He sports like the wave of water (*krīḍan ūrmā apām iva*). He unfolds to man the deities whose source or womb is "waters", giving birth to light of knowledge (*apām yat garbhaḥ āvṛṇīta devān ajanyan sūrye jyotiḥ*).[136]

130. 9.78.3.
131. 9.95.3.
132. 9.78.3.
133. 9.12.3.
134. 9.63.7.
135. 9.62.26.
136. 9.97.41.

Symbolism of "waters" is made clear by an expression in which Soma is said to inspire "waters" within man or of man (*hinvānaḥ mānuṣī āpaḥ*).[137] He moves along with or amidst the waves of "waters" revealing his final or highest abode (*apām ūrmim sacamānā samudram turīyam dhāma mahiṣaḥ vivakti*).[138] The "waters" follow or move according to the creative functions of Soma (*tava vratam anusacanti āpaḥ*).[139] This can also explain the meaning of the expression *indriyam rasam*. *Soma* is described as *indriyam rasam*.[140] Soma flows sustaining the faculties of man, as he is their inspirer, and also their fulfilment.

We now present some of the direct statements in which the symbolic meaning of Soma is stated clearly. Divine Soma finds delight in wisdom. The hero of the wise, Soma finds his increase or growth in the wisdom of the wise, or as the source and sustenance of wisdom in man he grows in and through the wisdom of the wise. He is born in the hearts of the wise, and grows there. He inspires divine speech in man, and reveals thereby the pathways to realise the truth. By inspiring divine speech in man he frees the wisdom of man.[141] As lord of speech, Soma flows through hymns. Divine speech of which the Veda is an expression in human language is the revelation of the divine. *Vāk* (speech) does not simply mean in the context of the Veda either the spoken or written word, but divine intelligence or wisdom as revealed in and through the intelligence of inspired seers. Being co-extensive and co-eternal with the divine, divine speech or wisdom is the supreme revelation of the divine to man, and *Soma* fills man with all-comprehensive speech or wisdom (*sahasra bharṇasam vācam*).[142]

Soma is described as the divine seed that is present within the worlds for providing divine strength and vigour to the

---

137. 9.63.7.

138. 9.96.19.

139. 9.81.5.

140. 9.47.3; 9.23.5; 9.86.10.

141. 9.95.5.

142. 9.64.25 and 26.

worlds. He moves within the speech for the fulfilment of man's existence (*antaḥ vāṇiṣu pracara su jīvase*).[143] Being born, he inspires the threefold speech or threefold Veda in man, or with the birth of Soma the threefold speech is revealed to man. Residing amidst waters — streams of inspiration — he generates speech, and seeks hymns (*go*) for his expression (*vācam janyan āpaḥ vasānaḥ abhi gāḥ iyakṣati*).[144] He blesses those whom he inspires with all-comprehensive speech (*sahasra bharṇasam vācam*). Divine Soma, the knower and lord or speech (*vacovid* and *vācaspati*) is even identified with divine speech or wisdom (*soma gaurī iti adhi śritaḥ*).[145] As inspirer of divine speech, which comprehends everything, Soma flows through hymns. The hymns that constitute the Veda are an expression of the wisdom that is inspired by Soma. He opens the doors of the minds of the singers, and by being within the intelligence or thoughts of the seers he sheds the essence of the divine (*dhīnām antariti sabaḥ dughā; apadvārāṇi matīnām prātnaḥ ruṇvanti kāravaḥ*).[146] Being within the cave of human heart he sustains the wisdom of the hymns (*guhācit dadhiśe girā*).[147] He milks the wisdom of a seer-poet (*kaveḥ āpatyam āduhe*), or he milks the offspring (hymns) of a *kavi*.[148] He is prayed to inspire wisdom, and sustain the vigour of the mind. The intelligent or conscious Soma moves or flows with the hymns of the seers (*cetana priyaḥ kavīnām matīpaviṣṭha*), or he inspires the speech of the seers that finds its expression through hymns (*vācam matibhiḥ kavīnām hinvānaḥ*).[149] He flows chiefly through speech, or as the leader of speech with wisdom bestowing wonderful gifts on the singers (*pavasva vācaḥ agriyā soma citrābhiḥ ūtibhiḥ abhi viśvāni kāvyā*).[150] He inspires the mind

143. 9.82.4.
144. 9.78.1.
145. 9.12.3.
146. 9.10.6.
147. 6.2.9.
148. 9.10.8.
149. 9.97.32.
150. 9.62.25.

of man, and achieves hymns (*vepate mati sādhate gira*).[151] He is eternally the inspirer of human minds or hymns (*sataḥ prasāviṣu matim*).[152] Being within the hearts of men he knows the wisdom or hymns that lay concealed within the creative waters of heart (*saḥ cit viveda nihitam yat apām apīcyam guhyam nāma gonām*).[153] Opening for man the paths leading to truth, he inspires or impels speech like oars a boat, and reveals the secret names of the deities. He plants the divine seed within the minds of men, and grows therein with wisdom. He is placed within the hearts of men and grows there, and gets expressed through the hymns fulfilling thereby the wisdom of man. He is prayed to inspire the intelligence of man to seek hymns (*jinva go iṣṭaye dhiyā*).[154]

The birth of Soma in man also indicates the birth of devotion in him. While inspiration in some form or other is at the source of all creativity leading to literary or other forms of creation, through which it is expressed, divine Soma as divine inspiration generates in man devotion leading him to a life of prayer and worship. He transforms man totally, and fulfils his existence supremely. He liberates man from his inner darkness by disclosing divine light. Brahma (devotion) is the chief form which *Soma* assumes.[155] The hymns also express Soma. As prayers and praises addressed to various deities, either individually or collectively, the hymns express man's devotion to the divine or the deities. Thus divine Soma finds his expression either through devotion or through hymns which express devotion.

Divine Soma is the delight or joy of the seers, of the wise and of the hymns (*anumādya manīṣibhiḥ, viprābhiḥ rukkābhiḥ*).[156] He is the maker of a *ṛṣi* (*ṛṣikṛt*), as well as the ultimate end or station of

151. 9.71.3.
152. 9.21.7.
153. 9.87.3.
154. 9.108.10.
155. 9.71.1.
156. 9.107.11.

them (*padavī kavīnām*). He inspires hymns, and is increased by them. Being born, Soma inspires speech consisting of threefold Veda (*prasavate udīrate tisraḥ vācaḥ*).[157] The Veda is an expression of the wisdom of the seers (*ṛṣi*) which is inspired by Soma (*yaḥ pavamāni adhieti ṛṣibhi sambhṛtam rasam*).[158] The seven metres of the Veda, which mean figuratively the Veda, express the one and never decreasing fountain of inspiration variously (*saḥ sapta dhītibhi hitaḥ nadyam ajinvat adruha ya ekaḥ akṣīṇam vavruduḥ*).[159] The hymns fulfil Soma and illustrate him (*śumbhanti*). They reveal and glorify the nature and substance of divine inspiration. They are the wonderful vehicles of its expression. The hymns that are full of devotion, and are the abode of truth clarify *Soma*, the divine child (*abhi brāhmi anuṣat yannaha ṛtasya mātarā marmujyante divaḥ śiśum*).[160] Soma is regulated or governed by the hymns (*śloka yantrāsa*). Soma who abides in all the regions of the world and is bound by the threefold Veda goes to the deities with seven metres by the vehicle of *ṛṣi*s. The seven metres milk for us the essence of truth from the highest (*asme sapta dhenavaḥ dudhuhe satyām āśiram prame vyomani*).[161] The speech of the seers is purified by Soma when he enters with his infinite streams the *pavitra* (filter) (*sahasra dhāre vitate pavitre avācam punānti kavayaḥ manīṣinaḥ*).[162] The metres, or the divine speech arranged or bound by the metres attain Soma amidst waters, the source of truth (*harim navante sapta dhenavaḥ apām upasthe kavim ṛtasya yonim*).[163] The seven (metres) offer laudation to their glorious and adorable parents (*Soma*). The seven metres (*saptavāṇī*) of the seers glorify Soma and praise him, the generator and leader of the hymns. While Soma is the inspirer of speech or hymns, the latter regulate him or articulate him,

157. 9.50.2; 9.108.12.

158. 9.67.31 and 32.

159. 9.9.4.

160. 9.33.5.

161. 9.70.1.

162. 9.73.7.

163. 9.86.25; see also 9.70.1.

and at the same time adorn him and glorify him. The hymns tend the infant Soma when he is born. The expression that Soma is a divine child, and the hymns help his growth (*śiśum panipatnam rihanti matayaḥ*), or the newly born child or Soma is taken care of by the hymns as mothers is significant.[164] The hymns are born due to divine inspiration or Soma as spontaneously as waves from a river, or as an arrow let loose from a bow.[165]

The hymns that milk truth (*ṛtasya dohanā*) shine with truth (*ṛatasya dīdhiti*), and glorify it. When Soma is awakened in man he fills or sanctifies the hymns with truth (*ajāgrivi vipra ṛtā matīnām soma punānaḥ*).[166] He is prayed to prepare the way for the creation of a new hymn. He shines through hymns (*ṛca śobhanta*) and is embodied or clothed by them. He seeks the hymns as the form of his expression, or the seers clothe him with hymns. The hymns hold within themselves Soma who is loved by all. After being purified Soma enters the hymns and dwells within or amidst them (*giraḥ soma āviveṣīda punānaḥ*), (*arkasya yonim āsadam*).[167] He finds delight in them and enjoys them. They are the means of his expression. Flowing in a stream or with knowledge (*dhāra*) that sanctifies, Soma the seer dwells in the prayer (*āpavasya pavitram dhārayā kave arkasya yonim āsadam*).[168] The intelligent and ever wakeful Soma flows through the hymns. He with his wisdom inspires all-comprehensive speech in man. Holy Soma enters the speech of the wise (*pavitravantaḥ parivācam āsata*). He is described as the source or father of the hymns. He is pleased with devotion and prayer, and flows with the speed of intellect. He is heavenly or divine light (*divyā suparṇa*) and flows as the chief or leader of speech and hymns (*agre vācaḥ agriyā goṣu gacchati*).[169] He prepares the path for the creation of a new hymn, and makes

164. 9.86.31.

165. 9.69.1.

166. 9.97.37.

167. 9.25.6; 9.50.4.

168. 9.50.4.

169. 9.86.12.

possible the attainment of that which is difficult to attain, that is creativity for composing a new hymn. The hymns rising like waves in a river long for Soma with reverence, and he also longs for them (*somam yanti matayaḥ vāvasānā*).[170] He reveals the thought or knowledge of Brahma that sustains *ṛta*. He is prayed to inspire a hymn as worthy as that of Ṛṣi Jamadāgni, or make the hymns worthy of a seer's recognition. By inspiring speech, and generating the hymns that are acceptable and pleasing to the deities, Soma is the best offering to them. Thus Soma is the essence of worship as well as the means of worship (*ātmā yajñasya; yajña sādhana*). Divine Soma, who is born in man as divine light or inspiration, the source of wisdom of the Vedic seers, is expressed by means of hymns which clarify him, articulate him. The hymns are an expression in language of the wisdom born of divine inspiration. They embody the splendour of truth, and are illumined by it. They express the truth as revealed to the seers under the divine influence of Soma. Truth is revealed to man when he is inspired by it. Thus what is received as a gift from the divine is offered back to the divine, and thereby man's existence is supremely fulfilled. He is liberated from the bonds of sin caused by his unawareness of the divine, and following the path of *ṛta* he attains immortality and bliss. In a word man is born a *kavi* or *ṛṣi*, and Soma accomplishes all this for man as divine light and inspiration.

The Veda, or the hymns constituting the Veda is an expression in human language of the divine speech or wisdom revealed to the seers during the moments of divine inspiration. They embody the light and wisdom of the divine as experienced by the seers. They also express the devotion of the seers experienced in response to their awareness of the divine. Now, the Vedic terms like *kratu*, *ṛta* and *dhīti* mean both wisdom and its expression either through religious acts of worship or through hymns. Similarly, the term *brahma* means both devotion and its expression in prayer. Likewise the term *kratu* means both wisdom

170. 9.97.34.

and all the acts that manifest it, especially *yajña*. *Ṛtam* as the dynamic side of the divine is truth itself as well as its manifestation in the universe either as cosmic order, or as moral order in man. It also means *yajña* which represents symbolically the process of the divine self-manifestation. It is also the supreme form of man's worship of the divine. To worship the divine is to participate in the divine process of creation and sustenance of the world. Likewise the terms *dhiyā*, *dhīti* and *mati* can mean either intellect or mind of man or their creation, the hymns. Thus the above Vedic terms are employed to convey the nature or essence of the divine, as well as the diverse forms of its manifestation in nature. When they are used substantively they refer to the divine, and when they are used adjectively they refer to the divineness of something, or indicate the presence of the divine either within man or in nature. According to the vision of the Vedic seers, the divine in itself is not an object of man's knowledge. It is known to man through its manifestations. And as nature is a self-manifestation of the divine it is a source of divine revelation to man. It is divine because of its capacity to inspire man divinely. Thus the phenomenal and the divine are experienced together and are, therefore, presented together in all the hymns of the *Ṛgveda*. The phenomenal reality reveals the divine, and the divine is not known independently of the phenomenal reality. How to express and communicate such a vision is a problem, and the apparent ambiguities in the usage of Vedic language are due to the nature of the vision of the Vedic seers. Thus every hymn describes the divine as revealed in and through nature. Therefore, the hymns can be interpreted naturalistically, but in doing so the wisdom of the Vedic seers which they convey is not grasped. Similarly, to interpret the hymns mystically or spiritually is to miss the nature of the divine which is not experienced by the Vedic seers independently of nature. Thus all the terms used to describe the divine refer to it in its dynamic aspect, or as it is revealed in and through its various manifestations. The divine as experienced by the Vedic seers is not an entity but a presence, and as presence it is everywhere, and unites all. To a divinely inspired seer nature is the abode of the deities, and hence a source of divine inspiration.

The Vedic hymns are not adequate to express the divinely inspired wisdom of the seers. As expressed in the *Ṛgveda*, and also in the later tradition, the hymns cannot reveal the nature of the divine to those who are not able to see through the words of the hymns the truth that is symbolically presented through them. They are helpless to convey their true sense to those who are lost in the words, and cannot grasp the truth expressed through them. It is due to the limitations of the language, as it is ordinarily used, that the deeper thoughts and vision of the Vedic seers cannot be communicated in a straightforward manner with its aid. Hence most of the time the Vedic seers resort to symbolic use of language. "Let not the power of men restrain the voice of the outpouring Soma."[171] Soma which flows spontaneously and playfully cannot be measured or determined by the hymns (*vṛdhā krīlantam mimate na gāvaḥ*).[172]

Although we intend to discuss the symbolic meaning of the terms *go* and *dhenu* in the next chapter, we present here the relationship between *go* or *dhenu* and Soma. In the passage just quoted above, the term *gāvaḥ* is used as a symbol for hymns or speech which cannot measure or determine the nature of divine inspiration, and express it adequately. In the *Ṛgveda*, the epithets *govinda* and *gopati* are commonly applied to several deities. In the post-Vedic Hindu tradition God is addressed as ê"Govinda" and "Gopati". Apart from *Nighaṇṭu*, according to which the words *go* and *dhenu* are synonyms of speech or hymns, these words reveal the same if we follow their usage in the *Ṛgveda*. Śaṅkara in his commentary on the *Viṣṇu Sahasranāma* explains the meaning of these epithets similarly. According to him, the words *go* and *dhenu* mean sacred knowledge or speech.[173] In several contexts

171. 9.101.13.

172. 9.97.9.

173. *Viṣṇu Sahasranāma* verses 33 and 71 and Śaṅkara's commentary thereon.

of their usage in the *Ṛgveda* these words can only mean sacred speech or hymns. As we are going to discuss the meaning of these terms, or their symbolic significance in the next chapter we do not enter into details here. For instance, the expression, "hath he (*Soma*) not purified and impregnated the cows who long to meet their lord, the cows who yield shining milk", will have no meaning in its direct sense, but reveals its meaning when the word *go* is taken to mean speech or hymns. Soma as bull impregnates with his divine seed the speech that sheds the shining essence of the divine. In another expression, *tam gāvaḥ abhyanuṣat sahasradhāram akṣitam indum dhartāram ādivaḥ*, it is said that cows (*gāvaḥ*) praise Soma.[174] They sing with joy to him even as a woman to her love. The cows (*dhenavaḥ*) adorn the new born child Soma. The cows (*dhenavaḥ*) run to Soma (*tubhyam dhāvanti dhenavaḥ*).[175] *Gāvaḥ* and *matyaḥ* go to Soma or approach him unitedly who is repeatedly born in the place of *ṛta* (*gāvaḥ matyaḥ yanti samyataḥ*).[176] *Soma* flows to the forms of cows (*dhāma gonām*). Generating divine light (Sūrya) and fulfiled by hymns (*apinvaḥ arkaiḥ*) or by devotion, *gāvaḥ* and *dhenavaḥ* desire Soma.[177] Soma flows along with *gonām*. He makes *gāḥ* as his robe or form. He knows and unfolds the secret names or forms of *gonām*. He comes to the hidden place of cows generated by the praises of the singers. He lives amidst *gāḥ* and *āpaḥ*. He discloses for the seers the place of "cows", and his inspiration is milked by those who desire *go* (*go iṣaḥ duhanti*).[178] He is prayed to inspire intelligence to seek *go*. He is enveloped by *go* (*gobhiḥ āvṛtam*), and is their discoverer and lord. He stands as a hero among the "cows". He goes round the group or heap of *go* and makes *gāḥ* as his robe (*gāḥ kṛṇvānaḥ nirnijam kaviḥ*).[179] These are some of the expressions

174. 9.26.2; 9.52.5; 9.80.2.

175. 9.66.6.

176. 9.72.6.

177. 9.97.31, 34 and 35.0

178. 10.76.7.

179. 9.107.26; 9.65.1; see also 9.104.4; 9.105.4.

in which Soma is described as closely related to *go* and *dhenu*, and as these terms are used symbolically for Vedic speech or hymns, their association with Soma is meaningful. Soma is also associated actively with the destruction of Vṛtra, and the resultant recovery or attainment of "cows". Thus Soma as divine inspiration is the source of Vedic wisdom. As inspiration of the poet-seers Soma flows through the hymns, or is expressed through them. Hence the supreme importance attached to the deity Soma in the *Ṛgveda*. And the hymns addressed to him in the whole of ninth *maṇḍala* of the *Ṛgveda* are known as purifying or sanctifying (*pavamāni*) hymns, and the Veda describes itself as a collection of wisdom (hymns) born of divine inspiration or Soma.[180]

180. 9.67.31 and 32.

7

Vṛtra

In this chapter we continue and conclude our discussion on the nature and meaning of divine inspiration, the source of Vedic wisdom. The object of this chapter is to present and interpret some of the important symbols associated with divine inspiration, and its expression. We begin with the myth of Vṛtra which runs throughout the *Ṛgveda*, and try to understand its significance in relation to the birth of divine in man. The destruction of Vṛtra and his allies is a theme which is central to the *Ṛgveda*, and all the deities aided by the Aṅgirasa seers fight and destroy Vṛtra and his allies to restore the precious things like light (*svaḥ*), "waters" (*āpaḥ*) and "cows" (*go* or *dhenu*) to the seers and mankind. The chief components of the myth are Vṛtra and his allies, the light that is enveloped by them, the "waters" whose flow they obstruct, and the "cows" which are concealed by them. These are the chief gifts of the deities to the seers. The seer-poets of the *Ṛgveda* pray for their attainment, or seek them as the chief gifts from the deities.

Several attempts have been made to interpret the Vṛtra myth, and almost all the interpreters have tried to understand its significance in terms of natural phenomenon. We are not going to consider and criticise those interpretations here. They will lose their validity and significance if our interpretation can throw light on the true significance of the myth. The interpretation attempted here is in tune with the general approach and method of interpretation followed in the various chapters. The soundness and validity of an interpretation depend more upon the thorough consultation of the facts interpreted, or a comprehensive view taken of them. The main purpose of our interpretation of the Vṛtra myth is to understand its significance in relation to the basic vision of the *Ṛgveda*, as well as to relate and reconcile the naturalistic and divine elements involved in it. Thus the problem is how to comprehend and reconcile all the elements involved in the story of the Vṛtra, and relate it to the total vision of the *Ṛgveda*. As the myth is central to the *Ṛgveda* its interpretation can help us in comprehending the central philosophy of the *Ṛgveda*. Before we set out to interpret the myth in its wholeness we propose to understand the meaning of the individual components involved in it.

Vṛtra and his allies Ahi, Paṇi, Vala, Namuci and Śambara are the forces that envelop and conceal light (*svaḥ*), obstruct the flow of "waters" (*āpaḥ*) and conceal the "cows" (*go* or *dhenu*), and with the destruction of Vṛtra and his allies light, "waters" and "cows" are restored to the seers, or are attained by them. These evil and dark forces are destroyed by the deities, either individually or collectively, and even the seers with the active help of the deities destroy them. And with the destruction of Vṛtra and his allies darknes is dispelled, and light or the sun is attained by the seers, the obstruction to the flow of "waters" is removed so that they flow into or from *samudra* (ocean) their goal, and the "cows" that are hidden by them are recovered or attained by the seers. Thus Vṛtra and his allies envelop the light, obstruct the flow of waters and conceal the cows, and the seers pray for the divine help in recovering or attaining them. In most of the hymns of the *Ṛgveda* the deities are either prayed for accom-plishing all these, or are praised in grateful acknowledge-ment for accomplishing them. The prayers are seen as effect-ive in encouraging and impelling the deities to destroy Vṛtra and his allies. They inspire the deities, and give them strength and vigour to destroy Vṛtra and his allies. The act of destroying Vṛtra is seen in the *Ṛgveda* as the major achievement of the deities, and the seers commonly pray for the recovery or attainment of light, waters and cows. The seers attach supreme value to their attainment, or to attain them is the highest aspiration of the seers. Therefore, a proper interpretation of the Vṛtra-myth can shed light on the meaning of the *Ṛgveda*. As the recovery or attainment of light, waters and cows is regarded as supreme by the seers, the destruction of Vṛtra and his allies, who stand in the way of their attainment, is given highest importance in the *Ṛgveda*. As we shall soon see the terms *svaḥ*, *āpaḥ* and *go* or *dhenu* refer to different facets of the same phenomenon, and Vṛtra and his allies are the manifestations of the same power. As the supreme purpose of human existence, as conceived in the *Ṛgveda*, is to attain divine wisdom or to be divinely inspired, or to be a *ṛṣi* or a *kavi*, any power that frustrates its attainment is seen as the greatest enemy of mankind and its elimination is sought wholeheartedly.

Vṛtra and his allies represent the same undivine power in its different manifestations, and conceal from man's vision what he ultimately longs for. Just as the deities, representing the various manifestations of the divine are given to man's experience, so also are Vṛtra and his allies. As the chief of the dark and undivine forces, Vṛtra by his very nature, or by the very definition of the term *vṛtra* is one who encompasses or envelops. He represents a growing phenomenon (*praviddha*), and manifests himself in various ways and forms, or assumes several forms. His existence is not historical, so that once destroyed he ceases to be for ever. He is ever growing and is, therefore, to be destroyed repeatedly by every man or generation. He increases himself and manifests himself in various forms (*puru varpāṁśī*). He has no fixed form, but represents a recurring phenomenon which is to be overcome by all. Although he represents a single phenomenon, through his manifestations he becomes many. The expressions like *daśa sahasrāṇi vṛtrāni* and *viśvavṛtrā* refer to his presence everywhere. By his *māyā* power he is present everywhere, and envelops all. Although he is described as abiding within *samudra* (ocean) and in waters (*āpaḥ*), or at the root or foundation of waters, he has no localised existence. He is present in heaven, as well as on earth. He torments or oppresses both the worlds, and Indra is prayed to destroy him from both the worlds. And with the destruction of Vṛtra all the three regions of the world become a safe abode for man. In a significant expression, Vṛtra is described as having no determinable or fixed form of existence (*atiṣṭhantīnām*) and fixed support or abode (*aniveśanānām*).[1] He is measureless and ever growing. He manifests himself in various forms, and the deities destroy him from all the corners of the world. Representing undivine or evil wisdom (*adevīmāyā* or *asura māyā*), he envelops the whole world, and is present everywhere (*sa imān lokān āvṛnot*).[2] Therefore, to overcome Vṛtra is to overcome undivine wisdom or power. We will soon explain this in detail when we discuss Ahi and Paṇi, the manifestations of Vṛtra. The Ṛgvedic comparison of Vṛtra with *aurṇavabham*, which according to Sāyaṇa means a spider, is significant in this connection. Like a spider Vṛtra weaves his web of delusion everywhere, and ensnares people. This must be the meaning of the expression *aurṇavabham* as in continuation Indra is prayed to destroy Vṛtra, and reveal or disclose the light to the wise (*apāvṛnu jyoti āryāya*).[3]

Vṛtra who envelops or covers (*vṛtram*) the divine waters (*āpaḥ*) resides or sleeps amidst them. He is also described as covering the rivers (*nadīvṛtam*); he envelops them from all sides. Ahi who is identified with Vṛtra is also described as staying in waters, and enveloping them. He remains concealed within waters.

Vṛtra is described as dwelling within darkness, and is even identified with darkness. To be enveloped by Vṛtra is to be enveloped by darkness. The "waters" that are enveloped by Vṛtra are enveloped by darkness (*tamasā parivṛtam*). Vṛtra, the enemy of Indra sleeps within darkness; and with his death the darkness is destroyed.[4] Paṇis also dwells in darkness. Now if we keep in view the other characteristics of Vṛtra, such as that he is the

1. 1.32.10.
2. 1.52.6. Sāyaṇa's commentary thereon.
3. 2.11.18.
4. 10.113.7.

source of undivine wisdom or knowledge and that he himself is undivine, the meaning of the darkness represented by Vṛtra as some undivine or unspiritual force or power becomes clear. This is also evident from the fact that in the destruction of Vṛtra the deities are inspired and helped by prayer and divine speech. Vṛtra is characterised as growing in his undivine *māyā* (*adevasya śūśuvānasya māyā*).[5] Vṛtra and his allies are described as the progeny of Bṛṣa, who, according to Sāyaṇa, is the creation of Tvastha, and that shows the common source of their origin (*prajām viśvasya bṛṣasya māyinaḥ*).[6]

Māyā which in the context of the *Ṛgveda* means either wisdom or power, is auspicious, creative and divine in relation to the deities; whereas it becomes oppressive, inauspicious or evil (*aśivam*) and undivine when it is employed by undivine forces or beings. In this sense *māyā* is possessed by human beings also, and manifests itself when they use their intelligence and other powers for evil purposes. "No mortal foe can ever prevail by *māyā* against him who worships (Agni) well."[7] It also refers to unillumined state of human understanding and speech (*adhenvā carati māyayā eṣaḥ vācam śuśruvān aphalam apuṣpam*).[8] Like a thin veil of mist it clouds human understanding so that man cannot see and hear truly though seeing and hearing.[9] And the prayers of the seers that the evil forces like Vṛtra should not rule over them indicate that Vṛtra represents an undivine force or power which is to be avoided and conquered. Vṛtra and his allies are seen as the enemies of mankind. They are unfriendly to man, and are of sinful nature (*vṛjinaḥ*).[10] The seers pray for the help of the deities to overcome or conquer Vṛtra, so that they can cross

5. 10.111.6.
6. 5.51.3.
7. 8.23.15.
8. 10.71.5.
9. 10.32.7.
10. 1.117.3; 3.34.6; 6.17.1; 2.11.10; 10.83.3. Vṛtra is identified as sin in *Śatapatha Brāhmaṇa*.

over all kinds of evil (*vṛtra hatyeṣu codaya viśvā tarema dūritāni*).[11] In another significant expression Paṇi is described as having his sway over human intellect, so that it cannot rise higher and higher to apprehend the divine.[12] And with his destruction the mind of man can soar high or rise upwards (*medhā ūrdhā bhavanti*).[13] In another expression the term *paṇi* is used to qualify the mind or understanding of man. The seers seek the destruction of evil or undivine wisdom in themselves (*paṇeḥ manīṣām*), which according to Sāyaṇa means evil mind or intellect (*āsurī buddhi*).[14]

The evil power which Vṛtra and his allies represent, prevents the seers from attaining precious things which they seek for the fulfilment of their understanding and existence. The Vṛtra power is described as inauspicious (*aśiva*), undivine (*adevī*), unilluminating (*guhyam* or *aprakāśyam*), sinful and dark.[15] It causes hatred for the divine or the deities (*devanīdaḥ*). It is unholy or opposed to devotion (*abrahma*), and hater of *āpaḥ* (*apadviṣa*). The Paṇis are described as unwise (*akratūn*) or are opposed to sacrifice. Vṛtra is one who offers food into his own mouth instead of offering it to the deities, and then partaking of it.[16] He is described as *gradhinaḥ* or tall talker, or whose speech has no foundation in truth.[17] He is *mṛdhravācaḥ* or one who hurts others by his speech, or unclear in his thoughts, or one who cannot see clearly.[18] Such men are faithless, and are without worship (*yajña*). They will not allow the promotion of divine life or its increase. They oppose the divine laws of Varuṇa. All these are the various forms of manifestation of undivine *māyā*, and all those in whom it manifests itself are the enemies of mankind. Thus Vṛtra — the

11. 7.33.15.
12. 3.58.2.
13. 3.58.2.
14. 3.58.2.
15. 7.1.10; 2.11.5.
16. 1.51.5; see also *Śatapatha Brāhmaṇa*.
17. 7.6.3.
18. 7.6.3.

word *vṛtra* also means an enemy — in whatever form he may manifest himself is the enemy of mankind. The enemity of Vṛtra is primarily at the spiritual level, for he is pre-eminently the enemy of the seers. The enemies of the Ṛgvedic seers are termed as *avratāḥ* or those who do not follow or observe divine laws. They are the haters of the deities. While Indra destroys Vṛtra and his allies, Varuṇa protects those who follow divine laws. Even if we take the terms *paṇi* and *dasyu* as referring to people who are opposed to Vedic way of life and religion, they are not necessarily people belonging to another race or nation, for the *avratāḥ* and *dasyu*s can be from among the Āryan people. *Dasyu*s are primarily those who are devoid of devotion (*abrahma dasyu*), or who are opposed to devotion and spiritual way of life.[19] Vṛtra can manifest himself either in one's own kinsmen or in others (*jāmi* and *ajāmi*) or among the Āryan and non-Āryan people. There are two kinds of *vṛtra*s or enemies (*ubhayāni vṛtrāni*). Therefore, the term *vṛtra* need not necessarily mean, in the context of the *Ṛgveda*, a racial or national enmity, or enmity based on religious beliefs and practices. Vṛtra and his allies essentially represent a power that manifests and grows itself either in nature or in man. So when certain people either belonging to one's own tribe or to another show the manifestations of undivine wisdom (*asura māyā*) they are known or termed as *vṛtra* or *dasyu*. They are primarily the enemies of the seers, and prevent man from growing spiritually. This becomes clear when we discuss the role of these forces in obstructing the flow of *āpaḥ* (waters) and in concealing *go* or *dhenu* (cows). One more significant point to note in this connection is that Vṛtra as spiritual darkness or undivine wisdom not only manifests and grows in nature and in man, but his manifestation allows degrees. This is indicated by the expression *vṛtrataram* or *vṛtratanam* (more or most *vṛtra* nature).

Vṛtra representing dark or evil power or wisdom resides within the hearts of men also. As undivine disposition of human heart or mind (*paṇeḥ manīṣā*) Vṛtra is unsatiable or unfulfilling

19. 4.16.9; 3.30.17.

(*asinvam*), and at the same time sweet (*madhu*).[20] It makes man indulge in pleasures, for in one expression Vṛtra is stated to dwell in *katpayam* or pleasure-seeking nature of man. He resides in pleasure-seeking nature of man (*katpayam śayānam*), and grows amidst undivine darkness (*asūryā tāmasī vavrīdhānam*).[21] Thus Vṛtra refers to pleasure-seeking undivine or unillumined nature of man which is opposed to divine and, therefore, the seers see in the destruction of Vṛtra the removal of the inner darkness that envelops their hearts (*hṛdā varadā tāmaṁsī*).[22] Ahi is described as residing within the hearts of men unmanifested and concealed (*guhā hitam guhyam gulham*). The powers represented by Vṛtra and his allies are seen as obstructing man's path to the divine (*ohānam*).[23] They obstruct man's search for truth or the divine, its revelation to man.

In the act of killing Vṛtra all the deities participate, though Indra is given the major credit. It is Indra who is mostly praised for the act of killing Vṛtra. However, the epithet *vṛtraghna* (Vṛtra killer) is not exclusive to Indra. Indra representing the inner spiritual strength of man is mostly responsible for overcoming Vṛtra who envelops man's intellect and vision. Agni is also addressed as ruling over all those who kill Vṛtra (*īśe vṛtra hadhānām*). He is also praised as the best of Vṛtra slayers (*vṛtra hantamam*) which epithet is equally applied to Indra and Soma. Agni destroys many a Vṛtra. Brahmaṇaspati mainly aids other deities in destroying Vṛtra, though he is also described as the slayer of Vṛtra. The epithet *vṛtra khādam* (devourer of Vṛtra) is applied to Brahmaṇaspati besides to Indra. Even Sarasvatī, the deity of divine wisdom and speech, is also involved in the destruction of Vṛtra. She is described as *vṛtrāghni*. The seers also participate in the act of destroying Vṛtra, and they are helped in that by their sacred speech or prayer, and their truthfulness.

20. 5.32.8.
21. 5.32.6.
22. 5.31.9.
23. 5.30.6.

They also inspire and strengthen the deities by their prayers to destroy Vṛtra. They furnish through their prayers Indra with power to kill Vṛtra. The seers also destroy Vṛtra aided by the deities. "Allied with Indra let us overcome Vṛtra (*indrena yujā taruṣema vṛtram*)."[24] "With your aid may we overcome both types of Vṛtra."[25] Indra is prayed to inspire the seers for killing Vṛtra (*vṛtra hatyeṣu codaya*) "For us make Vṛtra easy to be conquered."[26] Allied with Indra in friendship and following *ṛta* (*ṛtaṁ manvānaḥ*) or with the light of *ṛta* (*ṛta dītibhiḥ*), the seers wish to conquer Vṛtra. Seeking to win *go* the seers who are full of *ṛta* conquer Vṛtras. In the story of Saramā recovering "cows" from the Paṇis, it is said that Saramā is able to discover and win cows from the Paṇis not by means of its own power and strength but with the help of divine power and *ṛta* (*daivyena sahasā*).[27] Likewise Indra could conquer Vala and Paṇis, and win "cows" for the seers because of divine speech. Aśvins could recognise Vṛtra because of Soma. While being extolled for the act of killing Vṛtra, Indra is described as *sambhṛtam krato* or collected wisdom of the seers.[28] The rivers (*sindhu*) created by Viṣṇu flow to inspire Indra for killing Vṛtra. Agni kills Vṛtras with the aid of Brahmaṇaspati, the lord of devotion or prayer and sacred speech. The seers hope to become wise or attain wisdom by overcoming Vṛtra (*ghnanta vṛtrāni sūribhiḥ syāma*).[29] In a significant expression Indra is prayed to uncover Vṛtra (*indra vṛtram āvṛṇot*).[30] And the various terms employed to indicate the destruction of Vṛtra do not always mean the simple act of killing a physical enemy. They are: to devour, to kill, to overcome, to uncover, to make Vṛtra ineffective by making him to sleep or to lie quietly and to crush or tear him to pieces.

---

24. 7.48.2.
25. 6.19.13; see also 6.33.3.
26. 4.22.9.
27. 10.108.9.
28. 1.52.8.
29. 7.92.4.
30. 3.34.3.

The Ṛgvedic seers seek to recover or obtain three important and precious things as a result of Vṛtra's destruction. They are: winning of light, release or liberation of "waters" and recovery or attainment of "cows". Besides making the world a wise and happy place for man to live without fear, and dispelling the darkness from within the hearts of men, the seers seek to attain with the destruction of Vṛtra divine light. The seers pray that the light which remains covered because of Vṛtra be disclosed to them (*jyotiṣi kṛnu āvṛkāni* or *apāṛṇu jyoti āryāya*).[31] And with the winning of light Paṇis disappear, and the Sun or divine light is made to appear (*divi sūryam dṛśe*), or is won by the seers (*jaya svariti svaḥ*).[32] The Sun and the Dawn are generated with the destruction of Vṛtra (*ata sūryam janyan dhyām uṣasam*), and according to *Nighaṇṭu* the term "Sūrya" is a synonym of divine speech of wisdom.

The second precious thing that is sought to be won with the destruction of Vṛtra is the release of *āpaḥ* or *apaḥ* of *sindhu* (river). Vṛtra and Ahi stay in the "waters" or at their base, envelop them, and obstruct their flow; and with their destruction the flow of "waters" is restored, or the doors of *āpaḥ* are opened. After the death of Vṛtra the "waters" are impelled to flow to *samudra* (ocean) (*syandamānāḥ añjaḥ samudram avajagmu āpaḥ*).[33] The waters are impelled or inspired to flow to *samudra* (*āpaḥ samarya codayan; pra arṇāṁśī erayatam nadīnam*).[34] Then waters run with vigour, and Sarasvatī creates them or makes them spring up (*arṣantu āpaḥ javasā; sarasvatī āpaḥ sṛjat*).[35] In certain other expressions it is said that *āpaḥ* and *nadī* are created with the destruction of Vṛtra and his allies (*mānave viśvacandraḥ āpaḥ cakāra*). All blissful and well moving waters are made to flow with the destruction of Vṛtra (*sruja sindhūn saran āpaḥ; sṛjan samudrīya āpaḥ; āpaḥ asṛian anu vṛtra tūrye;*

31. 2.11.8; 1.55.6.
32. 8.89.4; 1.52.8.
33. 1.32.2.
34. 1.80.5; 6.82.3.
35. 8.89.4.

asṛja āpaḥ accha samudram).[36] By killing Ahi, Indra inspires the flow of seven rivers (*sapta sindhūn*), or unfolds them (*arināt sapta sindhūn apāvṛṇot*).[37] Vṛtra who dwells in the rivers is destroyed so as to allow them to flow. We shall explain the symbolic meaning of the terms *āpaḥ*, *samudra* and *nadī* or *sindhu* later. Meanwhile, it is interesting to note here that not only the flow of waters is restored with the destruction of Vṛtra, but they are even created as a result of Vṛtra's destruction.

The third and most commonly accomplished object with the destruction of Vṛtra is the recovery or attainment of *go* or *dhenu* (cows) by the seers. As we shall soon discuss, the recovery or winning of "cows" is regarded by the seers as the most precious gift from the deities. Finally, with the destruction of Vṛtra and his allies the path leading to the deities is made straight, and man is freed from the reign of evil. The deities are born or they manifest themselves in great *ṛta* (*mahā ṛte utajāyanta devāḥ*) when Vṛtra is destroyed by Indra.[38]

One of the important objectives accomplished with the destruction of Vṛtra and his allies, and for which the deities are constantly prayed for is the release of *āpaḥ* (waters). And at the same time, with the restoration of their flow the waters help in the destruction of Vṛtra. They are employed for the destruction of Vṛtra. Sindhu (stream) created by Viṣṇu flows for the inspiring Indra to destroy Vṛtra. In several other expressions it is stated that the "waters" which are enveloped by Vṛtra or darkness are released to flow with his death, and they in their turn participate in the act of killing Vṛtra. They flow with strength and vigour and kill Vṛtra to win light. The released or liberated "waters" flow either towards *samudra*, their end, or from *samudra* their source.

The use of the term *āpaḥ* or *apaḥ* is symbolic in several contexts of the *Ṛgveda*. Its symbolic meaning is evident from its usage in

---

36. 3.36.8; 8.76.3; 10.66.8.

37. 2.12.3.

38. 10.55.7.

close relation to the deity Sarasvatī, and *go* or *dhenu*. Therefore, to understand and appreciate its symbolic value we should understand its meaning in relation to Sarasvatī and *go* (cows). The meanings of these symbols are interrelated and to understand and appreciate the meaning of one we have to understand meanings of the other two symbols. While the symbolic character of the terms *go* and *dhenu* is transparent and clear, it is not so with regard to the term *āpaḥ*. However, as these two things are accomplished simultaneously with the destruction of Vṛtra, the meaning of each is related to the other. They symbolically represent two distinct but related aspects of the same phenomenon.

In the *Ṛgveda*, the term *āpaḥ, arṇaḥ, sindhu* and *nadī* are closely related to Sarasvatī, the deity of divine speech or wisdom, and in several contexts of the *Ṛgveda* they are employed synonymously. The term "Sarasvatī" means both a river, or the source of all rivers (*sindhumātā*), and the deity representing divine speech. Similarly, the term *akṣara*, literally what is imperishable, and *saraḥ* (flowing) can mean either waters or speech. Sarasvatī, who is described as *mahā arṇaḥ* (great ocean) is described as closely related to *āpaḥ* in the famous hymn of the first *maṇḍala* of the *Ṛgveda* (1.164). These two symbols or images are interrelated, and Sarasvatī is characterised as *apasām āpaḥ tamā*, or best among waters, which Sāyaṇa explains to mean best of action or full of action. In another expression She is described as *ambitama* which can mean either the best of waters or the best of mothers. The relationship between waters (*āpaḥ*) and speech (*vāk*), which is clearly indicated in various hymns of the *Ṛgveda* will also help us in knowing the symbolic value of the term *āpaḥ*, which plainly means water. The creative speech has the characteristic of flow, and on several occasions, divine inspiration which flows spontaneously, and is expressed through hymns is likened to the flow of waters. The spontaneous flow of inspired speech is like the self-impelled flow of waters. Thus the characteristic common to both waters and inspired or divine speech is spontaniety or self-impulsion (*sara*). As waters flow self-impelled or moved, so also divine inspiration which swells within the hearts of the poet-seers flow spontaneously in the form of Vedic hymns. The quality of self-impelled flow of waters or rivers has attracted the attention of the Vedic seers in describing symbolically, and at times even figuratively, the reality of divine inspiration and its spontaneous outflow in the form of hymns. Because of the striking similarity between the two, the flow of waters is taken as a symbol to describe the flow of divine inspiration. And what is intended as a symbol has at times become a means of expressing the reality of the flow of divine inspiration. In the post-Saṁhitā literature, especially in the Brāhmaṇas, the term *akṣara* which means both water and speech, is used to mean a reality which remains the same or retains its identity in and through its various forms of manifestation. Similarly, the term *saraḥ* which means either water or speech, and the term Sarasvatī (having flow as its characteristic) which also means either a river or divine speech, are used to describe a reality which is known for its spontaneous manifestation and expression. This characteristic similarity between the two realities, and for which reason the same term is employed to mean both is exemplified in the image of "Saramā"; and Saramā plays an important role in recovering "cows" from the Paṇis. Moreover, the Vedic seers have consciously employed the metaphor of flow of waters to describe divine inspiration, and its flow in the form of hymns. As we shall soon see the symbolic usage of the words *go* and *dhenu* also involves the same process.

A hymn is expressed or flows out like the flow of waters (*āpaḥ na pravate*). The hymns are created (*sṛja*) in the sense that they swell within the heart spontaneously. The word *sṛja* means spontaneous outflow or expression. Divine inspiration seeks expression as spontaneously as water seeks depth (*apām it ūrmayaḥ tarturāṇāḥ pramanīṣā īrate soma accha; pravi vipadvacā ūrmi na sindhuḥ giraḥ soma pavamāna manīṣā*).[39] Truthful speech sportively or spontaneously flows like waters (*āpaḥ na pravatāyati*). The hymns

39. 9.96.7.

flow forth like waters from a spring (*sargāḥ iva sṛjatam sustutiḥ*).[40] In a slightly altered form of metaphor, the prayers and praises to Indra are described as surging forth like joyous wave of water (*apām ūrmiḥ madan iva*). Likewise the seven Vedic metres are described symbolically as *sapta svasāraḥ* (seven self-flowing). Further, it is the primary characteristic of divine inspiration, which swells within the hearts of the seers, its seat, to flow out without any effort seeking expression in the form of hymns. And in the process it soaks or floods the entire person with its sweet delight. The words *sikta* or *siñca* are used in this sense within the *Ṛgveda*. Just as the waters drench as they flow, the flow of divine inspiration floods or soaks the inner being of man with divine light and joy. The flow of divine inspiration is pervasive in its influence, and informs the whole being of man before it finds its expression in the form of hymns. This interpretation is clearly borne out by several expressions of the *Ṛgveda*.

Before presenting such direct expressions we discuss some of the important qualities attributed to waters (*āpaḥ*), and also their relation to *Soma*. The divine waters addressed as *devī* or *divya* are full of light (*tejiṣṭhaḥ* or *svavatī*).[41] They adorn the deities, or are the best means of pleasing them (*deva avyam*). They are the source of delight to the deities as well as to human beings (*deva mādanam*). They are full of delight (*viśvacandrā*) or are delightful to all. They shed joy and delight to all (*madhumantam* and *madhuśchutam*).[42] The great waters (*mahi āpaḥ*) are seen as source of fulfilment of man's life (*jīvadhanyā*), or because of which man's existence is blessed. As, according to *Nighaṇṭu*, the term *mahi* is a synonym of speech the expression *mahi āpaḥ* can mean flow or waters of speech. The expression *Marutvatī jīvadhanyā* is also significant. Sarasvatī is also described as *Marutvatī*. Thus the epithet *Marutvatī* in relation to waters, which are the source of blessedness to man, may mean the flow of divine inspiration

40. 8.35.20.
41. 9.70.2; 8.40.8.
42. 10.30.6. and 9.

seeking expression in Vedic speech. The waters which purify man lead him to perceive the great (*mahe raṇāya cakṣase*).[43] They enable man to apprehend the beautiful splendour of the divine. In another expression the waters are described as conscious (*vicetasaḥ āpaḥ*), and are caused by Indra to flow to or through *go* (hymns).[44] The conscious waters which dwell within man are, therefore, something other than ordinary water or mid-region as interpreted by Sāyaṇa. The expressions like *āpaḥ vaiśvānaraḥ* (waters within all men), *kṣiyanti carṣanīnām* (dwelling in men) and *mānuṣī āpaḥ* (waters that are of man) can have no other meaningful explanation.[45] They can only mean, though symbolically, the flow of divine inspiration within man.

Waters are intimately connected with Soma, the state of being divinely inspired or divine inspiration. Soma who is described as the lord and leader of waters (*apām perum; apām rājā; apām netā*) lives amidst waters. The flow of *Soma* is likened to birth of waves in a river (*sindhu*) which literally means flowing, and is even identified with such flow (*sindho iva ūrmiḥ pavamāna arṣasi*).[46] He is shed within waters (*apsu ā suta*). He is at times identified with waters, and is described as growing within them (*apsu drapsam vavṛdhānam samudre*). He is their vigour (*apsu dakṣa*). He grows in *samudra* as well as in the waves of rivers. Soma is also intimately associated with *samudra*, and is even identified with it. And the destruction of Vṛtra is meant to release the waters of *sumudra* (*samudrīya āpaḥ*) which flows from it, and also into it. Soma who enters into waters lives within them and flows with them making them as the means of his expression, or enrobes himself with them. Soma the seer is created within waters. He flows enrobing himself with waters, or unfolds himself as he flows with waters, and thereby becomes a *kavi* (*āpaḥ vṛṇāna pavate kavīyan*).[47] He is

43. 10.9.1.

44. 1.83.1.

45. 7.49.4; 10.9.5.

46. 9.80.5.

47. 9.94.1.

anointed with the *rasa* of waters (*sam añjate rūpam apām rasena*).[48] The expressions *apām rasaḥ* and *apsu drapsam* are significant in this context. *Rasa* can mean either the essence of waters, or the divinely inspired emotion or feeling, and *Soma* is anointed with it, and also flows along with it. He is described as quickening or sharpening and even inspiring waters which dwell within man (*hinvānaḥ mānuṣī āpaḥ; āpaḥ śiśāsan*).[49] He impels them to flow (*āpaḥ sarmya codaya*). Dwelling amidst waters and flowing along with them or through them, Soma seeks *go* (hymns) as the means of his expression. The repeated assertion that *Soma* who dwells within waters, makes them as his form, and finally seeks *go* or Vedic speech as the means of his expression is highly significant (*āpaḥ vasāna abhi gāḥ iyakṣati*). It is further stated that Soma shedding divine flows by means of waters, and inspires human intelligence to seek *go* (*vṛṣṭhim divaḥ pavasva rītim apām jinva go iṣṭaye dhiyaḥ*).[50] He finds joy and delight in waters which are most auspicious. Soma who is wise or discerning (*vipaścita*) leads waters along waves (of inspiration) (*pra somāsaḥ vipaścitā apām nayanti ūrmayaḥ*).[51] Moving along with the waves of waters, Soma reveals or declares or seeks the final or real form of *samudra* (*apām ūrmim sacamānāḥ samudram turīyam dhāma mahiṣaḥ vivakti*).[52] He dwells amidst waters which remain concealed within the cave of heart (*guhā hitam guhyam gulham apsu vibhrīmasi prasravaṇena somam*).[53] He is described as the child of *sapta svasāraḥ*, seven principal metres of the Veda. He is the upholder or sustainer of waters (*apām gandharvam*). *Soma* is impelled by man within waters, or at their foundation which is also the seat of *ṛta* (*apām upasthe adhi āyavaḥ kavim ṛtasya yonā mahiṣaḥ aheṣata*).[54] He swells within the waves of rivers (*apām ūrmau sindhuṣu*

48. 9.97.57.
49. 9.63.7; 6.73.3; 6.50.7.
50. 9.108.10.
51. 9.33.1.
52. 9.96.19.
53. 10.148.2.
54. 9.86.26.

antaḥ ukṣita). The self-flowing (*svasāra*) waters giving birth to or surging forth with hymns (*go*) increase them in the ocean (*go vavṛdhānam samudre*).[55] Soma is prayed to flow from the seat of waters for the attainment of desirable and delightful wealth. The assertion that *Soma* generates Sūrya among waters, and dwells within *go* and *āpaḥ*, viewed in the light of the above expressions may, therefore, mean generating divine light within creative "waters" of man, Soma dwells within the hymns. Or as Sūrya is a synonym of speech, Soma generates divine speech within human waters. In another hymn it is stated more clearly that Soma inspires speech within the waters of the sea (*tvam samudrīyaḥ āpaḥ agriya vācaḥ īrayan pavasva viśvam ejaya*).[56] The seers discover Soma who pervades the waters of light (*tejiṣṭha*), or who enwraps himself with them. Soma makes or generates great waters, within whose womb the deities are revealed (*mahat tat soma mahiṣaḥ cakāra apām yat garbhaḥ āvṛṇot devān*).[57] The above expressions are meant to show that *āpaḥ* are intimately connected with divine Soma, and are the means of his expression. And as divine Soma represents divine inspiration, *āpaḥ* should mean its flow within man seeking expression through hymns.

The object of the following discussion is to consider some of the important expressions in which the symbolic meaning of *āpaḥ* is more evident and clear. They show clearly the symbolic character of the term *āpaḥ*, and reveal its meaning as the flow of divine inspiration, seeking hymns as its expression.

Āpaḥ which are the birthplace of Agni, and in which he places his divine seed or essence, are described as dwelling within man or as belonging to man. Indra impels the flow of waters which are within man, or which belong to man (*mānuṣi āpaḥ*). Dwelling within man, the waters rule over the mansion (of human body) (*īśānaḥ harmyānam kṣayanti carṣinīnām āpaḥ*).[58] Just as Agni is known

55. 9.6.15.
56. 9.62.26.
57. 9.97.41.
58. 10.9.5.

vaiśvānara as he is present within all men, so also are the waters addressed as Vaiśvānara, for they also dwell in man.[59] The conscious waters caused by Indra flow out seeking hymns. In several hymns of the *Ṛgveda* it is stated that the delightful wave of waters swell within, and flow forth from *samudra*, and as already pointed out, *samudra* (ocean) is used in the *Ṛgveda* as a symbol for human heart. The waters that are released with the destruction of Vṛtra belong to *samudra*. Now, keeping in view the symbolic meaning of *samudra* we can understand the meaning of the following expression: From the sea sprang forth the delightful or sweet wave, and by that light may we attain immortality (*samudrāt ūrmiḥ madhumān udārata upa amsunā sam amṛtatva mānasuḥ*).[60] The delightful wave of sweetness is experienced within the ocean of heart, as well as in the face or expression of waters (*apām anīke tam asyāma madhumantam ūrmim*). In another significant expression it is stated that the stream (of waters) flow as *dhenāḥ* (hymns) purified within the hearts and minds of men (*samyak sravanti saritāḥ na dhenā antaḥ hṛdā manasā pūyamānaḥ*).[61] It is from within the hearts of the wise spring forth waters of varied forms (*asmāt samudrāt bṛhatī divaḥ naḥ apām bhūmanam upa naḥ sṛja iha*).[62] Waters are to be impelled to flow from the depths of ocean (*āpaḥ pra īrayam sagarasya bhudhnāt*).[63] The heart of man is the seat of waters, or waters reside within the heart of man (*apām idam nyayanam sakrudasya niveśanam*), and they are to be kindled within the homes (*apām samidhyase durena*). The waters are prayed to join the hearts of the seers (*sam āpaḥ hṛdyāni nau*).[64] In the place of waters, which is also the place of *ṛta*, the singers kindle Agni, the seer, variously or rightly (*apām upasthe adhi āyavaḥ kavim ṛtasya yonā mahiṣaḥ aheṣata*).[65]

59. 7.49.4.
60. 4.58.1.
61. 4.58.6.
62. 10.93.12.
63. 10.89.4.
64. 10.85.47.
65. 9.86.2.

The ever alert waters, the chief creation of *samudra*, flow out being purified. They are prayed to approach the seers like the operations of the mind. "Let the prayer go to the deities, and let waters come towards us as if or like the object or operations of mind (*manasā prayukti*).[66] It is further stated that devotion is the guide to those who seek the meaning or object of waters (*apām ardham yatīnām brahmo bhavati sāradhiḥ*).[67] Varuṇa who rules over waters — almost all the deities are regarded and described as rulers of waters — is described as moving amidst or within them which are shining and purifying, and are able to discern between the truthfulness and untruthfulness of people.[68] This passage can be interpreted in the light of our approach to mean that Varuṇa who presides over the moral consciousness of man moves within the inspired consciousness of man, the seat of moral values. The waters of divine inspiration as they swell and flow enable man not only to discern between truth and falsehood, but lead him to perceive the highest (*maheraṇāya cakṣase*).

Agni who is seen and described as the child of waters (*apām napāt*), grows within them and is sustained by their strength or essence. He is kindled within them without any fuel.[69] Agni is also worshipped by the wise for granting them delightful waters. Deriving his strength from the waters Agni bestows divine riches on man. Agni is here identified with divine speech as in the Brāhmaṇa literature.

We now consider and discuss those expressions in which the waters are related to divine speech or the Vedic hymns. In the hymns of the *Ṛgveda* the waters are described as closely related to all the deities, and especially to Agni, Soma and Sarasvatī. Our concern here is to understand the significance of the relationship between the waters and Sarasvatī. As pointed out earlier, Sarasvatī means both a river and the deity of speech.

66. 10.30.1.
67. 1.158.6.
68. 7.49.3.
69. 10.30.4.

Likewise the expression *sapta svasāraḥ* can mean either the seven metres of Vedic speech, or the seven self-flowing streams. Similarly *samudra* is a symbol for human heart within which the waves of waters swell, or from whose foundation waters are inspired to flow. Here is an expression which is significant and relevant in this context. One divine light has entered the ocean of heart, and experiences all that is there, or all that has become. People with mature understanding experience it within, and the sacred speech caresses it, and it touches or caresses the sacred speech (*ekaḥ suparṇa samudram āviveśa idam viśvam bhuvanam vicaṣṭhe; tam pākena manasā apaśyam antariti tam mātā redīḥ ū iti redīḥ mātaram*).[70] The seers see him (*pataṅga*), which here means the same as *suparṇa*, the divine light, in the ocean's inmost depth, and seek its splendour (*samudraḥ antaḥ kavayo vicakṣate marīcīnām padam ichanti vedhasaḥ*).[71] The divine light holds within itself divine speech or wisdom which is held by *gandharva* within his womb (*pataṅgo vācam bibharti tam gandharvo avadat garbhe antaḥ*).[72] And Soma is described as the *gandharva* of waters. The seers also speak of light which is pure, and full of divine speech or wisdom (*mahā jyotiṣā śucata goarṇāsa*). The divine light descends into or enters the ocean of heart, the seat of divine inspiration and the birthplace of divine wisdom.

Sarasvatī is described as *mahā arṇā*, the mighty or great ocean, who inspires all knowledge or wisdom (*pracetayati ketuna*), and shines everywhere with intelligence (*dhiyā*).[73] She is best or supreme among waters (*ambitama, naditama* and *devitama*) or (*apsām apattamā*). Sarasvatī, the mother of flowing waters (*sindhu mātā*), flows with the streams of wisdom (*asuryā nadīnām sarasvatīm*).[74] Here the term *asurya* means wisdom. Sarasvatī, most dear among dear things with seven self-flowing streams or metres, is well

70. 10.114.4.
71. 10.177.1.
72. 10.177.2.
73. 1.3.11 and 12.
74. 7.96.1.

pleasing to the seers, and deserves our worship (*uta naḥ priyā priyāsu sapta svasā sujuṣṭhā sarasvatī stomyā bhūt*).[75] Or Sarasvatī who is well pleased with seven metres deserves our worship and praise. In another hymn Sarasvatī is identified with waters, or the term *āpaḥ* and Sarasvatī are used synonymously, and the waters described as holding within themselves auspicious wisdom (*bhadram kratum*), and immortality. Describing Soma as the collected wisdom of the Vedic seers, it is said that Sarasvatī sheds or sends delightful waters (*madūdakam*) for those who study the sanctifying hymns of Soma contained in the ninth *maṇḍala* of the *Ṛgveda*.[76]

Savitā, the deity of inspiration and creativity, is prayed to grant the worshippers precious and most desirable wealth which is to be conveyed to them by means of rivers or streams. "May the rivers hasten to convey it to us."[77] In another hymn Savitā, whose form is indescribable (*vapuḥ nirvacanam*) is described as the one from whom the rivers flow, and in whom the waters abide (*caranti yat nadyaḥ tastu āpaḥ*).[78] Divine inspiration flows in streams from within the heart of man, or spring up there in waves. Even Indra is identified with a well or spring (*utsa*) of inspiration.

In a more direct expression, it is asserted that the waters of the sea are the abode of Vāk (speech) which influences by her streams all that is.[79] Speech is described as moving with or within waters. It seeks them, and is increased by them. The divine speech with the help of seven Vedic metres milks the delightful wave of waters (*madhvā ūrmi duhate sapta-vāṇī*). The hymns by means of which the seers seek the protection of the deities, and hope to overcome all sin are upheld within the waters by the deities (*dhiyam vaḥ apsu dadhiṣe*).[80] It is frequently stated in the

---

75. 6.61.10.
76. 9.67.32.
77. 5.49.4.
78. 5.47.5.
79. 5.48.1.
80. 5.45.11.

Ṛgveda that the divine wave of waters, or the waters seeking the divine long for the deities (*devayanti* or *devayantaḥ*), and are created by Ilā, a deity representing speech (*devayantaḥ āpaḥ indrapānam ūrmim ākṛṇvati ilā*).[81] The divine wave of waters which gives delight to Indra is pure and sinless, and sheds *ghṛta* (light), and it is sought to be enjoyed by the seers also. The libations offered to the deities are the waters of the sea in which people rejoice. In another hymn it is stated that Varuṇa is praised by *āpaḥ*, and here Sāyaṇa explains the meaning of the word *āpaḥ* significantly as flowing speech or prayer (*stutivāk*).[82] Divine speech (*anuṣṭhubham*) is described in another hymn as moving friendly within divine waters, and Indra is apprehended by the seers as moving along with or within speech (*apām divyānām sakhye carantam anuṣṭhubham anucarcūyamānam indram nicikyuḥ kavayaḥ maniṣā*).[83]

Divine speech as expressed through the Vedic hymns, and the self-flowing waters are described as related (*jāmaya*). The self-flowing waters give birth to the hymns (*svasāraḥ āpaḥ abhi gāḥ utsaran*).[84] Saramā, the divine speech, is also described as self-flowing (*svasāram*). Divine waters flow to make sacrifice (*yajña*) acceptable to the deities, or make it a fit means of divine worship. They also generate devotion or prayer within man (*hinota brahma*). The hymns which embody divine wisdom attain the waters by their words (*asya vavṛm vasāna udakam padā āpuḥ*). The hymn "*gaurī mimāya salilāni takṣat ekapadī* . . ." should then be explained to mean that expressed speech determines or measures the waters into *ekapadī* (one footed), etc., instead of taking the word *mimāya* to mean "to low", as the waters in a way measure or determine the divine speech as they flow.[85] In a collection of hymns addressed to waters (*āpaḥ*) their symbolic character and spiritual significance are clearly indicated, by relating them to the inner

81. 7.47.1.
82. 8.58.11.
83. 10.124.9.
84. 9.82.2.
85. 1.164.41.

life of man. The divine waters that seek prayer come like the operations of the mind. The divine waters and speech know each other, and are in harmony with each other (*sam jānate sam cikitrai adhvaryavaḥ dhīṣānaḥ ca āpaḥ devī*).[86] Waters and prayers (*āpaḥ* and *dhīṣāna*) together attain the friendly Agni. Divine waters and speech of the seers knowing each other (*sam vidānaḥ*) hold Soma for Indra.[87] The waters that are born of truth (*pradhamajā ṛtena*), and spread by truth hold within themselves the seed of Prajāpati. Prajāpati places his seed within waters in whom all the deities move together observing the world. As we are not so much concerned here with the metaphysical conception, or the ontological status of waters as with their symbolic meaning, we do not go into a metaphysical explanation of "waters".

The most significant thing achieved or won with the destruction of Vṛtra and his allies is the recovery or attainment of "cows" (*go* or *dhenu*). Although the winning of light and the release of waters are significant, the recovery or attainment of "cows" is regarded by the seers as the most important thing achieved with the destruction of Vṛtra and his allies. The whole process of destroying Vṛtra is seen as culminating in the recovery or attainment of cows, or the recovery of "cows" is what is ultimately sought by the seers with the destruction of Vṛtra. The flow of divine inspiration that is released with the destruction of inner darkness seeks creative expression, and in that lies the supreme fulfilment of the inspired life of a seer. A person becomes a *ṛṣi*, or a *kavi*, or a *vipra*, or a *manīṣī*, or a *dhīra*, the supreme end of man's existence, when he is divinely inspired, and is able to give creative expression to divine inspiration. And the Vedic hymns, as an expression in language of divine inspiration, constitute man's response to the divine revealed in the state of inspiration. The devotion, which is a divine gift to man, is also the means of man's worship of the divine. Without it no religious act, including *yajña*, is meaningful. The inspired

86. 10.30.6.

87. 10.30.6 and 13.

existence of a seer finds its fulfilment in the creation of a hymn. Divine inspiration and creative ability to express it, which are essential for the creation of a hymn, are the two things which are earnestly prayed for by the seers.

The poet-seers of the *Ṛgveda* constantly pray to the deities to grant them that which makes the creation of hymns possible. Besides the material wealth, the seers pray for the divine wealth consisting of "cows" and light. In most of the hymns one thing that is earnestly prayed for by the seers is the most precious and desirable divine wealth consisting of "cows" (*goṃantam*). All the deities are prayed to help the seers in recovering or attaining the cows that are concealed by Vṛtra and his allies. The most important point to be noted in this connection is that prayer and devotion are regarded by the seers as effective in destroying Vṛtra, and in recovering the "cows". Now, the real significance of the myth of Vṛtra's destruction, which is a recurring phenomenon, and culminates in the recovery of cows can be comprehended by grasping the symbolic meaning of the terms *go* and *dhenu*. It also helps in revealing the true significance and symbolic character of the Vṛtra myth and its various components. Although the terms *go* and *dhenu* mean kine or cows in several contexts of their usage in the *Ṛgveda*, their symbolic usage is also made clear in several other contexts. We now propose to discuss the symbolic meaning of the terms *go* and *dhenu* with a view to comprehending the real significance of the Vṛtra myth.

Apart from the authority of *Nighaṇṭu*, according to which the terms *go* and *dhenu* are synonyms of speech or hymns, we have ample evidence to show that these terms are used in most of the hymns of the *Ṛgveda* to mean Vedic speech or hymns. These words cannot properly be defined etymologically to mean speech. So we do not try to understand their meaning etymologically. We treat them as symbols standing for the Vedic speech. As in the case of the word *āpaḥ*, so also in the case of the words *go* and *dhenu* the usage in most of the contexts of the *Ṛgveda* is symbolic, and even analogical. Most of the words that are given in *Nighaṇṭu* as synonyms of speech can mean it only symbolically.

Milking a cow, or a cow yielding milk is a metaphor used regularly in the *Ṛgveda* to describe various phenomena. The metaphor is used in various contexts of the *Ṛgveda* in all of which the idea sought to be conveyed with its help is the attaintment, either from the deities or from heaven and earth, of divine wisdom and blessings. Just as milk is regarded as the essence of cows (*payaḥ*), so also the essence of all the deities is truth which manifests itself in and through all of them and, therefore, all the deities can shed or reveal it to man, or man can milk it from the deities. In the introduction to *Bhagavad-Gītā* it is said that the *Bhagavad-Gītā* is the essence of all the Upaniṣads, and Kṛṣṇa milks it for Arjuna. As truth is the essence of all that is there, including the deities, the attainment of truth by man, or its revelation to him is compared to the milking of a cow. As a cow yields milk, its essence, the whole creation yields truth to man, its essence. Being the essence of all the deities, truth is inherent within them, and inspired speech or wisdom expressed through the Vedic hymns is that essence milked as it were by the seer-poets of the Veda. Inspired speech or wisdom is essence of the divine.

In the *Ṛgveda*, almost all the deities, heaven and earth, *ṛta*, and even speech and intellect are described figuratively as cows yielding truth, their essence, to man. The essence so milked is the divine speech expressed through the hymns of the Veda. The heaven and earth are likened to milk-yielding cows, and Soma milks their essence to man. The great earth, which fosters all, is like a cow to be milked (*mahīm avanīm viśva dhenām gām na dohase*).[88] The deity Indra, who is addressed as Gopati (lord of cows), and which epithet is applied to other deities also, is milked by the seer Vasiṣṭha to creat hymns. "Milking thee (Indra) as a milk cow, Vasiṣṭha has let loose his prayers. All proclaim you as Gopati."[89] Indra is like a cow, and easy to be milked, and in this

88. 4.19.6

89. 7.18.4; see also 8.1.10.

context he is described as *gāyatra vepasam* or having the form of inspiration. In another context it is stated that Indra's truth (*sūnṛta*) is like a milk-yielding cow to his worshippers, and there is none better than Indra who can disclose "cows" to the seers (*nākti tvā goṣu vṛṇvate*).[90] He is described as a great cow (*bhūri go*). Similarly Soma is also compared to a cow, who yields to man the essence of the divine. He is like a cow to be milked (*somam gām na dohase*). He milks the heaven and earth. He milks divine nectar to man (*divaḥ pīyūṣam duhate*). He milks for man the divine udder which is dear and delightful (*duhanā ūdhaḥ divyam madhupriyam*).[91] More significantly it is stated that the seven cows (Vedic metres) milk for Soma the essence of truth from the highest (*tri asme sapta dhenavaḥ duhe satyām āśiram pūrve vyomani*).[92] And he also milks the metres, and flows out as the chief of the rivers, speech and cows (*agre sindhūnam, agre vācaḥ, agriyaḥ goṣu*). He flows like the milk of the cows (*arṣanti payasā iva dhenavaḥ*). Him the twenty-one (metres) milk, and he (Soma) the delightful flows within the hearts of men (*ayam tri sapta duduhānaḥ āśiram soma hṛde pavate cāru matstaraḥ*).[93]

The metaphor of milking a cow is used in relation to the deities Uṣas and Agni also. The cows of truth have brought Agni into existence as they flow (*ṛtasya dhenā*). Heaven and earth are the cows that milk the nectar of Agni. Uṣas is described as the milkmaid of the divine (*duhitā divasya*), or the daughter of the divine, for she sheds divine light to man, or milks for him auspicious light (*bhadram ghṛtam duhāna*).

The cows of *ṛta* (*ṛtasya dhenā*) milk or shed their essence for the sake of *ṛta*, and *ṛta* is also actively associated with the process of recovering cows. *Ṛta* seeks cows, and they yield their milk to *ṛta*. The cows that yield the milk of *ṛta* enter into *ṛta*, their source. The wisdom that is born of *ṛta* seeks *ṛta* as its object or end (*ṛtena*

90. 7.32.16.
91. 9.107.5.
92. 9.70.1.
93. 9.86.21.

gāvaḥ ṛtam āviveśuḥ).[94] The seers pray that the cows of *ṛta* manifest or shine as in the past (*ṛtasya sudughā purāṇa vat virocatām*).[95] All the deities and the entire phenomenal reality shed the essence of *ṛta* (*ṛtasya dhāra sudughā duhānaḥ*). This can mean either that the deities milk the streams of *ṛta*, or if we take the meaning of the word *dhara* as speech, then the deities are the means of revealing the speech that is born of *ṛta* or truth. The same idea is expressed differently when it is said that the adorable and divine mind of the deities is like a milk cow which milks or yields for man speech of thousand (countless) forms.[96] Finally the metaphor of cow yielding milk is used to describe speech also. The intellect of man is like a cow which can be milked for nectar. Human intellect is to be milked like a cow for the attainment of divine riches.[97] Being in the minds or intellect of men, Soma milks nectar for man. The threefold speech or the threefold Veda (*trisraḥ vācaḥ*) having light as its leader (*jyoti agrā*) milks (divine) udder which sheds sweetness. Divine speech (*vāk*) milks in all the four directions strength and essence of truth to one who knows its highest form (*vāk satasra ūrjam duduhe payāṁsi kvasvit asyāḥ paramam jagāma*).[98] The expression that the "hymns milk Indra" (*dohase gira*) shows that the Vedic speech, representing the creative or divine principle within man, is the means whereby man milks the truth. Thus intellect of man is compared to a cow that is to be milked, and similarly speech is also likened to a cow that yields for man worldly and divine riches. And being as comprehensive as the divine, or being co-extensive with it speech or wisdom is the chief means of revealing the divine to man.

We now discuss those passages of the *Ṛgveda* in which the speech in the form of hymns is symbolically identified with a cow, or the terms *go* and *dhenu* are symbolically used to mean

94. 4.23.9.
95. 10.43.9.
96. 10.101.9; see also 10.133.7.
97. 2.2.9; see also 7.94.4.
98. 8.89.10.

sacred speech. In the hymns addressed to *vāk* (divine wisdom or sacred speech), she in clear terms is identified with *go* or *dhenu*. Divine speech is (like) a cow which is to be milked for delightful food and power (*sā naḥ mandra iśam ūrjam duhānā dhenu, vāk asmān upasystutā āetu*).[99] Divine speech which comprehends within herself all the deities is regarded and addressed as a cow whom only fools abandon (*vācaḥ vidam vācam udīrayantīm viśvābhiḥ dhībhiḥ upatiṣṭhamānam devīm devebhyaḥ paryoyuṣīm gām mā vṛka marto dabhra cetāḥ*).[100] In another hymn in which the divine or inspired speech is seen as the mother of all the deities, and the centre of immortality is identified with a cow which is not to be hurt or destroyed. Although the words *go* and *dhenu* means symbolically speech in general, they stand to mean in numerous contexts of their usage in the *Ṛgveda* the sacred speech that is embodied in hymns. They are often used as synonyms of hymn or *mati*. The expressions like *dhiyā dhenā* and *manīṣām dhenum* indicate that. In these expressions the terms *dhīyā* and *manīṣā* which can mean either intellect or thought or wisdom, or their expression through hymns are identified with *dhenu* (cow). In two of the Soma hymns the terms *go* and *dhenu* are used as synonyms of hymns. In certain other contexts they are used together to mean the same reality. Cows go to Soma worshipping him, and hymns go to Soma longing him (*gāvaḥ yanti gopatim pṛchamānāḥ, somam yanti matyaḥ vāvasanāḥ*).[101] *Gāvaḥ* and *dhenavaḥ* (hymns) long for Soma, and the enlightened worship him with hymns (*somam gāvaḥ dhenavaḥ vāvasanāḥ somam viprāḥ matibhiḥ pṛcchmānāḥ*).[102] The word *pṛccha*, according to *Nighaṇṭu*, is a synonym of worship. Further the symbolic significance of the terms *go* and *dhenu* is made clear in several hymns of the *Ṛgveda* in which it is stated that "cows" sing to or praise the deities. In such expressions the term *go* is used to mean a hymn or a prayer (*dhenavaḥ anonavaḥ abhyanuṣat;*

---

99. 8.89.11.
100. 8.101.16.
101. 9.97.34.
102. 9.97.35.

dhenāḥ īdhe). "Cows" sing to Soma as a woman to her lover. *Gāvaḥ* and *matyaḥ* approach Soma together, and here the "cows" are described as *punarbhava* or born again and again in the place of *ṛta*, (*sam īmiti gāvaḥ matyaḥ yanti samyataḥ ṛtasya yonā sadane punarbhava*).[103] The hymns move commingled with *go* (*antaḥ matiḥ carati niṣpidam go*). The hymns (*dhenavaḥ*) serve Indra with reverence. Agni is awakened by "cows" (*gāvaḥ*) that are enkindled (*agnim samidhyamānam gāvaḥ prati bodhayanti*). The seven cows or metres (*sapta dhenavaḥ*) attain Soma. The expression *go ohena* or by the vehicle of *go* Indra is invited to attend the worship of the devotees is also significant. Indra is prayed to manifest *gāḥ* (hymns) in his worshippers (*abhi gāḥ Indra trundi*).[104] Indra hears and enjoys the hymns (*go*), and also desires them (*agorudhāye* or *goīṣe*). He notices or observes the prayers addressed to him (*dhenāḥ indra avacākasat*). His truthful speech (*sūnṛta*) which is rich in "cows" (*gomati*) is like a branch with ripe fruits to his worshippers (*sūnṛtā viraśmī gomatī mahi pakvā śākhā na dāsuṣe*).[105] Here the expression *gomatī mahi* can mean speech expressed through hymns, or hymns containing sacred speech, as the term *mahi* is a synonym of speech. Indra is praised and worshipped with the "cows" (hymns) when they are born and which are quick moving and great. Indra, who dwells within every person, witnesses their prayers (*dhenā*) (*viśam viśam maghavā pari āsayat janānām dhenā avacākasat*).[106] People become protected by Indra when he inspires in them sacred speech in various forms (*asmābhyām purudhā gāḥ iṣanya; kṣemena dhenām maghavā yat invati*).[107] Indra knows by his wisdom the prayers (*gāḥ*) of men (*tvam gāḥ indra śacyā it avinda*).[108] He increases wisdom (*supramatim*) in those who seek "cows" (*gavyantam*). In this context it is stated that Indra helps them to

103. 9.72.6.
104. 6.17.3.
105. 1.8.8.
106. 10.43.6; see also 8.32.22.
107. 3.50.3; 1.55.4.
108. 8.96.17.

attain supreme knowledge consisting of speech (*gavām ketam parām*). "Let us approach Indra seeking 'cows' or hymns (*gavyantam*) who will increase in us wisdom (*supramatim*)."[109] Indra is pleased with "cows" and prayers (*dhenābhiḥ mādayasva dhībhiḥ viśvebhiḥ*).

Apart from these expressions in which the terms *go* and *dhenu* are used to mean hymns or prayers, there are expressions of different kind in which the deities are prayed to inspire *go* or *dhenu* in the worshippers. "Inspire my thought or intellect which desires to creat a hymn (*jinva goṣthaye dhiyā*)."[110] The thought or intellect is guided by hymns, or it has the hymns as the chief means of its expression (*dhiyā go agre; dhenu jinvatam uta jinvatam viśaḥ*).[111] Soma milks divine nectar within the intellect of man (*dhīnām antariti sabaḥ dugaḥ*). Pleased by Soma, Indra inspires in us many a hymn or hymns of varied forms (*asmābhyām purudhā gāḥ iṣan*).

In the story of Ṛbhus, the sons of Sudhanvan, it is stated that their attainment of divine status is due to their ability to creat hymns (*gāḥ araṇīta carmanaḥ*). Here it is significant to note that Sāyaṇa takes the word *carmanaḥ* as a form of the word *śarmanaḥ*. If this is allowed then the story of Ṛbhus attaining divinity gains its real significance. Then the expression (*dhiyā gām araṇīta carmanaḥ tena devatvam ṛbhavaḥ sam ānasuḥ*)[112] can mean that Ṛbhus out of bliss gave birth to a hymn or formed a hymn out of their inspired intellect, and thereby attained divinity. This interpretation gains further confirmation in the use of the word *tvaca* (ordinarily meaning skin) which can mean form, as for instance in the expression *sūryasya tvacaḥ* (the form of the Sun). At times the terms *carma* and *tvaca* are used to mean the same thing. Moreover, in the context of the *Ṛgveda* to attain divine status is to be a *ṛṣi* or a *kavi* or

109. 1.33.1.

110. 9.108.10.

111. 1.90.5; 8.35.18.

112. 3.60.2; 1.60.7. Consider the following expressions: *citānaḥ goḥ adhi tvaci* (knowing the form of the hymns (cows) 9.101.11; *tvacaḥ budhne rajasaḥ asya yonau* 4.17.14; often the term *tvacaḥ* is used in relation to Soma meaning thereby the form of Soma.

be able to create a hymn. And Ṛbhus attained the highest end of their lives by receiving divine inspiration, the source of their wisdom. They formed a hymn, or to them the divine speech is revealed which can milk nectar for them (*takṣat dhenu sabardugām*).

The "cows" are often described as having or consisting of three elements, and of being threefold or abiding in three forms (*tridhātu gāvaḥ* or *tridhāhitam*). And in the context of the Veda the expression can mean the threefold collection of Vedic hymns. Thus it is said that the "cows" carry within their udders a great light, the light of truth, which is drawn by the seers and expressed in the form of hymns.[113]

The following expressions show clearly the symbolic meaning of the terms *dhenu*. In the place of *ṛta*, Uṣas shines as the flow of "cows" (*gavām na sargāḥ uṣasaḥ vibhāti*). As the hymns (cows) are born spontaneously out of an inspired intellect, the divine dawn, the first appearance of divine light, flows as or through the hymns. The flow of "cows" can only mean the spontaneous outflow of inspired speech purified within the heart and mind of man (*samyak sravanti saritāḥ na denāḥ antaḥ hṛdā manasā pūyamanāḥ*). Soma flows as the flow of *dhena* (hymns) purified within the heart and mind of man.

As shown in the previous chapter, Soma seeks "cows" (hymns) as the chief form of his expression, or the seers embody him, as soon as he is born, with "cows" or hymns. The essence of Soma is milked by those who seek hymns (*go*) (*ni asya rasam go īṣaḥ duhanti*).[114] In all such expressions the terms *go* and *dhenu* can only mean a hymn, as otherwise the meaning of the expressions remains utterly unintelligible. In the following assertions the intention of the seers is made completely clear. Making sacred speech (*gāḥ*) as his own form, Soma generates hymns with his power (*nrībhi yataḥ kṛṇute nirnijam gāḥ ataḥ matiḥ janayanta svadhābhiḥ*).[115]

113. 3.30.14.

114. 10.76.7.

115. 9.95.1; see also 9.86.26; 9.107.26.

In another hymn it is stated that Soma, the finder of light (*svavidam*), is increased by the essence of *gāvaḥ*, and they (cows) adorn him with hymns (*abhi tyam gāvaḥ payasā payaḥ vṛdham somam śrīnanti matibhiḥ svavidam*).[116] Such expressions can be multiplied to show that Soma flows seeking "cows" (hymns) as the best form of his expression. He flows to them, or seeks them, and is enriched by them. He knows the form of the hymns (*citānaḥ goḥ adhi tvaci*), and is fulfilled by them.

Goyūdha or the abode of "cows" is identified with Ilā (*ilā yūdhasya mātā*), the deity of speech. Ilā, the deity of speech, is the source of cows. She is described as *dhenu mātā* (mother of cows). Similarly Uṣas is also identified as the mother and leader of cows. In this context we find a hymn expressing the same idea in a significant manner. "Let us make a hymn whose mother will open for us the stall of cows" (*ā it dhiyam kṛṇvāma sakhāyaḥ asya mātā ruṇuta vrajam goḥ*).[117] Here the mother of hymns (*dhiya*) who opens up the stall of cows is divine speech in its unexpressed state, or before it is expressed in the form of hymns. The flowing cows with udders full of speech hold the form of Soma (*vacanāvantaḥ ūdhabhiḥ parisritam usriyā nirnijam dhire*).[118]

The above discussion, and the hymns cited clearly show the symbolic employment of the terms *go* and *dhenu* by the Vedic seers to mean sacred speech or hymns. We now discuss certain factors involved in the process of winning cows to justify and confirm further our interpretation. Firstly we discuss the nature of the cows recovered or attained with the destruction of Vṛtra and his allies, and then the means of their recovery. In both the cases the symbolic meaning of the words *go* and *dhenu* is evident. However, all the expressions in which the words *go, dhenu, usriya* and *adhna* are used, do not mean sacred speech or hymns. In certain contexts the term *go* is used to mean a ray either of the Sun or of Dawn. Here we are concerned only with those passages in which

116. 9.84.5.

117. 5.45.6.

118. 9.68.1.

the terms *go* and *dhenu* are symbolically used to mean sacred speech, and these passages are invariably connected with the myth of Vṛtra's destruction, and the consequent recovery of cows.

The seers themselves proclaim that the term *go* is not always used by them in its ordinary sense of a cow. "Even to the wise let that still be a wonder to which the ordinary or general name of cow is given."[119] While the ordinary cows are born for milking, Pṛṣṇi the cow has drained but once her fair bright udder. The real meaning of "cow" is hidden to ordinary understanding. The secret names of cow are known to Agni, and they are revealed to the seers by Varuṇa. The real cows are created by Aṅgīrasa seers by their austerity or penance (*yāḥ aṅgirasāḥ tapasā cakruḥ*).[120] Soma knows all the forms and names of the cow. The sage, seer and thinker Uśna knew by his wisdom the secret or hidden meaning or name of cows (*ṛṣiḥ viprāḥ dhīra uśna kāvyena saha cit viveda nihitam yat āsan apīcyam guhyam nāma gonām*).[121] The cows, whose place of origin is the highest, or who dwell in the realm of *ṛta* (truth) (*paramāt antaḥ; ṛtasya pade* or *sadane*) are of infinite forms (*viśvarūpa*) and impel or inspire all (*viśvajuvam*). The exhaustless udder of the cow of speech, as the term *mahi* is a synonym of speech, sheds infinite streams of milk that fulfil the existence of man (*sahasra dhārā payasā mahi gau*).[122] The cows that are in the highest realm, or in the realm of truth shed their essence to reveal and fulfil truth. *Ṛta* seeks cows as means of its expression or manifestation, and they milk for it in the highest. The idea may be that the sacred speech, the source of revelation of the divine to man reveals the divine to man, and again seeks the divine as its ultimate object. Truth is the source, as well as the end of sacred speech (*ṛtena gāvaḥ ṛtam āviveśuḥ*). By revealing *ṛta* or truth to man, divine speech leads man to religious or spiritual life. The expression that by means of "cows" we shall

119. 6.56.1.

120. 10.169.2.

121. 9.87.3.

122. 10.101.9; see also 10.133.7.

overcome all evil (*gobhiḥ tarema amatim*) also shows the relation between "cows" and *ṛta*.[123] They reveal truth and righteousness to man, and thereby save him from all evil and sin. From the beginning the flowing "cows" live or move in the highest realm. Agni is prayed to protect the hidden cows with that which is in the station of Viṣṇu; and that which is in the loftiest station of Viṣṇu, the highest aspiration of the seers, is either perfect bliss or the highest truth. The real place of origin of cows, or the real realm of their existence is also the source of *ṛta*. The expression that at the first shining of the earliest dawn in the *pada* of *go* (place of cows) is born (*mahat akṣaram*) the great imperishable, and then the worshippers perform the religious rites or worship the deities,[124] may, therefore, mean, according to our interpretation, that the inspired intellect or divinely illumined consciousness (*goh pade*) is the seat or the source of devotion and hymns. Or if we take the expression *goh pade* to mean words of a hymn, then the statement that the great imperishable or truth is born in *goh pade* may mean that the hymns of the Veda are the source of revelation of truth, or contain it. The divinely illumined or inspired consciousness of man is the source of hymns. This interpretation gains further support or confirmation in the statement that the divine Uṣas, the first revelation of truth to man, is the mother and leader of cows (hymns). The cows or hymns are the creative expression of the truth that is revealed to the seers. The cows or hymns seek Uṣas, and bear her, or they are the vehicles of its expression. The divine dawn breaking forth finds out for man the great light, and opens the place of cows for him. She is intimately connected with the recovery of cows. She is described as best of Aṅgīrasa seers (*aṅgirattamā*), and full of truthful speech (*sūnṛtā vati*).

The cows milk the essence of the highest or the divine, and bearing its form they attain the waters, or hold within themselves the flood of divine inspiration (*kṣīram duhate gāvaḥ asya vavrim vasānaḥ*

123. 10.42.10.

124. 3.55.1.

udakam padā āpuḥ).[125] Being the creative expression of truth, the cows (sacred speech) are identified with all the deities and Aditi, the mother of the deities. They are described as related to all the deities by kinship. They are mothers of Rudra, and are worshippable. They are identified with Indra, and are described as the chief food or enjoyment of Soma. The deities are often described in the *Ṛgveda* as born of "cow" or sacred speech or divine wisdom (*gojā* or *gojātā*). They are, therefore, its protectors (*gopati*). Most significantly, the deities are addressed as *govinda,* that is, they are to be known or attained by sacred speech or divine wisdom. Agni who knows his Father from his birth generates divine wisdom or speech (*asya dhāra asṛjat*) which is expressed through hymns. In the hymn: "let us go to Indra seeking cows; he will develop in us divine mind (*supra-matim*) and bless us with his wealth of supreme knowledge related to or consisting of cows" (*asya rāyaḥ gavām ketam parām āvarjate naḥ*), hymns or sacred speech are explicitly identified with cows.[126] Indra milks with light sacred speech or hymns (cows) from darkness. The seers seek the divine mind of Indra (*daivyā pramatim*) which is full of vigour, and having as its chief (manifestation) cows (*go agrayā*). Cows (hymns) measure in terms of metres the flow of divine inspiration. In this context it is significant to note that the mother cow bears twenty-one names. The twenty-one names of the mother cow are identified even by Sāyaṇa with the twenty-one metres of the Veda. At times the metres are counted as seven which are the principal ones. The cows as divine speech milk for man all as soon as they are born. Ilā, a deity of speech, representing *mādhyamika vāk,* is described as the mother of cows, and is characterised as *dhenumati* or hymn-minded or full of hymns (*ilā dhenumatī duhe*). The Vedic speech or hymns are regarded in the Vedic tradition as representing *mādhyamika* stage of *vāk*. In the expression *gobhiḥ vāṇaḥ ajāyate*, it is stated that the Vedic hymns (*gobhiḥ*) are born of divine speech, as the word *vāṇaḥ* is a synonym of speech, according to *Nighaṇṭu*.

---

125. 1.54.7.

126. 1.33.1.

The cows are recovered or attained by breaking open the rock or mountain (*adri*) in which they are concealed by Vr̥tra, and in the recovery of them almost all the deities, especially Brahmaṇaspati, Indra and Agni, are involved. In the process of recovering cows, man's devotion and prayer are also helpful. Most of the deities, who are described as protectors of cows, help man in finding them out. The epithets *gojit* (winner of cows), *gopati* or *gopā* (protector of cows) and *govit* or *govinda* (known or attained by cows) are applied to Indra, Soma, Agni and Brahmaṇaspati. Winning of cows is regarded by the seers as a supreme achievement, and most of the hymns are an invocation to the deities seeking their benevolence and active help in winning them. The ancient seers (Aṅgīrasas) were the first to win them with divine aid, or with the gracious help of the deities. And the divine aid is sought by the seers of the *R̥gveda* to recover or win the cows. Thus the process of recovering cows is a continuous one, and every seer wants to win them. And the deities are prayed to repeat the act of recovering the cows in the case of the present seers also as it was done in the case of ancient seers.[127] The place of cows, or the place where they are hidden is identified with speech or Ilā. The rock (*adri*) in which the cows are concealed by the dark forces represented by Vr̥tra and his allies has a symbolic meaning. It is not an ordinary rock or mountain. Although it is not our concern here to explain the symbolic meaning of the word *adri* in which the cows are concealed by Vr̥tra, it is sufficient to point out here that *adri* is defined in the *R̥gveda* itself as the form of *yajña* or *adhvara* (*adri adhvarasya peśa*).[128] Therefore, we may be right in interpreting *adri* as meaning some latent feeling or sense of divine in man seeking clarity and expression. It is the place wherein the cows lay concealed. The *adri* is somewhere in the highest in which the cows remain concealed (*paramāt antaḥ adre kūcit sat urvi gāḥ viveda*).[129]

127. 1.132.4.

128. 7.42.1.

129. 9.87.8.

It is further stated that the cows remain concealed within the cave of darkness, and the deities are prayed to disclose the great light and the cows to the seers by destroying the concealing darkness of the cave. The cave of darkness is interpreted by Sāyaṇa as the darkness of ignorance residing latently within human heart (*hṛdaye bhāva rūpam ajñānam*).[130] And the cows symbolising divine speech or wisdom that is born of divine light lay concealed within the cave of heart. Thus it is said that Indra by disclosing the cows, made manifest the true light of the sun in darkness of the cave. According to *Nighaṇṭu* the term *sūrya* is a synonym of knowledge. It is by destroying the inner darkness with light the cows are milked (*nirjyotiṣā tamasā gāḥ adukṣata*).[131] Maruts destroy the darkness with great pure light that is flood of cows (*mahājyotiṣā śucatā goarṇasa*). Divine Uṣas, the mother and leader of cows, is made manifest when the darkness within the cave is destroyed, or she is born destroying the darkness, and spreads her rays of light. As the mother of cows she manifests herself in the place of cows. It is further stated that she rises scattering the clustered darkness, and sets open the doors of man. Thus the appearance of divine dawn, and the manifestation of cows are interrelated. With the rise of divine dawn the cows (hymns) are made manifest to the seers. Aṅgīrasa seers have discovered the cows with the rise of divine dawns who diffuses knowledge (*vayunāni*), which is to be comprehended by the pious.[132] "All-embracing black darkness has approached me, discharge it Uṣas as if it were a debt."[133] "In this world our forefathers departed after instructing us *ṛtam*. When calling upon the Uṣas they extricated the milk yielding cows concealed among rocks in the darkness."[134] Great light is inherent within the udders of the cows (*mahājyotiḥ nihitam vakṣanāsu*), and the seers

130. 1.06.10 and Sāyaṇa's commentary thereon.

131. 1.33.10.

132. 5.48.2.

133. 10.127.7.

134. 4.1.13; see also 7.90.4; 6.55.5; 7.75.7; 1.92.4.

long for it. "Indra with the aid of Maruts when contending with Vṛtra perceived a great light issuing from darkness. The conscious dawns recognising him arise, and Indra became the single lord of cows."[135] And Uṣas moves as the flow or upsurge of hymns (*ṛtasya sadasaḥ devī gavām na sargāḥ usasaḥ jaranti*).[136] She is described as full of cows or hymns (*gomati*). These expressions show that the place wherein the cows lay hidden is the cave of darkness, or the unillumined heart of man, and *adri* may, therefore, refer to this state of man's existence. The manifestation of divine light within man is obstructed or prevented by the presence of inner darkness, and its destruction with the rise of divine Uṣas is the moment of manifestation or discovery of divine speech or cows. With the appearance of divine Uṣas man is awakened to the divine treasure hidden within, or within the cave of his heart. It means the birth of divine consciousness in man in the light of which man sees the presence of the divine, within himself, and in nature; or the various deities are revealed in nature. To see the presence of the divine in nature is to see each phenomenon of nature as a phenomenal manifestation of the divine, or as represented by a deity. "Awakened they (seers) looked around when first they beheld the heaven allotted treasure. The universal deities then came to all their dwellings. May my vision be true."[137] And the Vedic hymns express that vision in language, or the hymns are created when the seers give expression to that vision in language.

In the process of recovering or attaining cows or divine speech man has an important role to play. Here we have to assume that man naturally has some dim awareness of the divine, and that urges him to realise it more fully and clearly. Natural man is not utterly devoid of the sense of the divine. Divine help and guidance are required to make man realise the divine fully and clearly. Truth is governed by truth, or truth is self-governed.

135. 3.31.4.

136. 4.51.8.

137. 4.1.18.

Since truth is self-governed, self-luminous and self-evident, it is the means of its own revelation and realisation. The truth that is within man is the reason for his quest to realise it fully or to comprehend it clearly. It is truth that inspires man to know it more fully and clearly. The struggle for attaining "cows" is man's spiritual struggle to realise fully and clearly the divine treasure hidden within himself by overcoming the inner darkness that obstructs its manifestation and realisation. In this struggle divine help is valuable, and is constantly prayed for, by the seers.

The process of recovering or attaining cows also helps us in comprehending the true meaning of cows. The rocky place which conceals cows is to be pierced through or broken to recover the cows, and that is achieved by means of truthfulness, prayer and divine speech or wisdom. The ancient seers with a mind desirous of attaining cows (*gavyatā manasā*) forced open the compact solid rock enclosing or concealing the cows with divine or inspired speech (*daivyena vacasā*).[138] The seers meditating deeply on the essential nature (*name*) of cows found out the twenty-one names of the mother cow which dwells in the highest (*manavata pradhmam nāma dhenoḥ trisapta mātuḥ paramāṇi vindan*).[139] They then glorified the conscious dawns, and sang the prayers prepared to free the cows, and found the light. "Our forefathers, celebrators of holy rites, proceeded to the region of pure light, and reciting prayers, dispelling darkness, they made manifest the cows."[140] Aṅgīrasa seers by their truthfulness (*ṛtena*) cleft or broke open the rock and won the cows or discovered them, achieving thereby great bliss to themselves. The seers that won the cows are men of holiness, righteous action, and above all longing for the vision of the divine (*devayantaḥ*). They are also known as *padajña* which may mean either the knowers of word or the place of cows, and *svavidāḥ* or who have attained light. Thus one who has attained divine light knows the place of cows,

138. 4.1.15.

139. 4.1.16

140. 1.62.2; 4.2.16.

or is able to create a hymn. Therefore, the Vedic hymns are the repository of truth, or they are the expression of truth in language. In or through the words of the sacred speech (*goḥ pade*) is born the imperishable or truth. In another hymn it is stated that the wisdom concealed in the words of hymns is spoken or revealed to the seers by Agni (*padam na go apāgulham vividvān agni mahyam pra it vocata manīṣām*). "Wisdom hidden in the words of hymns is revealed to me by Agni, the wise."[141] Aṅgīrasa seers through the grace of Uṣas won the cows from the summit of the mountain by worship, and divine speech or wisdom (*arkeṇa* and *daivyena vacasā*). Śaramā found out the cows with the help of *ṛta*.

Brahmaṇaspati, the deity representing devotion and sacred speech, is also closely connected with the recovery of cows. Most divine among the divine being (*devānām devatama*), Brahmaṇaspati by the power of sacred prayer destroyed Vala and released cows, or dispelled darkness and disclosed light. The cows so released or recovered flew in all directions as streams of a mighty river. Indra with the help of the prayers of Aṅgīrasa seers recovered the cows. The seers with their truthful minds (*satyena manasā*) seeking cows approached Indra, the lord and protector of cows, with their thoughts or prayers (*dhībhiḥ*). Śaramā, who is appropriately identified by Sāyaṇa on occasions as flowing speech, is the messenger of Indra sent to recover the cows, and she, following the path of *ṛta*, and by means of it discovered them (*ṛtam yāti saramā gāḥ avindata; ṛtasya padhā śaramā vidat gāḥ*).[142] And then to Aṅgīrasa seers is revealed the truth of all, or they came to know the truth of all that is there (*viśvāni satya aṅgiraḥ cakāra*). The glory by which the seers have won the cows is a gift of Indra. The seer and thinker Uśna discovered the hidden cows by means of his wisdom (*kāvyena saḥ cit viveda*). Divine Uṣas, who is described as true among the truthful (*satyā satyebhi*) and great among the great and worshippable, shaking the firm place holding the cows, helped the recovery of cows. And Uṣas

141. 4.5.3.

142. 5.45.7. and 8.

symbolising the dawn of divine light, the source of all wisdom, is appropriately described as Aṅgirattamā, full of inspiration. It is by following the path of *ṛta* the place of cows is broken; and their recovery is for the sake of manifesting *ṛta,* and its glorification. Cows express *ṛta,* and it is their ultimate goal as well. Truth manifests itself for its own sake, and its realisation is an end in itself.

The way the cows are hidden in the rock, as well as the manner of their recovery are also highly significant, and reveal the symbolic meaning of the cows. The metaphors employed in this context are equally significant, and throw light on the meaning of the terms *go* and *dhenu*. The recovery and winning of cows by Brahamaṇaspati is compared to taking grain from a granary which is full of grain.[143] It is like a bird emerging from an egg, or like a bowl is made out of wood.[144] He found the cows as one sight fish in scanty water, or in a shallow pool of water.[145] The use of these metaphors to describe the manner of recovery of cows from the rock clearly indicates that the cows are not alien to the place where they are hidden, or from where they are discovered. They do not give the meaning that the cows are stolen by someone, and hidden in the rock. The relation of the cows to the place of their concealment is not unnatural. The cows belong to the place inherently, or the place contains them intrinsically. Therefore, to win them or attain them is to discover them. Their attainment is a matter of recovery. In another significant metaphor it is said that the cows are recovered from the place of their concealment as marrow is extracted from bones.[146] Although the metaphors are not so apt, they sufficiently convey the idea that the cows belong to the place intrinsically and, therefore, their attainment by the seers is only a matter of discovery or realisation. The cows are there within man, but are

143. 10.68.3.

144. 10.68.7. and 8.

145. 10.68.8.

146. 10.68.9.

concealed or hidden from his vision because of inner darkness and, therefore, all his efforts and divine help to attain them are meant to uncover them. "Dissipate the concealing darkness of the cave, drive away every devouring foe and show us the light we long for."[147] The recovery of cows is not, therefore, an achievement of something new, as their recovery or attainment is simultaneous with the destruction of concealing darkness which keeps them hidden from the vision of man. As a bowl is carved out of wood, and as a bird emerges breaking the egg shell, so also the divine speech or wisdom that is there within man, but remains unrevealed because of concealing inner darkness gets revealed to man the moment the inner darkness is destroyed. Then the wisdom flows out spontaneously seeking its expression in the form of hymns. Thus the hymns are created. This process is initiated and quickened by divine inspiration which is mediated to man through the deities or nature. He whom the deity Indra inspires to devotion wins divine wealth, and becomes a winner of cows. Aṅgīrasa seers have made the world shine in its real or divine glory by discovering the cows with the aid of Śaramā.[148] They discovered truth, and in its light they could see nature as the dwelling place of the deities, or nature has revealed to them its divine meaning. The divine speech or wisdom, the source and centre of immortality (*amṛtasya nābhi*) is expressed through hymns, and comprehends within itself all the deities (*viśvebhiḥ dhībhiḥ upatiṣṭhamānam devīm devebhyaḥ pari paryuṣīm gām*).[149]

The speech which the terms *go* and *dhenu* symbolically represent is not the ordinary speech meant to convey ordinary experiences of man about the world. If we follow the traditional Vedic classification of speech (*vāk*) into *parā* (supreme or highest) *paśyantī* (that which is seen), *madhyamā* (middle) and *vaikharī* (the ordinary speech), the Vedic speech or the speech contained in

147. 1.86.10; see also 7.80.2; 4.52.4; 1.113.16.

148. 5.45.7.

149. 8.90.16.

the hymns of the Veda refers to *madhyamā* stage of speech. But at the same time it derives its authority and validity from *parā* and *paśyantī* stages of speech. *Parā vāk*, the self-revelatory aspect of the divine or divine wisdom is co-extensive and co-eternal with the divine. Its extension is the same as the extension of the Divine. Its limits are the limits of the divine, or it is limitless and unmeasured; whereas *paśyantī* speech is that stage of *vāk* which is revealed to the seers, or as seen or known by them. It is the *parā vāk* as revealed to the seers. It refers to the inspired vision of truth. It is the highest wisdom as revealed to the seers. And *vāk* is known as *madhyamā*, when the divinely inspired wisdom of the seers is expressed in human language, or the language of the Vedic hymns. It is the expressed form of *paśyantī vāk*. *Paśyantī vāk* is *parā vāk* as revealed to the seers, and *madhyamā vāk* is the expression of the latter in the form of Vedic hymns. When the truth or divine wisdom as revealed to the seers is expressed in human language, Veda in its literary form comes into existence. Thus the Veda represents divine wisdom as revealed to the seers, and expressed in human language. And the process of recovering cows symbolises the process of attaining divine speech or wisdom. This also explains the Śruti character of the Veda. Hence the constant seeking of the Vedic seers for the attainment of divine speech or wisdom in which they see the ultimate fulfilment of their lives. This also explains the divine and all-comprehensive nature of the cows, and the supreme value and meaning attached to their recovery or attainment. To recover or win the cows is the supreme quest of the Vedic seers, and it is expressed throughout *Ṛgveda*. In the later Hindu tradition the epithets Gopati and Govinda are applied to God or Viṣṇu as He is the lord and ultimate source of sacred knowledge, as well as its ultimate object. He is the ultimate source of sacred knowledge, and is also attained by it.[150]

---

150. *Viṣṇu Sahasranāma* verses 33 and 71 and Śaṅkara's commentary thereon.

The divine wisdom or sacred knowledge of the Veda, as a divine gift to man, is mediated to him through the deities who dwelling in nature inspire in him divine speech and devotion, and awaken him to the divine. And the wisdom so attained is made an offering in worship to the divine, thereby completing and fulfilling the creative process involved in the self-manifestation of the divine. Man offers back in worship to the divine what he receives from it as a gift, and realises thereby the ultimate meaning of his existence, as well as the divine purpose revealed through creation. He also realises thereby the true meaning of *yajña*, and sees in his divine life its extension and fulfilment. The *Ṛgveda* records this process in a language of devotion and worship. Thus the hymns of the *Ṛgveda* — the word *ṛk* means to worship — are essentially prayers inspired by the divine, and are offered in worship to the divine in and through its diverse manifestations in nature or the deities.

Bibliography

In this work the *Ṛgveda Saṁhitā* with the commentary of Sāyaṇācārya published in five volumes by Vaidic Samsodhana Mandal (Vedic Research Institute), Poona, is followed. And in translating the hymns into English the translations of the *Ṛgveda* by Ralph T.H. Griffith, and published by Motilal Banarsidass, Varanasi, and by H.H. Wilson, and published in seven volumes by Cosmos Publications, New Delhi, are consulted. On occasions the translations of Griffith are quoted either partly or fully.

Vedic Saṁhitās (Text)

Ṛgveda Saṁhitā with the commentary of Sāyaṇācārya, five volumes, Vaidika Saṁśodhana Maṇḍala, Poona, 1946.

Vājasaneyī Saṁhitā (*Śukla Yajurveda*), Chowkhamba Sanskrit Series, Varanasi, 1972.

Taittirīya Saṁhitā (*Kṛṣṇa Yajurveda*) with the Commentary of Sāyaṇācārya, Vaidika Saṁśodhana Maṇḍala, Poona, 1970.

Sāmaveda Saṁhitā, Samskrit Samsthan, Khvaja Kutub, Bareilly, 1969.

Atharveveda Saṁhitā, with Sāyaṇa's Commentary, Vishveshvarananda Vedic Research Institute, Hoshiarpur, 1961.

Translations (English)

Ṛgveda Saṁhitā (*The Hymns of the Ṛgveda*), Ralph T.H. Griffith, Motilal Banarsidass, Varanasi, 1973.

———, H.H. Wilson, in seven volumes, Cosmo Publications, New Delhi, 1970.

Vājasaneyī Saṁhitā (*White Yajurveda*), Ralph T.H. Griffth, E.J. Lazarus and Co., Varanasi, 1957.

Taittirīya Saṁhitā (*Black Yajurveda*), A.B. Keith, two vols., Harvard Oriental Series, Authorised Reprint by Motilal Banarsidass, Varanasi, 1967.

Sāmaveda Saṁhitā, Ralph T.H. Griffith, Chowkhamba Sanskrit Series, Varanasi, 1963.

Atharvaveda Saṁhitā, (*The Hymns of Atharvaveda*), Ralph T.H. Griffith, two vols., Chowkhamba Sanskrit Series, Varanasi, 1968.

———, W.D. Whitney, two vols., Motilal Banarsidass, Varanasi, 1952.

Other Vedic Literature

Aitareya Āraṇyaka, text with translation by A.B. Keith, Oxford University Press, London, 1969.

Aitareya Brāhmaṇa (text), ed. Vinayaka Ganesa Apte, Anandasrama Series.

Bṛhaddevatā (text), ed. Macdonell, Harvard Oriental Series, vol. 5, Cambridge, 1904.

Nighaṇṭu and *Nirukta*, edited and translated by Laksman Sarup, Panjab University, 1927.

Śāṅkhāyana Āraṇyaka, translated by A.B. Keith, Oriental Books Reprint Corporation, New Delhi, 1975.

Śatapatha Brāhmaṇa, translated by Julius Eggeling, 5 vols., Sacred Books of the East, Motilal Banarsidass, Varanasi (reprint), 1964.

Other Works

Aurobindo, *On the Veda*, Pondicherry, 1956.

Barth, A., *Religions of India*, Chowkhamaba Sanskrit Series, Varanasi, 1963.

Bloomfield, M., *The Religion of the Veda*, Indological Book House, Delhi, 1972.

Bergaignes, A., *Vedic Religion*, one volume edition, Motilal Banarsidass, Varanasi, 1978.

Cole Brooke, H.T., *Essays on the Religion and Philosophy of the Hindus*, Ashok Publications, New Delhi, 1976.

Dayananda Saraswati, *Commentary on the Ṛgveda*, tr. Dharmadeva Vidya Martanda, Sarvadeshik Arya Pratinidhi Sabha, New Delhi, 1974.

Gonda, J., *The Vision of the Vedic Poets*, Mouton and Co., The Hague, 1963.

Max Müller, F., *Lectures on the Origin and Growth of Religion*, Longman's Green and Co., London, 1898.

———, *On the Science of Religion*, Longman's Green and Co., London, 1898.

Mcdonald, K.S., *The Vedic Religion*, Sanskrit Pustaka Bhandar, Calcutta, 1982.

Purani, A.B., *Sri Aurobindo's Vedic Glossary*, Pondicherry, 1962.

———, *Studies in Vedic Interpretation on the lines of Sri Aurobindo*, The Chowkhamba. Varanasi, 1963.

Renou, L., *The Destiny of the Veda in India*, Motilal Banarsidass, Varanasi, 1965.

———, *Religions of Ancient India* (Jordan Lectures, 1951), University of London, London, 1953.

Index